Codex 4/604

Fiat 132 1972–80 Autobook

By the Autobooks Team of Writers and Illustrators

Fiat 132 1600, Special 1972–74
Fiat 132 1600 GL 1974–76
Fiat 132 1600 GLS 1974–77
Fiat 132 1800 Special 1972–74
Fiat 132 1800 GLS 1974–76
Fiat 132 1800 ES   1976–77
Fiat 132 2000, GLS 1977–80

Autobooks Ltd. Golden Lane Brighton BN1 2QJ England

The AUTOBOOK series of Workshop Manuals is the largest in the world and covers the majority of British and Continental motor cars, as well as the majority of Japanese and Australian models.

Whilst every care has been taken to ensure correctness of information it is obviously not possible to guarantee complete freedom from errors or omissions or to accept liability arising from such errors or omissions.

CONTENTS

ISBN 0 85146 113 1

First Edition   1975
Second Edition, fully revised   1976
Reprinted   1978
Third Edition, fully revised   1978
Fourth Edition, fully revised   1980

856

Printed in Brighton England for Autobooks Ltd by G. Beard and Son Ltd   E
Bound in Hove England for Autobooks Ltd by Jilks Ltd

INTRODUCTION

This do-it-yourself Workshop Manual has been specially written for the owner who wishes to maintain his vehicle in first class condition and to carry out the bulk of his own servicing and repairs. Considerable savings on garage charges can be made, and one can drive in safety and confidence knowing the work has been done properly.

Comprehensive step-by-step instructions and illustrations are given on most dismantling, overhauling and assembling operations. Certain assemblies require the use of expensive special tools, the purchase of which would be unjustified. In these cases information is included but the reader is recommended to hand the unit to the agent for attention.

Throughout the Manual hints and tips are included which will be found invaluable, and there is an easy to follow fault diagnosis at the end of each chapter.

Whilst every care has been taken to ensure correctness of information it is obviously not possible to guarantee complete freedom from errors or omissions or to accept liability arising from such errors or omissions.

Instructions may refer to the righthand or lefthand sides of the vehicle or the components. These are the same as the righthand or lefthand of an observer standing behind the vehicle and looking forward.

CHAPTER 1

THE ENGINE

1:1 Description

Three different size engines of 1600, 1800 and 2000 cc have been fitted in the Fiat 132. They are basically similar in construction and most maintenance and repair operations are common. Where differences occur they will be covered separately in the appropriate section. Specifications and dimensions are given in the **Technical Data** section of the **Appendix** at the end of this book.

The engines are in-line, four cylinder, twin overhead camshaft units with crossflow induction and exhaust. The camshafts are driven by a toothed belt that also drives an auxiliary shaft connected to the distributor, oil pump and fuel pump, as shown in **FIG 1:1**. A vee belt drives the alternator and water pump. Cars with power steering have a second vee belt driving the hydraulic pump.

The camshafts are mounted in two separate housings bolted to the top of the cylinder head. Valve clearance adjustment is carried out by the selective fitting of shims to the valve tappets.

The cast iron cylinder block includes the upper half of the crankcase and houses the bearings for the crankshaft. The cylinder bores are bored directly in the block and house the aluminium pistons which may be in any one of five sizes to ensure correct matching.

The five bearing counterbalanced crankshaft is a special steel casting. Crankshaft end thrust is taken by thrust half-rings at the rear main bearing position. The main and big-end bearings are provided with renewable shell-type inserts. **FIG 1:2** shows a longitudinal section of the engine.

A gear-type oil pump draws the oil from the sump under the engine and supplies it to the system under pressure. A relief valve is fitted to the system to limit the maximum oil pressure when the engine is cold. Pressured oil is fully filtered before being passed to the main oil gallery running along the righthand side of the engine. From this point the oil is routed to the main and big-end bearings and to the camshaft support bearings. The valve gear is lubricated by oil draining from the camshaft bearings, the pistons and cylinders being lubricated directly by supply jets and indirectly by oil splash from the big-end bearings. Oil passages in the crankcase supply oil to the auxiliary shaft bearings.

1:2 Removing the engine

The normal operations of decarbonising and servicing the cylinder head can be carried out without the need for engine removal, as can the majority of engine servicing procedures. A major overhaul, however, can only satisfactorily be carried out with the engine removed and transferred to the bench. For some overhaul work, certain special tools are essential and the owner would be well advised to check on the availability of these factory tools or suitable substitutes before tackling the items involved. If the operator is not a skilled automobile engineer, it is suggested that he will find much useful information in **Hints on Maintenance and Overhaul** at the end of this manual and that he read it before starting work. It must be stressed that the lifting equipment used to remove

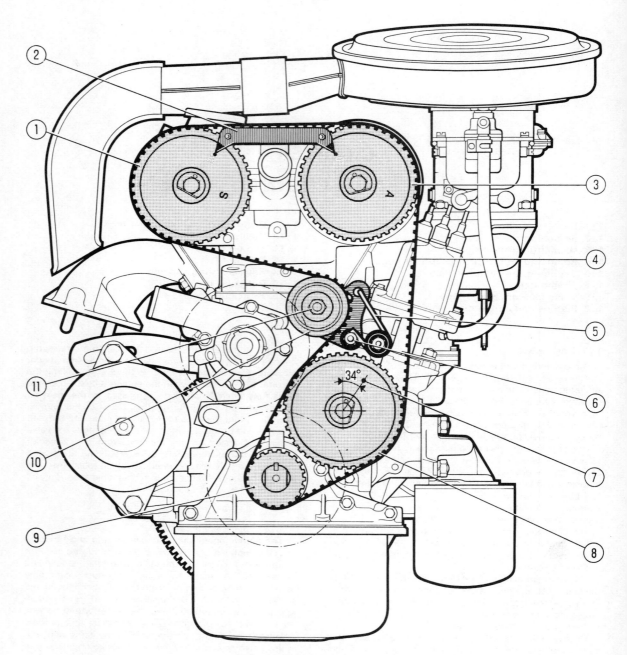

FIG 1:1   The timing gear drive

Key to Fig 1:1   1 Exhaust camshaft sprocket   2 Bracket with timing pointers   3 Inlet camshaft sprockets   4 Timing belt
5 Tensioner pulley spring   6 Pulley (lockscrew)   7 Timing mark for auxiliary shaft sprocket   8 Auxiliary shaft sprocket
9 Crankshaft sprocket   10 Tensioner pulley   11 Tensioner pulley locknut

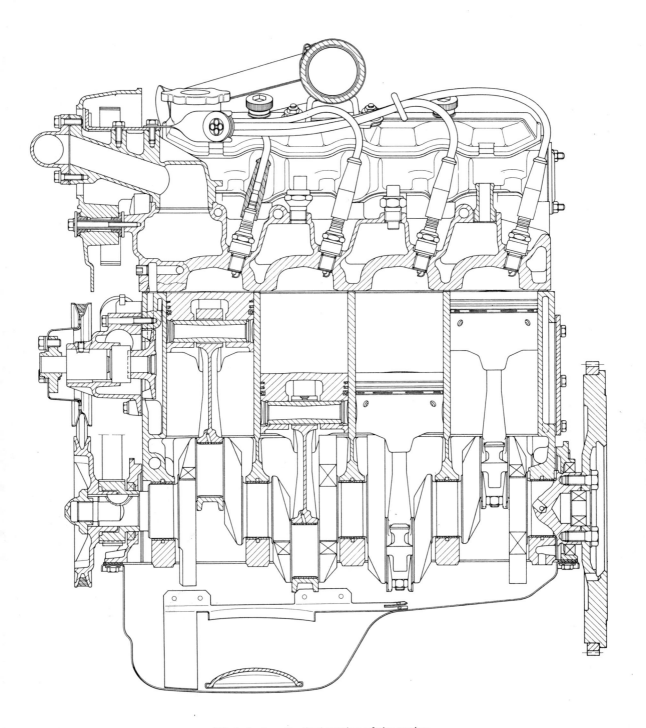

FIG 1:2 Longitudinal section of the engine

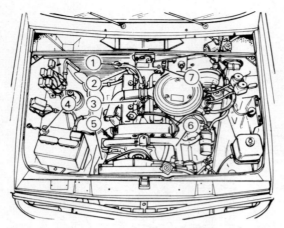

FIG 1:3 Parts to be disconnected before removing the engine

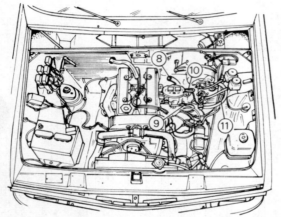

FIG 1:4 Parts to be disconnected before removing the engine

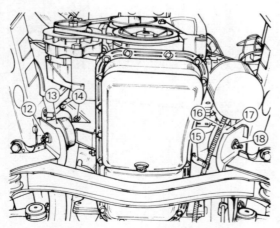

FIG 1:5 Parts to be disconnected beneath the car

the engine from the car should be sound, firmly based and not likely to collapse under the weight it will be supporting. Note that it will be necessary to remove the gearbox or automatic transmission separately before the engine can be removed from the car.

Removal:

Apply the handbrake and chock the rear wheels against rotation. Raise the front of the car and securely support it on stands. Alternatively, drive the car over a pit to provide the necessary access to the underside.

Remove the bonnet as described in **Chapter 13**. Drain the engine oil. Drain the cooling system as described in **Chapter 4**.

Refer to **FIG 1:3** and disconnect the heater hoses 1 and 2, the air cleaner bracket 3, the battery negative terminal 4, the radiator hoses 5 and 6 and the accelerator control rod 7.

Refer to **FIG 1:4** and remove the hose 8, fuel line 9, and hoses 10 and 11. Remove the air cleaner as described in **Chapter 2**. Disconnect the choke cable and accelerator control rod from the carburetter. Disconnect the exhaust pipe from the exhaust manifold.

Disconnect the wiring from the starter motor and alternator and from all connections on the engine unit.

Remove the gearbox or automatic transmission as described in **Chapter 6** or **7**.

From beneath the car, remove the engine shield and refer to **FIG 1:5**. Remove the nuts 12 and 18 from the engine mounts 13 and 17. The nuts securing the exhaust pipe to the manifold are shown at 14. Disconnect the clutch cable support 15 and the cable 16. The engine and gearbox supports are shown in **FIG 1:6**.

Attach the special sling A.60511 or a suitable substitute to the engine, then carefully raise the engine until it is clear of the engine compartment and transfer it to the bench.

1:3 Dismantling the engine

The engine main castings and gaskets are shown in **FIG 1:7**. Remove the engine mounting brackets from the crankcase. Remove the oil dipstick. Remove the clutch assembly as described in **Chapter 5**.

Disconnect and remove the sparking plugs and unbolt and remove the distributor. Store these items in a clean dry place. Extract and store the oil pressure and water temperature transducers.

Unbolt and remove the alternator and drive belt. Remove the water pump as described in **Chapter 4**.

Lock the crankshaft against turning by suitable means (see **FIG 1:8**) then unbolt and remove the drive pulley from the opposite end of the crankshaft. Note that this pulley is keyed to the shaft so that the timing mark will be properly located. Unbolt and remove the flywheel from the crankshaft.

Unbolt and remove the water outlet cover housing the thermostat, remove the thermostat then unbolt the lower half of the outlet from the cylinder block.

Remove the carburetter and fuel pump as described in **Chapter 2**. Loosen and remove the oil filter cartridge. Remove and dismantle the cylinder head as described in **Section 1:4**.

Invert the engine and remove the sump and front timing gear cover. Unbolt and remove the drive sprocket from the

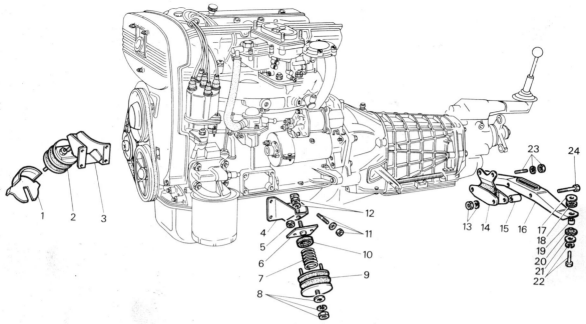

FIG 1:6 Engine and gearbox mountings

Key to Fig 1:6   1 Insulator shield   2 Insulator   3 Right bracket   4 Left bracket   5 Insulator support nut   6 Insulator support   7 Spring   8 Nut, lockwasher and flat washer   9 Insulator   10 Spring cup   11 Nut, flat washer and stud   12 Nut and flat washer   13 Nut and spring washer   14 Transmission rear insulator   15 Spacer   16 Rear crossmember   17 Flat washer   18 Grommet   19 Spacer   20 Grommet   21 Flat washer   22 Screw and lockwasher   23 Stud, lockwasher and nut   24 Screw

crankshaft, then withdraw the bearing with the Fiat special tool or similar as shown in **FIG 1:9**.

Remove the oil pump upper drive gear from its spindle, unscrew the bolts attaching the pump to the crankcase and withdraw the pump complete with its suction pipe.

Before unbolting the connecting rod caps, make sure that they are numbered in order to ensure that they are refitted in their original positions. Remove the bolts and caps, then remove the connecting rods and pistons through the tops of their cylinder bores.

Remove the fixing bolts and detach the rear cover plate from the crankcase (see **FIG 1:10**). Mark the main bearing caps so that they will be refitted in their original positions, then take out the fixing bolts and lift off the caps and shell bearing shell halves. Lift out the thrust bearing half rings from the rear main bearing (see **FIG 1:11**).

1:4 Removing and refitting cylinder head

Drain the cooling system as described in **Chapter 4**. Remove the air cleaner as described in **Chapter 2**. Disconnect the exhaust pipe from the manifold flange (see **FIG 1:5**). Disconnect the sparking plug leads from the sparking plugs. Before proceeding any further, the engine should be turned to the timing position for the crankshaft and the two camshafts. See **FIG 1:17** and **Chapter 3 FIG 3:6**.

Disconnect the accelerator and choke linkages from the carburetter and the hoses and electrical wiring from

the cylinder head connections. Refer to **Section 1:6** and remove the timing belt (see **FIG 1:12**). Do not turn the crankshaft or camshafts after the belt has been removed, otherwise the valves will hit the pistons and cause internal damage. Slacken the cylinder head securing bolts in the order shown in **FIG 1:13**, then remove the bolts. Lift off the cylinder head, gently tapping it with a soft-faced hammer if it sticks. Remove and discard the cylinder head gasket.

Refitting:

The camshafts must be correctly positioned before the cylinder head is refitted. After this, the crankshaft and camshafts must not be turned until the timing belt has been installed otherwise the valves will contact the pistons and cause internal damage.

Turn the crankshaft until pistons Nos. 1 and 4 are at Top Dead Centre.

Turn each of the camshafts until each reference dot is against its respective pointer on the double timing bracket at the front of the cylinder head, see item 2 in **FIG 1:1**. Note also that each camshaft sprocket has a small hole in its rearward side which lines up with an embossed pointer on the front camshaft bearing.

Check that the auxiliary shaft is correctly aligned as shown in the illustration. The engine is now set for cylinder head refitting.

Fit two suitable dummy studs into two of the cylinder head bolt holes in cylinder block. Fit a new cylinder head

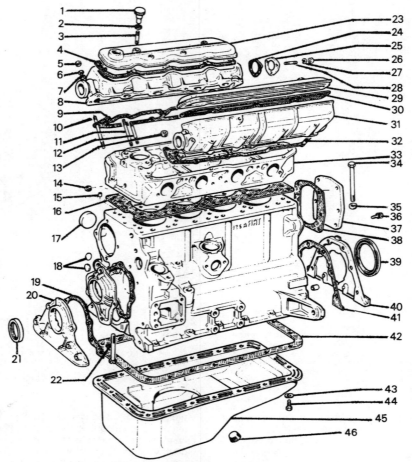

FIG 1:7   The engine main castings and gaskets

Key to Fig 1:7   1 Cover the retaining screw   2 Washer   3 Stud   4 Gasket   5 Nut   6 Circlip   7 Washer   8 Camshaft housing   9 Gasket   10, 11, 12 Stud   13 Core plug   14 Screw plug   15 Locating pin   16 Gasket   17, 18 Core plugs   19 Gasket   20 Cover   21 Seal   22 Bolt   23 Cover   24 Gasket   25 Coverplate   26 Nut   27 Spring washer   28 Stud   29 Cover   30 Gasket   31 Camshaft housing   32 Gasket   33 Cylinder head   34 Bolt   35 Washer   36 Screw   37 Coverplate   38 Gasket   39 Seal   40 End plate   41, 42 Gaskets   43 Washer   44 Screw   45 Sump   46 Drain plug

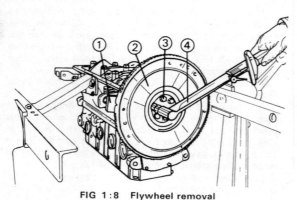

FIG 1:8   Flywheel removal

Key to Fig 1:8   1 Locking tool   2 Flywheel   3 Mounting bolts   4 Wrench

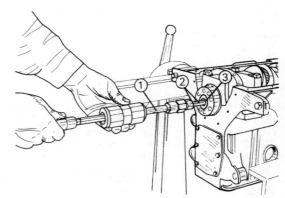

FIG 1:9   Removing the ballrace from the rear of the crankcase

gasket over the dummy studs. Carefully position the cylinder head on the block using the dummy studs as pilots. Fit the cylinder head securing bolts by hand only, removing the dummy studs to refit the last two bolts.

The cylinder head bolts must now be progressively tightened according to the sequence shown in **FIG 1:13**, in not less than two stages. At the first stage tighten to a torque of 29 lb ft (4 kgm) and then to the final figure of 61 lb ft (8.5 kgm).

Refit the timing belt as described in **Section 1:6**, then refit the ancilliary items that were disconnected from the cylinder head during removal. Refill the cooling system as described in **Chapter 4**.

1:5 Servicing the cylinder head

Remove the cylinder head as described in **Section 1:4** and transfer it to the bench, taking care not to damage the light-alloy surface. **FIG 1:14** shows a split section through the cylinder head assemblies.

FIG 1:10   Removing the rear crankcase coverplate

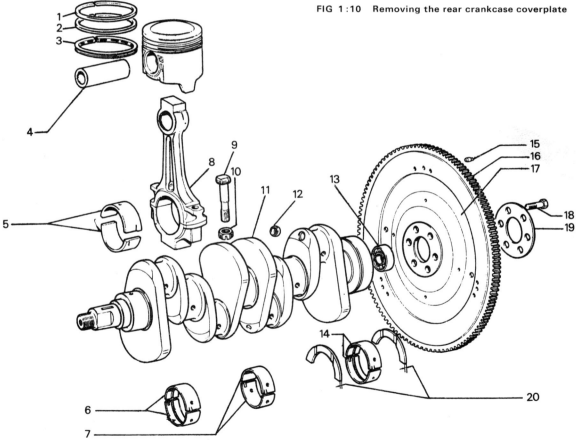

FIG 1:11   The crankshaft, connecting rod and flywheel components

Key to Fig 1:11   1 Top ring   2 Second ring   3 Oil control ring   4 Gudgeon pin   5 Big-end bearing shells   6, 7 Main bearing shells   8 Connecting rod   9 Connecting rod bolt   10 Nut   11 Crankshaft   12 Plug   13 Spigot bearing   14 Main bearing shells   15 Alignment pin   16 Starter ring gear   17 Flywheel   18 Bolt   19 Flange ring   20 Thrust bearings

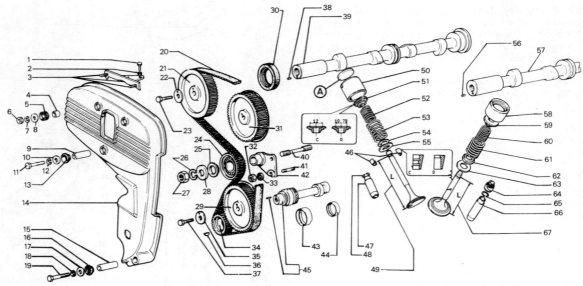

FIG 1 : 12   The camshaft drive gear and valve components

Key to Fig 1 :12   1 Screw   2 Washer   3 Timing plate   4 Collar   5 Bush   6 Nut   7 Spring washer   8 Washer
9 Spacer   10 Washer   11 Bolt   12 Spring washer   13 Bush   14 Coverplate   15 Spacer   16 Bush   17 Washer
18 Spring washer   19 Bolt   20 Timing belt   21 Exhaust camshaft sprocket   22 Washer   23 Screw   24 Idler pulley
25 Spacer   26 Circlip   27 Nut   28 Washer   29 Auxiliary shaft sprocket   30 Seal   31 Inlet camshaft sprocket   32 Nut
33 Washer   34 Crankshaft sprocket   35 Washer   36 Woodruff key   37 Bolt   38 Dowel pin   39 Exhaust camshaft
40, 41 Studs   42 Bearing plate   43, 44 Bearings   45 Auxiliary shaft and key   46 Collets   47 Valve guide   48 Circlip
49 Exhaust valve   50 Bucket tappet   51 Spring retainer   52 Inner spring   53 Outer spring   54 Spring retainer   55 Washer
56 Dowel pin   57 Inlet camshaft   58 Tappet   59 Spring retainer   60 Inner spring   61 Outer spring   62 Spring retainer
63 Washer   64 Valve stem seal   65 Circlip   66 Valve guide   67 Inlet valve

Remove the camshafts and the housings complete, loosening the fixing bolts alternately and evenly to avoid straining the housings. Extract the tappets and adjusting shims from each valve position, storing them in the correct order for refitting in their original positions. Remove the inlet and exhaust manifolds as shown in **FIG 1 :15**.

Valve removal :

Use a suitable valve spring compressor to remove the valve gear from the cylinder head. With the spring compressed, remove the split taper collets, then remove the compressor tool and collect the valve, springs, spring seats and washers. Keep all valve gear components in the correct order for refitting in their original positions.

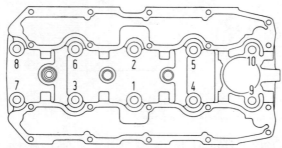

FIG 1 :13   Cylinder head bolt tightening and loosening sequence

Valves :

When the valves have been cleaned of carbon deposits, they must be inspected for serviceability. Valves with bent stems or badly burned heads must be renewed. Valves that are pitted can be re-cut at a service station, but if they are too far gone for this remedial treatment, new valves will be required. Valves that are in serviceable condition can be ground to their seats as described later.

Valve guides :

Valve guides that are worn or scored must be renewed. As the guides must be pressed into or out of place, reamed, then the valve seat re-cut for concentricity, this work should be carried out by a service station having the necessary special equipment.

Valve seat inserts :

Valve seat inserts that are pitted or burnt must be re-faced or, if they are too far gone for remedial treatment, renewed. As either operation requires the use of special equipment, the work should be carried out by a service station. If the valve seat inserts are serviceable, they should be ground to the valves as described later.

Valve springs :

Test the valve springs by comparing the efficiency of the old springs against that of the new spring. To do this, insert both the old and new springs end to end with a metal plate between them into the jaws of a vice. If the old

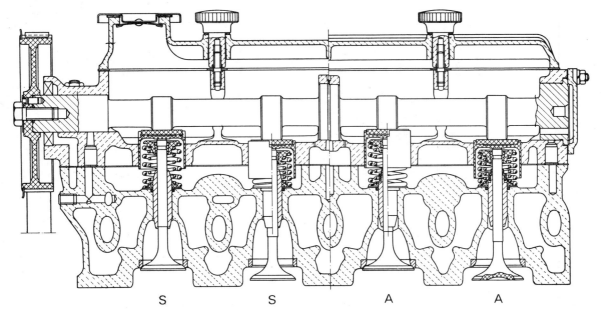

FIG 1:14 Longitudinal sections through the cylinder heads showing: A, inlet; and S, exhaust valves

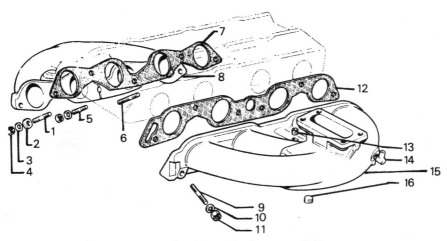

FIG 1:15 The inlet and exhaust manifolds

Key to Fig 1:15 1 Stud   2 Nut   3 Washer   4 Circlip   5, 6 Studs   7 Gasket   8 Exhaust manifold   9 Stud
10 Washer   11 Nut   12 Gasket   13 Nut   14 Vacuum union   15 Inlet manifold   16 Screw plug

spring is weakened, it will close up first when pressure is
applied. Take care that the springs do not fly out of the
vice under pressure. Any spring which is shorter or
weaker than standard should be renewed.

Decarbonising and valve grinding:

Avoid the use of sharp tools which will damage the
light-alloy cylinder head or piston surfaces. Remove all
traces of carbon deposits from the combustion chambers,
inlet and exhaust ports and joint faces. If the pistons have
not been removed and cleaned during previous engine
dismantling, plug the waterways and oil holes in the top

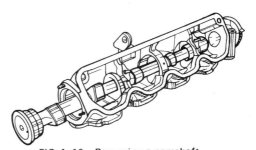

FIG 1:16 Removing a camshaft

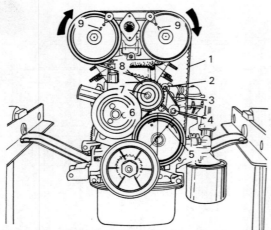

FIG 1:17 Aligning the timing marks on the camshaft and auxiliary shaft sprockets

For key see Fig 1:18

surface of the cylinder block with pieces of rag to prevent the entry of dirt, then clean the carbon from the piston crowns.

To grind-in valves, use medium grade carborundum paste unless the seats are in very good condition, when fine grade paste can be used at once. A light spring under the valve head will assist you in the operation and allow the valve to be lifted from its seat without releasing the grinding tool. Use a suction cup tool and grind with a semi-rotary movement, letting the valve rise off its seat occasionally by pressure of the spring under the head.

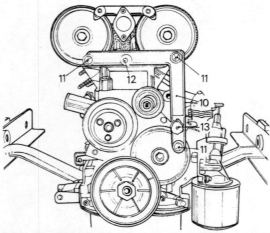

FIG 1:18 Installing the special tool to prevent sprocket rotation

Key to Figs 1:17 and 1:18   1 Timing belt   2 Pulley support   3 Return spring   4 Spring spacer attachment screw   5 Index hole in auxiliary shaft sprocket   6 Tensioner pulley support screw   7 Tensioner pulley support nut   8 Tensioner pulley   9 Index holes in inlet and exhaust camshaft sprockets   10 Special tool A.60319   11 Tool securing screws   12 Tool to cylinder head attachment screw   13 Tool to crankcase attachment screw

Use paste sparingly. When both seats have a smooth, matt-grey finish, clean away every trace of grinding paste from port and valve.

Reassemble the valves to the cylinder head in the reverse order of removal, making sure that all parts are fitted in their original positions, and fitting new oil seals on the valve guides if necessary. Lubricate the valve stems with engine oil before reassembling.

Camshafts:

Refer to **FIG 1:14** and remove the fixing bolts and camshaft sprockets. Remove the covers from the rear of the camshaft housings and withdraw the camshafts to the rear as shown in **FIG 1:16**. Check the camshaft lobes and bearing journals and the bearing bores in the camshaft housing for wear or scoring, renewing parts as necessary. Refitting the camshaft to the housing is a reversal of the removal procedure, lubricating the bearing surfaces with engine oil.

Refit the camshaft housings complete with camshafts to the cylinder head, tightening the fixing bolts alternatively and evenly to avoid straining the housings. Use new gaskets between the housings and cylinder head.

When cylinder head servicing is complete, refit the cylinder head as described in **Section 1:4** then check and adjust the valve clearances as described in **Section 1:7**.

1:6 Timing belt

Renewal:

The timing belt should be changed at intervals of 37,000 miles (60,000 km). **Care should be taken when handling the belt to avoid bending it to acute angles, as this could cause permanent damage to the belt fabric.**

Drain the radiator as described in **Chapter 4**, then remove the upper radiator hose and the alternator drive belt. Remove the timing gear cover.

Turn the engine until the camshaft timing holes on the sprockets align with the pointers on the index and the timing hole on the auxiliary shaft sprocket is 34 deg. from the vertical axis (towards distributor), as shown in **FIG 1:1** and **FIG 1:17**. Install tool A.60319 as shown in **FIG 1:18** to prevent the camshaft and auxiliary shafts from rotating after they have been correctly positioned. Also note that the crankshaft must not be rotated during the remaining belt renewal procedure.

Refer to **FIG 1:19** and loosen nut 3 and bolt 4. Exert pressure on the tensioner and pulley support 5 to relieve the belt tension and hold in this position while firmly retightening the bolt and nut. Remove the timing belt from the pulleys.

Refitting:

Carefully fit the timing belt over the pulleys. Loosen nut 3 and bolt 4 then firmly retighten them, so that the tensioner can tighten the belt. Remove the special tool used to prevent sprocket rotation, then turn the engine approximately three-quarters of a revolution forwards. Again loosen and firmly retighten nut 3 and bolt 4. Repeat this procedure two or three times, turning the engine approximately three-quarters of a turn each time.

This should correctly tension the timing belt.

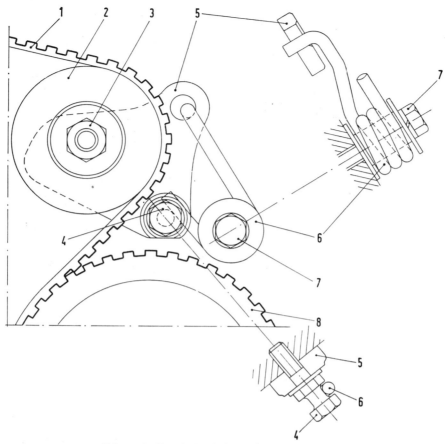

FIG 1:19   The timing belt tensioner components

Key to Fig 1:19   1 Timing belt   2 Idler   3 Clamp nut   4 Belt tensioner pulley support bolt   5 Belt tensioner
6 Tensioner spring   7 Spring retaining bolt   8 Auxiliary drive sprocket

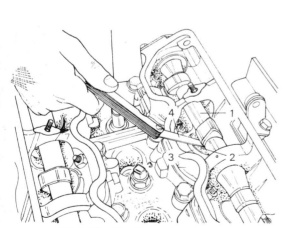

FIG 1:20   Checking valve clearances

Key to Fig 1:20   1 Camshaft   2 Tappet shim   3 Tappet
4 Feeler gauge

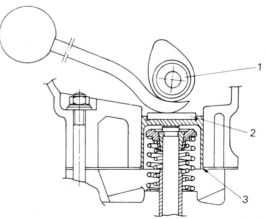

FIG 1:21   Using the pressure lever to push the tappet
away from the camshaft

Key to Fig 1:21   1 Camshaft lobe   2 Tappet shim
3 Tappet

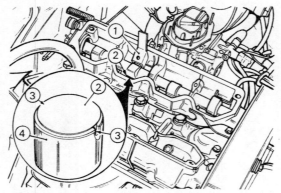

FIG 1 : 22 Fitting special tool to hold the tappet down for shim removal

Key to Fig 1 : 22   1 Tool A.60422   2 Tappet shim
3 Notches for shim removal   4 Tappet

FIG 1 : 23 Removing the shim from the tappet

Key to Fig 1 : 23   1 Tool A.60422   2 Camshaft   3 Tappet
shim   5 Tappet   6 Pliers

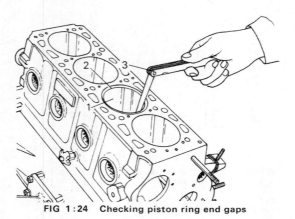

FIG 1 : 24 Checking piston ring end gaps

When belt tension is correct, the belt should deflect .31 to .35 inch (8 to 9 mm) when a load of 22 lb (10 kg) is applied at the centre of the belt run between the two camshaft pulleys. A special tool, A.95749/2 is available to check belt tension.

On completion, re-check the alignment of the camshaft and auxiliary shaft sprocket marks to ensure that the timing is still correct. Refit the parts removed and refill the cooling system.

If the timing belt is removed in the course of engine servicing or if it has become slack, always fit a new belt. Do not attempt to take up slackness by means of the tensioner.

1 : 7 Valve clearance adjustment

The correct adjustment of valve clearances is important as they affect engine timing and performance considerably. Excessive clearance will reduce valve lift and opening duration and reduce engine performance, causing excessive wear on the valve gear components and noisy operation. Insufficient or zero clearance will again affect engine timing and, in some circumstances, can hold the valve clear of its seat. This will result in much reduced performance due to lost compression and the possibility of burned valves and seats. Valve clearances should be checked and adjusted every 6000 miles (10,000 km) as routine maintenance and, additionally, whenever the cylinder head has been serviced.

Unscrew the knurled nuts and remove the camshaft cover plates from the top of the engine. Turn the engine until the cam lobe over the valve to be checked is pointing upwards, away from the tappet. Use feeler gauges to check the clearance between the cam and the tappet as shown in **FIG 1 : 20**. The correct clearance for inlet valves is .018 inch (.45 mm), for exhaust valves .023 inch (.60 mm). The engine must be cold when checking valve clearances. If adjustment is needed, use pressure lever A.60443 to lever the tappets away from the camshaft as shown in **FIG 1 : 21**. With the tappet held down, insert tool A.60422 and remove the pressure lever, as shown in **FIG 1 : 22**. Use a suitable pair of pliers to extract the shim from the tappet as shown in **FIG 1 : 23**.

If the clearance previously measured was greater than the correct measurement, it will be necessary to fit a new shim which is thicker by the amount of the difference and vice versa. For example, if an inlet valve clearance was found to be .65 mm, the clearance is .2 mm greater than the correct clearance of .45 mm and a shim must be used which is .2 mm thicker than the shim just removed. Shim thickness is marked on each shim, but it is recommended that this figure be checked by the use of a micrometer to ensure accuracy.

When the correct thickness of shim has been selected, fit it into place in the tappet and use the pressure lever to hold down the assembly while removing the second special tool. Recheck the clearance with feeler gauges to ensure that it is correct. Repeat the checking and adjustment procedure for each of the remaining valves. On completion, refit the parts removed in the reverse order of removal.

1 : 8 Pistons and connecting rods

Clean carbon deposits from the piston crowns, then gently ease the rings from their grooves and remove them over the top of the pistons. Clean carbon from the piston ring grooves, for which job a piece broken from an old piston ring and ground to a chisel point will prove an ideal tool. Inspect the pistons for score marks or any signs of seizure, which would dictate renewal.

Fit the piston rings one at a time into the bore from which they were removed, pushing them down with the inverted piston to ensure squareness. Measure the gap between the ends of the ring while it is positioned in the bore, using feeler gauges as shown in **FIG 1:24**. Compare the measurement with the figures given in **Technical Data**. Hold the ring in the piston groove from which it was removed as shown in **FIG 1:25**, then measure the side clearance with feeler gauges. Compare the measurement with the figures given in **Technical Data**. If the clearance measurements in either test are at or near the wear limits, new rings must be fitted. Excessive ring clearance can be responsible for high oil consumption and poor engine performance.

Check the cylinder bores for score marks and remove glaze and carbon deposits. Badly scored or worn surfaces will dictate a rebore to accept new pistons, this being a specialist job. The fitting of new pistons to connecting rods must be carried out by a Fiat service station, due to the need for special heating and press equipment to remove and refit the gudgeon pin.

Check the clearance of each piston in its bore, measuring with feeler gauges at right angles to the gudgeon pin and at 2 inch (52 mm) from the piston crown for 1600 and 2000 engines, or at 1.2 inch (30 mm) from the piston base for 1800 engines, as shown in **FIG 1:26**. Correct clearance is .0027 to .0035 inch (.070 to .090 mm) for 1600 and 2000 engines, or .0016 to .0024 inch (.040 to .060 mm) for 1800 engines. Excessive clearance will dictate the fitting of new pistons and, possibly, reboring of the cylinder bores.

Connecting rods:

If there has been a big-end bearing failure, the crankpin must be examined for damage and for transfer of metal to its surface. The oilway in the crankshaft must be checked to ensure that there is no obstruction. Big-end bearing clearance can be checked by the use of Plastigage, which is the trade name for a precisely calibrated plastic filament. The filament is laid along the bearing to be measured for working clearance as shown in **FIG 1:27**, the bearing cap fitted and the bolts tightened to the specified torque. The bearing is then dismantled and the thickness of the flattened filament measured with the scale supplied with the material. The figure thus measured is the actual bearing clearance.

Requirements for the use of Plastigage:

1 Each main bearing must be measured separately and none of the remaining bearing caps must be fitted during the operation.
2 The bearing surfaces must be clean and free from oil.
3 The crankshaft must not be turned during measuring procedure.
4 The point at which the measurement is taken must be close to the respective dead centre position.
5 No hammer blows must be applied to the bearing or cap.

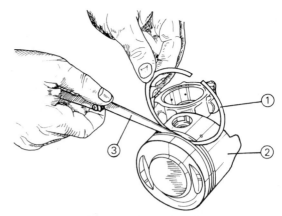

FIG 1:25 Checking piston ring side clearances

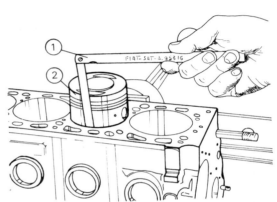

FIG 1:26 Checking piston clearance in the cylinder bore

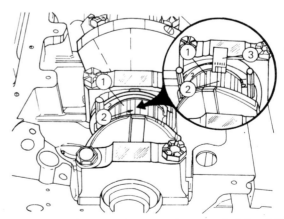

FIG 1:27 Using Plastigage to measure shell bearing clearances

Key to Fig 1:27   1 Crankpin   2 Plastigage
3 Measuring scale

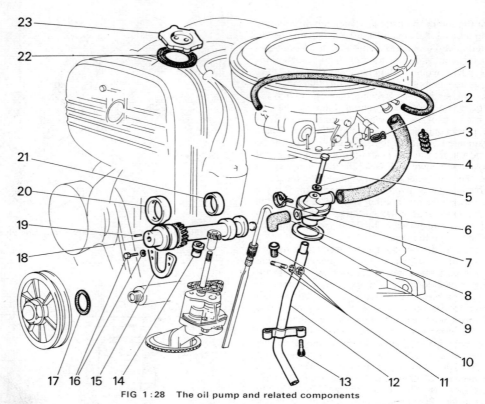

FIG 1:28 The oil pump and related components

Key to Fig 1:28   1 Vapour hose   2 Collar   3 Backfire suppressor   4 Breather hose   5 Screw and flat washer   6 Breather
7 Collar   8 Hose   9 Breather seal   10 Vapour return connector   11 Stud, lock washer and nut   12 Breather tube
13 Screw   14 Oil pump drive gear bush   15 Auxiliary shaft retaining plate   16 Screw and lock washer   17 Spring washer
18 Auxiliary shaft   19 Locating dowel   20 Auxiliary shaft front bush   21 Auxiliary shaft rear bush   22 Seal   23 Oil
filler cap

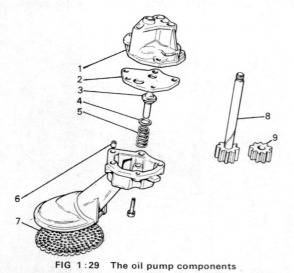

FIG 1:29 The oil pump components

Key to Fig 1:29   1 Housing   2 Plate   3 Valve   4 Washer
5 Spring   6 Locating pin   7 Filter   8 Drive shaft
9 Gearwheel

Procedure:

Place a length of plastic filament identical to the width of the bearing on the crankshaft journal, then fit the main or big-end bearing cap with liners and tighten to the specified torque. Remove the bearing cap and measure the width of the flattened filament to obtain the running clearance for that bearing. Check the figure with those given in **Technical Data** in the **Appendix**. If the bearing running clearance is too high, new bearing shells must be selected by the measurement procedure to bring the running clearance to within the specified limits.

1:9 Crankshaft and main bearings

If there has been a main bearing failure, the crankshaft journal must be checked for damage and for transfer of metal to its surface. The oilways in the crankshaft must be checked to ensure that there is no obstruction. Main bearing clearance can be checked by the use of Plastigage, in the manner described in **Section 1:8** for big-end bearings, the procedure being the same. If there is any doubt about the condition of the crankshaft it should be taken to a specialist for more detailed checks.

Examine starter ring gear on the flywheel. If the teeth are broken or worn, a new ring gear must be fitted by a Fiat service station. When reassembling the engine, check the crankshaft end float as described in **Section 1:13**.

1 : 10 Cylinder block

Thoroughly degrease the cylinder block and crankcase unit and blow through all the oilways until they are clear. Inspect the block for any signs of cracks or other damages that would dictate renewal. Make sure that the mating surfaces on the castings are clean and free from old gasket material. Do not use sharp tools for cleaning purposes as these could damage the mating surfaces.

If the cylinder liners require reboring or renewing, the work should be entrusted to a Fiat service station as special equipment is required to carry out the work.

Use a straightedge laid across the mating surfaces and the top of the block to ensure that they are flat and square. If the surface is found to be out of true, regrinding by a Fiat service station will be necessary.

1 : 11 The oil pump

The oil pump and related components are shown in **FIG 1 : 28**. The oil pump is gear-driven from the auxiliary shaft.

With the drive shaft downwards, clamp the oil pump in a vice having padded jaws and remove the fixing bolts to separate the casing halves. Dismantle the pump into the order shown in **FIG 1 : 29**, then thoroughly clean all parts.

Refit the pump gears and check the clearance between the tip of the gear teeth and the inside of the housing as shown in **FIG 1 : 30**. This clearance should be .0043 to .0070 inch (.110 to .180 mm). Lay a straightedge across the pump joint face, over the gears as shown in **FIG 1 : 31** and use the feeler gauge to check the clearance between the straightedge and the gear faces. The clearance should be .0012 to .0045 inch (.031 to .116 mm). If the clearance is excessive in either test, renew the gears and/or the pump housing as necessary.

Inspect the oil pressure relief valve spring for cracks or weakening. The load needed to compress the spring to a length of .88 inch (22.5 mm) must not be less than 12.2 lb (5.8 kg). If the spring is weakened, damaged or distorted it should be renewed.

On completion reassemble the oil pump and evenly tighten the securing screws. Make sure that the gears can rotate freely when the pump is assembled.

1 : 12 The oil filter

The oil filter is of the renewable cartridge type and should be renewed every 6000 miles (10,000 km). To do this, unscrew the oil filter cartridge as shown in **FIG 1 : 32** and discard it.

Clean the filter mounting face on the engine then lightly coat the new seal with engine oil. Make sure that the seal is correctly fitted, then screw the new filter into place until it just contacts its seating. From this point tighten a further three-quarters of a turn by hand only. Do not over-tighten the filter or oil leaks may result. A strap type tool may be used to remove the filter unit if it is too stiff to be unscrewed by hand, but never use anything but hand pressure to tighten the unit. On completion, check the engine oil level, start the engine then check for oil leaks around the filter unit.

1 : 13 Reassembling the engine

Reassembly of the engine is a reversal of the dismantling procedure, noting the following points. Use new

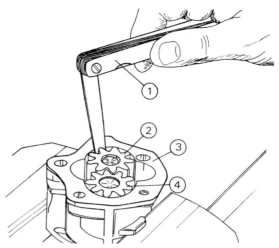

FIG 1 : 30   Checking oil pump gear side clearance

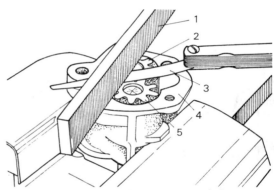

FIG 1 : 31   Checking oil pump gear end clearance

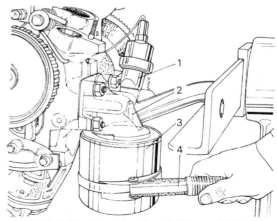

FIG 1 : 32   Removing the oil filter cartridge

Key to Fig 1 : 32   1 Oil pressure sender unit   2 Oil filter support   3 Oil filter cartridge   4 Strap tool for removal

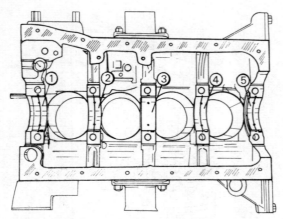

FIG 1:33 The crankshaft bearing shell positions

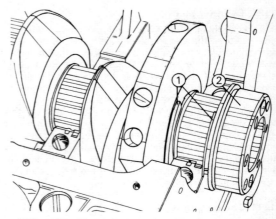

FIG 1:34 The thrust bearings 1 and crankshaft 2

gaskets throughout and lubricate all moving parts with engine oil during reassembly. Observe the torque wrench settings given in **Technical Data** when tightening the various fixtures.

Clean and dry the main bearing shells. Fit the shells to their respective cylinder block and cap positions as shown in **FIG 1:33**, then lightly lubricate the bearing surfaces with engine oil. Carefully fit the crankshaft into position. Make sure that the thrust rings are correctly located at the end main bearing position as shown in **FIG 1:34**. Evenly tighten all the crankshaft bearing cap bolts and make sure that the crankshaft can rotate freely. Use a suitable dial gauge to check crankshaft end play which should be between .0021 and .012 inch (.055 and .305 mm). If end play is above these limits, new thrust bearings should be fitted. These are available in standard size or .005 inch (.127 mm) oversize.

Fit new oil seals to the front and rear coverplates. Oil the pistons before inserting them in the cylinder bores, noting that the reference number on the connecting rod faces the left and the oil hole in the rod towards the auxiliary shaft. Use a suitable clamp when entering the piston rings into the bores. Make sure that the big-end caps are fitted to their correct respective connecting rods, noting the reference numbers stamped on each part. Use new big-end cap nuts.

When installing the oil pump to the crankcase, temporarily refit the distributor to ensure that the oil pump drive shaft is flush with the distributor drive shaft.

Tighten the sump fixing bolts diagonally to avoid distortion, making sure that the gasket is not displaced. Follow the instructions given in **Sections 1:4** and **1:6** to refit the cylinder head and timing belt. When refitting the distributor, follow the instructions given in **Chapter 3** to ensure correct ignition timing.

1:14 Refitting the engine

This operation is a reversal of the removal procedure detailed in **Section 1:2**. Refit the gearbox as described in **Chapter 6**.

On completion, the sump and cooling system should be refilled and the engine started. Check the operation of the various warning lights and for water, oil and fuel leaks.

After a period of running at normal operating temperature, the engine should be allowed to cool right down and the cylinder head fixing bolts retightened to the correct torque figure and the valve clearances checked.

1:15 Fault diagnosis

(a) Engine will not start

1 Defective coil
2 Faulty distributor capacitor
3 Dirty, pitted or incorrectly set contact points
4 Ignition wires loose or insulation faulty
5 Water on spark plug leads
6 Battery discharged, corrosion of terminals
7 Faulty or jammed starter
8 Sparking plug leads wrongly connected
9 Vapour lock in fuel pipes
10 Defective fuel pump
11 Overchoking or underchoking
12 Blocked fuel filter or carburetter jet
13 Leaking valves
14 Sticking valves
15 Valve timing incorrect
16 Ignition timing incorrect

(b) Engine stalls

1 Check 1, 2, 3, 4, 5, 10, 11, 12, 13 and 14 in (a)
2 Sparking plugs defective or gaps incorrect
3 Retarded ignition
4 Mixture too weak
5 Water in fuel system
6 Petrol tank vent blocked
7 Incorrect valve clearances

(c) Engine idles badly

1 Check 2 and 7 in (b)
2 Air leak at manifold joints
3 Carburetter adjustment wrong
4 Air leak in carburetter
5 Over-rich mixture
6 Worn piston rings
7 Worn valve stems or guides
8 Weak exhaust valve springs

(d) Engine misfires

1 Check 1, 2, 3, 4, 5, 8, 10, 12, 13, 14, 15 and 16 in (a)
2 Weak or broken valve springs

(e) Engine overheats (see **Chapter 4**)

(f) Compression low

1 Check 13 and 14 in (a); 6 and 7 in (c) and 2 in (d)
2 Worn piston ring grooves
3 Scored or worn cylinder bores

(g) Engine lacks power

1 Check 3, 10, 11, 12, 13, 14, 15 and 16 in (a); 2, 3, 4 and 7 in (b); 6 and 7 in (c) and 2 in (d). Also check (e) and (f)
2 Leaking joint washers
3 Fouled sparking plugs
4 Automatic advance not working

(h) Burnt valves or seats

1 Check 13 and 14 in (a); 7 in (b) and 2 in (d). Also check (e)
2 Excessive carbon round valve seats and head

(j) Sticking valves

1 Check 2 in (d)
2 Bent valve stem
3 Scored valve stem or guide
4 Incorrect valve clearances

(k) Excessive cylinder wear

1 Check 11 in (a)
2 Lack of oil

3 Dirty oil
4 Piston rings gummed up or broken
5 Badly fitting piston rings
6 Connecting rod bent

(l) Excessive oil consumption

1 Check 6 and 7 in (c) and check (k)
2 Ring gaps too wide
3 Oil return holes in piston choked with carbon
4 Scored cylinders
5 Oil level too high
6 External oil leaks

(m) Crankshaft and connecting rod bearing failure

1 Check 2 in (k)
2 Restricted oilways
3 Worn journals or crankpins
4 Loose bearing caps
5 Extremely low oil pressure
6 Bent connecting rod

(n) Internal water leakage (see **Chapter 4**)

(o) Poor water circulation (see **Chapter 4**)

(p) Corrosion (see **Chapter 4**)

(q) High fuel consumption (see **Chapter 2**)

(r) Engine vibration

1 Loose generator bolts
2 Engine mountings loose or defective
3 Misfiring due to mixture, ignition or mechanical faults

NOTES

CHAPTER 2

THE FUEL SYSTEM

2 : 1 Description

Fuel is drawn from a rear mounted tank by an engine driven pump and delivered to a dual-barrel downdraught carburetter. The Weber or Solex carburetters, which are similar in operation and construction, are fitted with a manual choke on early models. On later models the Weber carburetter is fitted with an automatic choke operated by coolant temperature. Details are given in the **Technical Data** at the end of this manual.

2 : 2 Air cleaner

The air cleaner is fitted with a paper element which should be renewed at 6000 miles (10,000 km) intervals. Detach the cover plate from the air cleaner casing and lift out the old element. Wipe the inside of the casing and cover to remove dirt and grease, then reassemble the air cleaner using a new filter element.

To remove the complete air cleaner assembly, remove the cover and filter element then detach any hoses attached to the air cleaner casing. Remove the nuts securing the air cleaner casing to the carburetter then lift the unit from the car. It is a good plan to use pieces of clean rag to cover the intake throats of the carburetter when removing the air cleaner casing to avoid dropping small components into the carburetter and to avoid the entry of dirt.

The position of the air intake to the air cleaner should be set so that the seam lines up with the blue or letter **E** reference mark in warm climates or summer, for cold climates or winter the intake should be turned so that the seam lines up with the red reference mark or letter **I**.

2 : 3 Fuel pump

The fuel pump, shown in **FIG 2 : 1**, is mounted on the lefthand side of the engine. The filter screen 5 is accessible with the pump installed. Take out the screw 1 and lift off the cover 3 complete with its seal and the sealing washer 2. It may be necessary to disconnect the supply line to the pump and plug it so that fuel does not syphon through. Lift off the filter 5 and wash it in clean fuel. Wash or scrape out any sediment from the bowl on the fuel pump. Dry the filter with compressed air and check that the gauze is unbroken. Compressed air can be used to clean out the bowl but take care not to blow down the inlet port in the bowl. Check that the seals for the cover are satisfactory. Fit the filter back into position followed by the cover. Tighten the screw until the cover is very lightly nipped and partially rotate the cover to ensure that it is fully and squarely seated before fully tightening the screw.

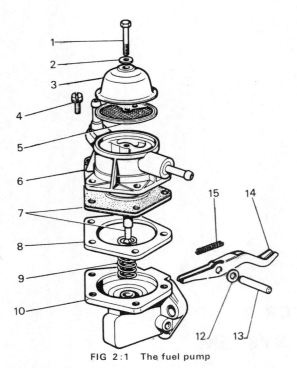

FIG 2:1 The fuel pump

Key to Fig 2:1 1 Cover fixing screw 2 Washer 3 Cover
4 Cover body screw 5 Filter 6 Upper body 7 Diaphragm
8 Spacer 9 Spring 10 Lower body 12 Washer 13 Pivot
pin 14 Operating lever 15 Lever return spring

To remove the fuel pump, first disconnect the two fuel
supply pipes, inlet from the tank and outlet to the
carburetter, plugging the pipe leading from the tank to
avoid loss of fuel. Unscrew the two bolts securing the
pump to the crankcase and lift off. Clean off all external
dirt and oil and dismantle completely.

Wash all parts in fuel and see that all sludge is removed
from the filter gauze and the casing. Examine the
diaphragm for any trace of cracking or hardening and
check that the return spring and that of the operating
lever are not weak or deformed. Renew any defective
parts.

When reassembling always use new seals and gaskets
and smear them lightly with grease before fitting. Place
gaskets and insulator over the studs on the crankcase,
then fit the pump, checking that the lever is free on its
spindle and making correct contact with the face of the
cam. Refit the fuel pipes. Start the engine and check for
fuel leaks.

2 : 4 Weber DMS adjustments

Note that an accurate tachometer, connected in
accordance with the manufacturer's instructions, is
needed to set the idle speed accurately. When the idle
speed and mixture adjustments have been completed, the
CO (carbon monoxide) content of the exhaust gas should
be checked, and further fine adjustments made, as necessary, to bring CO content within legal limits where these

apply. If suitable analytical equipment is not available, the
car should be taken to a service station for a final check.

The idle adjustment screws for the Weber 34 DMS are
shown in **FIG 2:2**. Note that the throttle stop screw 3
is locked in position and should not be disturbed for normal
routine adjustments. If the carburetter has been dismantled, screw 3 should be carefully tightened until it just
contacts the linkage with the throttles fully closed. Then
tighten the locknut to retain this position.

If no improvement results from the following adjustments, service the carburetter and check float level as
described in **Section 2 : 7**. These adjustments will only be
effective if the sparking plugs, contact points and other
systems are in good order. The engine must be at normal
operating temperature, and the air cleaner removed,
before starting these adjustments.

Start the engine and allow it to idle. Carefully adjust the
mixture screw 1 to obtain the smoothest possible idle.
Adjust idle speed screw 2 to obtain the correct idling
speed. If necessary make fine adjustments to screws 1
and then 2 to obtain a smooth idle at the correct speed. On
completion lightly lubricate the carburetter linkages and
refit the air cleaner.

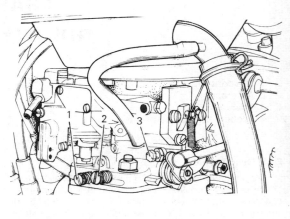

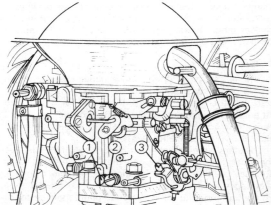

FIG 2:2 The idle adjustment screws on Weber (above)
and Solex (below) carburetters. Service adjustments
are made with screws 1 and 2 only, screw 3 being locked
in the correct position

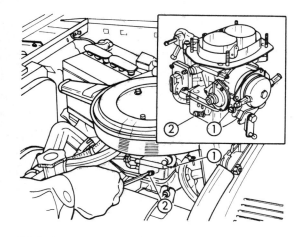

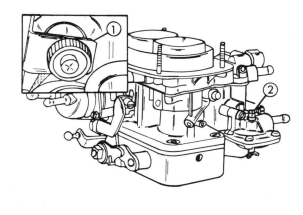

FIG 2:3 Idle speed screw 1 and mixture screw 2 on the Weber 32 ADF carburetter

FIG 2:4 Emission control button 1 and fast-idle adjustment screw 2

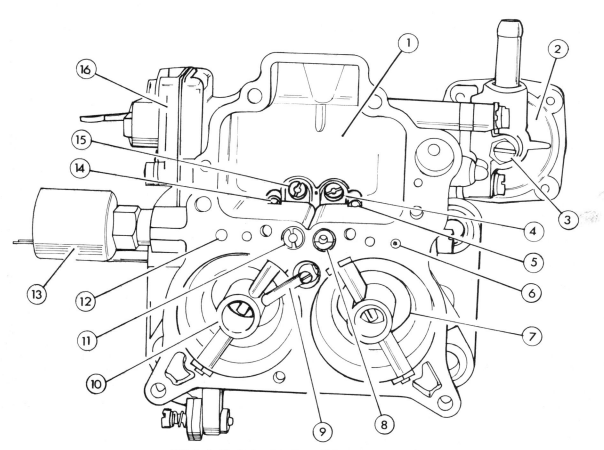

FIG 2:5 Typical carburetter with top cover removed

Key to Fig 2:5   1 Float chamber   2 Fast-idle diaphragm assembly   3 Fast-idle adjustment screw   4 Secondary main jet 5 High speed gas inlet   6 High speed air passage   7 Secondary venturi   8 Secondary air correction jet   9 Accelerator pump nozzle   10 Primary venturi   11 Primary air correction jet   12 High speed air passage   13 Idle shut-off solenoid   14 High speed gas inlet   15 Primary main jet   16 Accelerator pump housing

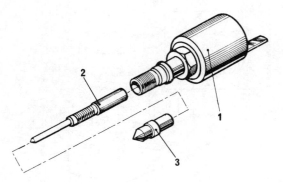

FIG 2 : 6   Idle shut-off solenoid 1, plunger 2 and idle jet 3

2 : 5 Weber ADF adjustments
Slow idle adjustment :

Refer to **Section 2 : 4** and note the comments regarding an accurate tachometer. This is particularly important when setting the fast-idle speed as described later. The idle speed adjustment screw and idle mixture adjustment screw are shown in **FIG 2 : 3**. On later cars the idle mixture screw is sealed with a plastic cap; this should be removed only if a satisfactory idle cannot be obtained by the use of the idle speed screw alone.

With the engine at normal operating temperature and the air cleaner **in position**, allow it to idle and adjust screw 1 to obtain a slow but even idling speed. Now adjust screw 2 to obtain the fastest possible idling speed then re-adjust screw 1 to return the idling speed to the correct figure. A further fine adjustment of screw 2 may then be necessary to obtain a smooth idle at the correct speed.

On models fitted with automatic transmission, apply the footbrake and select **D**. Check that the engine does not hesitate or stall when drive is engaged. If it does increase the idling speed slightly by adjusting screw 1.

On models fitted with air conditioning the carburetter is fitted with a vacuum operated device which increases the idle speed to compensate for additional loads. With the idle speed correctly adjusted, switch on the air conditioning system and check that the idle speed is maintained correctly. If not leave the system switched on and adjust the screw fitted over the vacuum tube connection.

Fast-idle adjustment :

Ensure the gear lever is in neutral, or **N** on automatic transmission cars, start the engine and allow it to idle. Refer to **FIG 2 : 4**, depress and hold the emission control button 1. Accelerate the engine to 2000 rev/min then allow it to return to idle. The fast-idle speed should now be 1600 ± 50 rev/min for manual transmission models or 1300 ± 50 rev/min for automatic transmission models. If the fast-idle speed is outside these limits, adjust by turning fast-idle adjustment screw 2. On models fitted with air conditioning refer to **Section 2 : 4** for the method of adjustment.

2 : 6 Solex C34 adjustments

The adjustment screws are shown in **FIG 2 : 2**. Adjustments are carried out in the same manner as described in **Section 2 : 4** for the Weber DMS carburetter.

2 : 7 Servicing the carburetter

If poor running characteristics are traced to the carburetter and the adjustment procedures described previously do not cure the fault, the unit should be removed and the top cover detached. The float mechanism should be checked and the float chamber, jets and passages cleaned. If this does not cure the faults, the carburetter assemblies and automatic choke mechanism should be checked by a service station.

Removal and refitting :

Remove the air cleaner as described in **Section 2 : 2**. Disconnect the accelerator linkage from the carburetter lever and the water hoses from the automatic choke, if applicable. Disconnect the fuel and vacuum pipes, noting the position of each pipe so that it can be refitted correctly. Plug the fuel and water hoses to prevent leakage and entry of dirt. Remove the four nuts securing the carburetter to the manifold and lift off the carburetter and gasket.

Refitting is a reversal of the removal procedure, using a new flange gasket. Tighten the securing nuts alternately and evenly to avoid distortion of the flange.

On completion, start the engine and check for fuel or water leaks at the hose connections. Check the coolant level as described in **Chapter 4**. If necessary carry out the slow-running adjustments described in the previous sections.

Dismantling and servicing :

Remove the fixing screws and detach the top cover assembly from the carburetter body, taking care not to damage the float mechanism which remains connected to the top cover. Empty the fuel from the carburetter float chamber into a suitable container. Remove and discard the cover gasket. The locations of jets and passages in the body of a typical carburetter are shown in **FIG 2 : 5**. The unit illustrated shows the idle shut-off solenoid at 13 fitted to some models. Individual components of the solenoid are shown in **FIG 2 : 6**. The layout of all carburetters is similar although the idle shut-off valve may not be used.

Carefully remove the jets, noting the position of each one so that it may be refitted in the correct position. Clean all jets and passages using clean petrol and compressed air or a tyre pump. Use a small brush for cleaning purposes. **Do not use cloth or a wire probe.**

Refer to **FIG 2 : 7** or **2 : 8**, unscrew and remove the hexagonal plug from the fuel inlet casing and carefully remove the wire gauge filter. Wash the filter in clean petrol. Renew the filter if it is damaged or will not clean properly. Carefully refit the filter, then fit and tighten the plug.

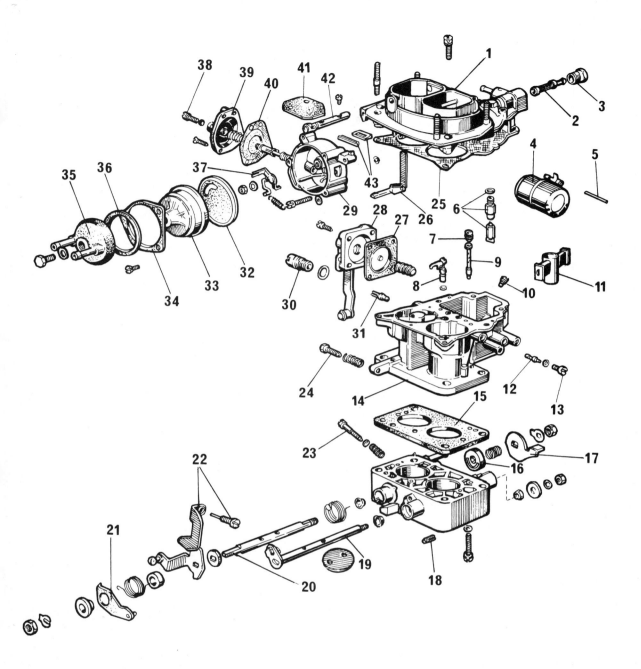

FIG 2 : 7   Weber ADF carburetter components

Key to Fig 2 : 7   1 Top cover   2 Fuel filter   3 Filter plug   4 Float   5 Float pivot   6 Needle valve assembly
7 Air correction jet (2)   8 Pump injector   9 Emulsion tube (2)   10 Main jet (2)   11 Venturi   12 Secondary idle jet
13 Idle jet carrier   14 Main body   15 Insulating flange   16 Shutter   17 Pump cam   18 Secondary throttle stop screw
19 Secondary throttle spindle   20 Primary throttle spindle   21 Throttle lever   22 Choke lever and screw   23 Idle mixture control
screw   24 Primary throttle stop screw   25 Gasket   26 Choke linkage   27 Accelerator pump diaphragm   28 Pump cover
29 Automatic choke housing   30 Idle jet carrier   31 Primary idle jet   32 Heat shield   33 Bi-metal spring and housing
34 Gasket   35 Water jacket cover   36 Seal   37 Bi-metal spring lever   38 Choke stop screw   39 Choke diaphragm cover
40 Choke diaphragm   41 Choke plate   42 Choke spindle   43 Dust cover

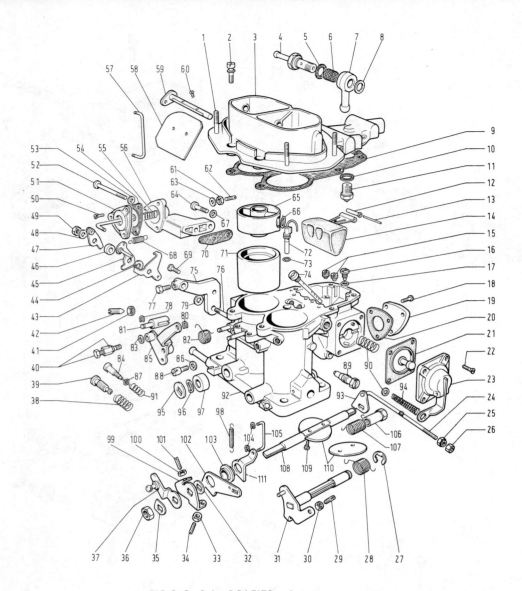

FIG 2:8   Solex C 34 EIES carburetter components

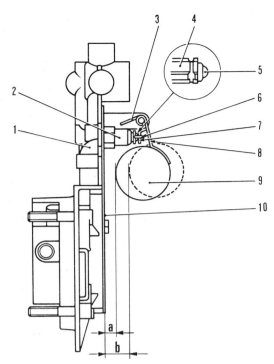

FIG 2 : 9   Weber carburetter float setting diagram

Key to Fig 2 : 9   1 Carburetter cover   2 Needle valve
3 Float lug   4 Needle   5 Moveable ball   6 Return hook
7 Tongue   8 Float arm   9 Float   10 Gasket

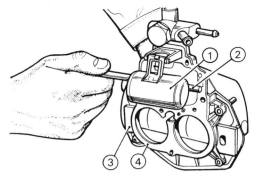

FIG 2 : 10   Setting the Weber carburetter float level

Key to Fig 2 : 10   1 Float   2 Gauge A.95121
3 Carburetter cover   4 Cover gasket

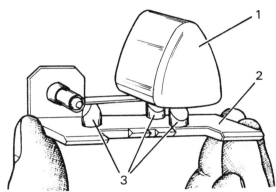

FIG 2 : 11   Checking the Solex carburetter float arm
setting

Key to Fig 2 : 11   1 Float   2 Gauge A95134   3 Gauge
setting points

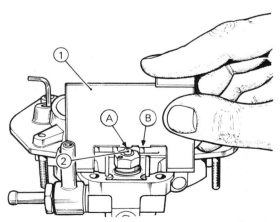

FIG 2 : 12   Checking the Solex carburetter needle valve
setting

Key to Fig 2 : 12   1 Gauge A95134   2 Needle valve

Carefully detach the hinge pin to remove the float from
the carburetter top cover. Check the float for leaks by
immersing it in fairly hot water and watching for a stream
of air bubbles. Any leaks may also be detected by shaking
the float and listening for fuel splashing inside. If the float
leaks or is damaged at all, it should be renewed.

Unscrew and remove the needle valve assembly shown
as 2 in **FIG 2 : 9**. If a washer is used between the valve
body and the top cover, this must be retained for correct
refitting as it governs the float level. Check the assembly
for wear or damage and inspect the tapered seat of the
needle for any sign of a ridge. Renew complete assembly if
any faults are found. Install the needle valve assembly with
the sealing washer, if fitted, then fit the float and ensure
that it moves freely on its hinge pin.

Float level setting :

Weber 34 DMS :

In order to set the float level correctly a special gauge,
A95121, or suitable .27 inch (7 mm) bar or drill will be
required.

With the gasket in position on the top cover, hold the
cover vertically as shown in **FIG 2 : 9**, so that the float arm
rests lightly against the needle valve. In this position check
that measurement **a** is .27 inch (7 mm) by using the
special tool or a suitable drill or round bar. If the
measurement is incorrect, carefully bend the float arm as
necessary making sure that the float is kept square to the

upper face. The maximum distance of the float from the cover, when the float is allowed to hang free with the cover horizontal, should be .57 inch (14.5 mm) as shown at **b** in **FIG 2 : 9**.

Weber 32 ADF :

Refer to **FIG 2 : 9**. Check the level in the same way as described for the Weber 34 DMS carburetter but note that measurement **a** should be .24 inch (6 mm) and distance **b** should be .55 inch (14 mm).

Automatic choke :

This device is regulated by a bi-metal spring influenced by the temperature of the coolant in the engine. When starting from cold, the accelerator pedal must be fully depressed and then slowly released to set the choke. When the engine is running, the depression below the throttle plate is used to open the choke and so prevent strangulation. As the engine warms up the bi-metal spring progressively opens the choke plate. Two special tools are required for the correct setting of the automatic choke and the procedure is as follows :

Refer to **FIG 2 : 13**. Screw in the tool 1 into the hole provided and set the adjusting screw 3 on the second step of the cam 4. Screw out, but do not remove, the stop screw 5. Press the small lever 6 in the direction of the arrow and then turn the tool 1 until the choke plate 7 is opened to the dimension given by tool 2; this is .177 inch (4.5 mm). Now screw in the stop screw until it contacts the diaphragm spindle. This sets the minimum choke opening.

To set the maximum opening, with the tool 1 still screwed in, release the tag 6 from the bi-metal spring and check that the choke plate is now open by .263 inch (6.7 mm) as shown by tool 2a. If this dimension is not achieved, fit a new choke mechanism.

In the absence of the special tool a suitable gauge rod or drill could be used for this operation.

Solex C 34 :

In order to set the correct level special tool gauge A95134 will be required. Fit the float assembly to the gauge, as shown in **FIG 2 : 11** and ensure the float rests on the points 3 with no gap at any point. If not, carefully bend the float arm to obtain the correct settings. Invert the top cover and use the gauge to check the needle valve setting, as shown in **FIG 2 : 12**. With index **A** in line with the valve needle, the needle should not interfere with the gauge. Slide the gauge along so index **B** is aligned with the valve needle. In this position the needle should contact the gauge. If the index **A** contacts the needle, or the needle does not contact index **B**, the sealing washer should be changed to one of appropriate thickness to set the needle assembly in the correct position.

The checking and adjusting of the automatic choke requires special tools and gauges. If the operation of the choke is unsatisfactory the car must be taken to a suitable service agent to enable the checks and adjustments to be carried out.

2 : 8 Fault diagnosis

(a) Leakage or insufficient fuel delivered

1 Air vent to tank restricted
2 Fuel pipes blocked

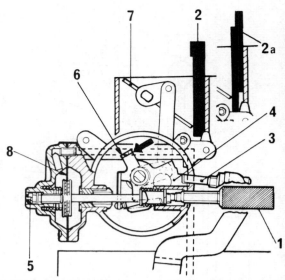

FIG 2 : 13 Sectional view of the automatic choke, showing method of adjusting the minimum plate opening (ADF carburetter)

Key to Fig 2 : 13 1 Tool No. A65502 2 and 2a Tool No. A65506 3 Adjusting screw 4 Stepped cam 5 Stop screw 6 Lever tag 7 Choke plate 8 Diaphragm

3 Air leaks at pipe connections
4 Fuel filter blocked
5 Pump gaskets faulty
6 Pump diaphragm defective
7 Pump valve sticking or seating badly

(b) Excessive fuel consumption

1 Carburetter requires adjustment
2 Fuel leakage
3 Sticking choke unit
4 Float level too high
5 Dirty air cleaner
6 Excessive engine temperature
7 Brakes binding
8 Idling speed too high

(c) Idling speed too high

1 Incorrect idle speed adjustment
2 Rich fuel mixture
3 Throttle control sticking
4 Choke unit sticking
5 Worn throttle valves or shafts

(d) Noisy fuel pump

1 Loose pump mountings
2 Air leaks on suction side of diaphragm
3 Obstruction in fuel pipe line
4 Clogged fuel filter

(e) No fuel delivery

1 Float needle valve stuck
2 Tank vent blocked
3 Defective pump diaphragm
4 Pump valve stuck
5 Pipe line obstructed
6 Bad air leak on suction side of pump

CHAPTER 3

THE IGNITION SYSTEM

3 : 1 Description

The ignition system may be either conventional, or an inductive discharge electronic system.

The conventional system comprises an ignition coil, distributor and contact breaker system. The distributor incorporates automatic timing control by means of a centrifugal mechanism. The ignition coil is wound as an auto-transformer. The primary and secondary windings are connected in series, the common junction being connected to the contact breaker, with the positive feed from the battery going to the opposite terminal of the primary winding via the ignition switch.

When the contacts are closed, current flows in the coil primary winding, magnetising the core and setting up a strong magnetic field. When the contacts open, current is cut off and the magnetic field collapses. This induces a high current in the primary winding and a high voltage in the secondary. The primary current is used to charge the capacitor connected across the contacts, the flow is high and virtually instantaneous. It is this high current peak which induces the surge in the secondary winding and produces the sparking voltage across the plug points.

The high energy inductive discharge electronic system consists of an electronic pulse generator, and electronic module/ignition coil assembly and an ignition distributor. Pulses are generated in a coil wired to a magnetic circuit of the variable gap type. It consists of a permanent magnet, fixed plate with stator pole, coil and reluctor integral with the distributor shaft. As the reluctor rotates inside the distributor a magnetic pulse is generated each time a point of the reluctor passes the stationary magnet. The pulse is then processed by the transistorised electronic module which interrupts the circuit of the coil primary winding and generates high voltage current in the secondary winding. This in turn produces the spark across the plug points.

3 : 2 Routine maintenance

The attachment of the distributor to the engine and the cap to the distributor is shown in **FIG 3 : 1**. The distributor with the cap removed is shown in **FIG 3 : 2**.

Always keep the distributor cap, HT leads, and the top of the ignition coil clean and free from dirt or moisture. Wipe the parts with a soft clean cloth, not forgetting to wipe the inside of the distributor cap occasionally as well.

Lubrication:

This should be carried out at intervals of 6000 miles (10,000 km). Take out the screws which secure the distributor cap and lift off the cap. Remove the rotor from the top of the distributor shaft and wipe clean the cam which opens the contact breaker points. Apply a very

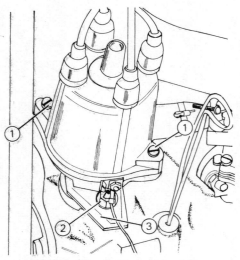

FIG 3:1 The distributor installation

Key to Fig 3:1 1 Cap attachment screws 2 Securing nut
3 Clip

thin smear of grease to the cam, a few drops of oil to the shaft and weights, then refit the rotor. Avoid allowing grease or oil to contaminate the contact breaker points, lubricating sparingly for this reason.

Adjusting the contact points:

Turn the engine until one of the cams has opened the points to the fullest extent, then check the gap between the points with a clean feeler gauge. The correct gap is .015 to .017 inch (.37 to .43 mm). To adjust the gap, slacken the screw B in **FIG 3:2** so that the points can be altered but do not move on their own. Insert a screwdriver into the slot D and by rotating the screwdriver the points gap can be altered. Slide a feeler gauge of the correct thickness between the unworn portions of the contacts A and adjust them until the feeler gauge is just

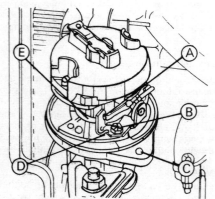

FIG 3:2 The distributor with the cap removed

Key to Fig 3:2 A Points B Screw C Housing D Slot
E Capacitor lead

lightly nipped and slight drag is felt on it as it is moved. Tighten the screw B and check that the adjustment has not altered.

Cleaning the contact points:

Use a fine carborundum stone or a special contact point file to polish the points if they are dirty or pitted, taking care to keep their faces flat and square. On completion, wipe away all dust with a cloth moistened in petrol, then set the points gap as described previously. If the points are badly pitted or burned and would require excessive removal of material to clean up, a new contact point set should be obtained and fitted.

3:3 Ignition faults:

If the engine runs unevenly, set it to idle at about 1000 rev/min and, taking care not to touch any metal part of the plug leads, remove and replace each lead from its sparking plug in turn. Doing this to a plug which is firing properly will accentuate the uneven running but will make no difference if that plug is not firing. To avoid shocks during this test, it is advisable to wear a thick glove or use a pair of insulated pliers to pull off the leads.

Having located the faulty cylinder, stop the engine and remove the plug lead. Remove the plug connector from the lead so that the end of the lead is exposed. If the plug connector cannot be removed, insert a drill or suitable metal bar into the connector to act as an extension. Start the engine and hold the lead carefully to avoid shocks so that the end is about $\frac{1}{8}$ inch away from the cylinder head. A strong, regular spark confirms that the fault lies with the sparking plug, which should be cleaned as described in **Section 3:7** or renewed if defective.

If the spark is weak and irregular, check the condition of the lead and, if it is perished or cracked, renew it and repeat the test. If no improvement results, check that the inside of the distributor cap is clean and dry and that there is no sign of tracking, which can be seen as a thin black line between the electrodes or to some metal part in contact with the cap. Tracking can only be rectified by fitting a new cap. Check that the carbon brush in the centre of the cap is clean and that it moves freely against its spring to make good contact with the rotor arm.

Testing the low-tension circuit:

The low-tension circuit connects the battery, ignition switch, coil primary winding and the contact breaker assembly and provides timed pulses of current to the coil primary windings as the contacts open and close. These pulses control the secondary coil winding which provides current at high voltage to the distributor, where the distributor rotor arm directs it through the high-tension leads to the sparking plugs.

Remove the distributor cap and position it out of the way, without disconnecting any of its leads. Check that the contact breaker points are clean and correctly set. Disconnect the thin wire from the coil that connects to the distributor. Connect a 12-volt test lamp between these terminals to complete the circuit, switch on the ignition and turn the engine slowly. If the lamp lights and goes out as the points close and open, the circuit is in order. If the lamp fails to light, there is a fault in the low-tension circuit. Remove the lamp and reconnect the wire to the coil and distributor.

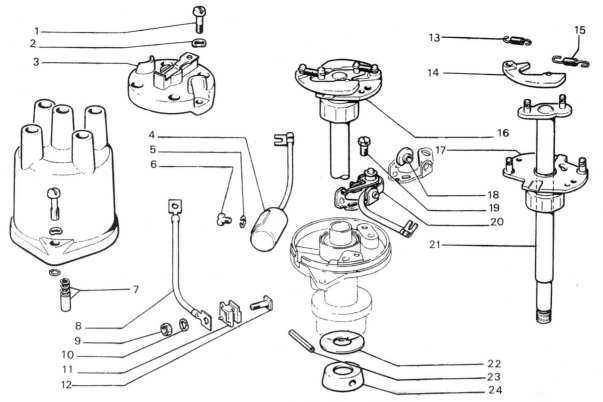

FIG 3:3 The conventional distributor components

Key to Fig 3:3   1 Screw   2 Washer   3 Rotor   4 Capacitor   5 Circlip   6 Screw   7 Carbon brush   8 Primary lead
9 Nut   10 Circlip   11 Terminal clip   12 Bolt   13 Spring   14 Centrifugal weight   15 Spring   16 Cam   17 Cam
plate   18 Insulating bush   19 Screw   20 Contact assembly   21 Shaft   22 Washer   23 Pin   24 Collar

If the fault lies in the low-tension circuit, use the lamp
to carry out the following tests with the ignition switched
on. Remove the wire from the ignition switch side of the
coil and connect the lamp between the end of this wire
and earth. If the lamp fails to light, it indicates a fault in
the wiring between the battery and the coil, or in the
ignition switch. Reconnect the wire if the lamp lights.

Disconnect the wire from the coil that connects to the
distributor. Connect the lamp between the coil terminal
and earth. If the lamp fails to light it indicates a fault in the
coil primary winding and a new coil must be fitted.
Reconnect the wire if the lamp lights and disconnect its
other end from the distributor. If the lamp does not light
when connected between the end of this wire and earth it
indicates a fault in that section of wire.

Capacitor:

The best method of testing a capacitor (condenser) is
by substitution. Disconnect the original capacitor and
connect a new one between the low-tension terminal on
the distributor and earth for test purposes. If a new
capacitor is proved to be required, it can then be properly
fitted.

An alternative check for the capacitor is to charge it
from a DC source, such as the car battery, then leave it for
about five minutes. The terminal and case of the capacitor
should then be shorted with a piece of wire and, if the
capacitor is in good condition, a noticeable spark should
result.

If a new capacitor is required, the capacity of the
replacement unit should be .2 to .25 microfarad at 50 Hz.

3:4 Removing and refitting distributor

To remove the distributor from the engine, first disconnect the HT leads to the sparking plugs and unscrew
and remove the distributor cap. Disconnect the LT lead to
the contact breaker terminal which can be seen above the
securing nut 2. Remove the nut 2 and clip shown in
FIG 3:1 securing the distributor in place on the engine
and lift the distributor clear of the shaft bearing hole.

Time may be saved in setting up after maintenance if
the precise position of the rotor in relation to one of the
terminals is noted and the engine crankshaft is not turned
while distributor maintenance is being carried out.

Cover the distributor mounting hole with a clean, lint-
free rag to prevent the entry of dirt or swarf while the
distributor is being serviced.

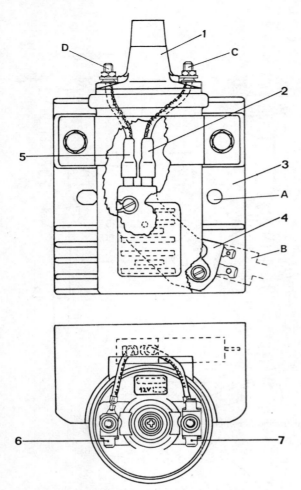

FIG 3:4 Coil, heat dissipator and electronic module

Key to Fig 3:4 1 Ignition coil 2 Connector between coil and electronic module 3 Heat dissipator 4 Electronic module 5 Connector between coil and electronic module 6 Tachometer terminal 7 Ignition coil terminal A Heat dissipator earthing point B Connector to electronic module C Coil +B terminal D Primary winding output terminal

Refitting:

If the crankshaft position has not been altered since the distributor was removed, turn the rotor to the approximate position it was and insert the spindle into the skew gear at the bottom of the distributor shaft housing. Correctly set the ignition timing as described in **Section 3:7**.

Should the crankshaft position have been altered, it is necessary to first set piston No. 1 at the top of its compression stroke. To do this, remove the cylinder head covers and examine the position of the cams. Turn the engine until both cams for No. 1 cylinder have their lobes pointing upwards away from the valves (valves closed). Now turn the engine a little from this position until the timing marks are correctly aligned as described in **Section**

3:7. Turn the rotor of the distributor until the rotor arm is pointing towards terminal 1 on the distributor cap. Insert the distributor shaft home in the skew drive gear and set the ignition timing as described in **Section 3:7**. Refit the cylinder head covers.

On completion, refit the distributor cap to connect the HT leads to the respective sparking plugs. Finally, reconnect the capacitor lead and the LT lead from the ignition coil, terminal D, to the LT terminal on the distributor.

3:5 Distributor overhaul

The distributor components are shown in **FIG 3:3**. Remove the two fixing screws and remove the distributor cap. Dismantle the centrifugal weights and springs. Beneath the distributor mounting is a collar secured by a pin. Remove the pin and slide the collar off the shaft. The shaft may now be withdrawn from the distributor. Disconnect and remove the capacitor. Dismantle the contact breaker assembly. Wash all metal parts in a suitable cleaning fluid and dry them.

Examine the shaft and rotor for signs of excessive play or wear. Renew parts as necessary. Examine the fixed and moving contacts of the contact breaker assembly, cleaning the contact faces as described in **Section 3:2** if necessary. **Never use emerycloth when cleaning the points as particles of emery may become embedded in the contact surface.**

Check the cam faces for signs of wear or scoring. Polish out light scores with a smooth carborundum stone or renew the parts if they are too badly worn.

Examine the insulation of the rotor cap and distributor cap for signs of tracking or carbonisation and renew any faulty part. Check the condition of the rotor contact arm, distributor cap internal carbon brush and HT contact in the distributor cap. Renew the cap if the contacts are badly burned or if the carbon brush is worn or damaged.

Check the condition of the cam follower on the moving contact arm of the contact breaker assembly and renew if the wear is such as to alter the dwell angle by more than 2 deg. This is difficult to check without a special meter but, if follower wear is such that the setting of the contact gap necessitates the fixed plate being close to the limit of adjustment, ignition timing will almost certainly be affected and a new contact point set should be fitted.

Examine the condition of the weights and springs. The springs must not be stretched, which would mean that the coils do not close tightly when the springs are at rest, and the weights must be an easy, but not sloppy, fit on the pins. Renew parts as necessary.

Reassemble the distributor and set the contact points gap as described in **Section 3:2**. If a small spring balance is available with a scale of up to 2 lb, check the pull of the moving arm pressure on the fixed contact. This should be about 20 oz.

Before refitting the rotor, check that the movement of the flyweights about their pins provides the necessary movement to the cam on the distributor shaft and that the action is free. Apply a spot of oil to the pivot points and to the shaft before insertion in the mounting bushing. Insert the shaft into the bushing and refit the collar, securing it with the pin. Check for end play which should not be

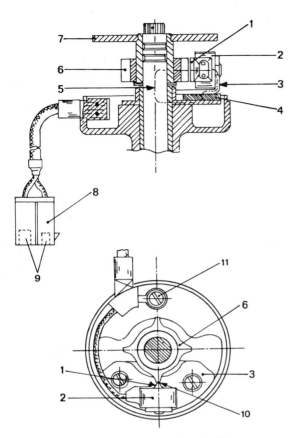

FIG 3 : 5   Cross-sections of the distributor

Key to Fig 3 : 5   1 Stator pole   2 Coil   3 Fixed plate
4 Permanent magnet   5 Magnetic field   6 4-pole
reluctor   7 Timing plate   8 Connector to electric module
9 Terminals   10 Air gap   11 Earth cable retaining screw

noticeable. Fit and reconnect the capacitor across the
contact breaker points.

Examine the HT leads from the distributor cap and, if at
all perished, replace them fitting the rubber covers at the
cap end and the shrouded connectors at the sparking
plug end, with the cable-bunching washers at the intermediate positions.

3 : 6 Electronic ignition

It is essential that, when checking the electronic system
the correct procedure and tools are used. The instruments
required are DC voltmeter and ohmmeter, and if these are
not available the car should be taken to a service station
with the correct facilities. Due to the nature of the system
it is particularly important to avoid certain situations. Do
not disconnect the HT terminal of the coil with the engine
running and do not earth the LT lead to the tachometer. If
the instrument panel is disconnected, do not start the
engine. Ensure that the heat dissipator is properly earthed
before turning on the ignition circuit, and never short out
the LT signal from the coil to the tachometer.

Installation and wiring :

Turn the ignition on and carefully inspect all wiring and
connections. Ensure that the earth connection of the heat
dissipator, engine and battery are clean and tight.
Resistance of the connections should not exceed .2 ohm.
Check that the connector **B** in **FIG 3 : 4** is fully inserted
and locked against the stop on the dissipator.

To check the input to the coil, fit the voltmeter between
the +B terminal of the coil and a good earth. With the
ignition switched on the reading should be 12 volts. Check
that the reading at coil terminal +D is not more than .3 volt
different to the reading at terminal +B. If the readings are
incorrect check the coil primary winding. Resistance
across the coil LT terminals should be approximately .8
ohm.

Checking the distributor :

The following operation must be undertaken with great
care to avoid injury to the operator or damage to the
components. Switch on the ignition and disconnect one
HT lead from a spark plug. **Do not disconnect the
central HT lead from the coil to the distributor.** Using
insulated pliers, hold the end of the HT lead about 5 mm
from the engine block and start the engine. A strong spark
should cross the gap between the lead and the engine.
Repeat this test for each spark plug in turn. If no spark
appears check the distributor.

With the ignition switched off disconnect the terminal 8
in **FIG 3 : 5** from the coil. Insert the probes of the ohmmeter into the terminals 9 and check the reading which
should be 700 to 800 ohms. Remove the distributor cap
and check the air gap 10 between the reluctor and stator
pole, which should be .012 to .016 inch (.3 to .4 mm).

If the above checks are satisfactory, any further trouble
will be due to a faulty electronic module which should be
renewed by a service station.

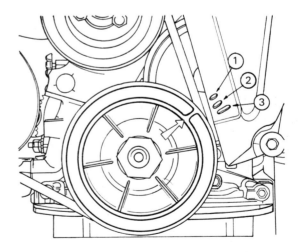

FIG 3 : 6   The ignition timing marks

Key to Fig 3 : 6   1 10 deg. BTDC   2 5 deg. BTDC   3 TDC.
Timing mark on pulley is arrowed

FIG 3 : 7 Adjusting the sparking plug gap. The electrodes should always be filed clean and parallel

3 : 7 Timing the ignition

The piston in No. 1 cylinder must be at TDC on the compression stroke in order to set the ignition timing. To set the piston in this position, either remove the camshaft covers and turn the engine until both cam lobes for No. 1 cylinder are pointing away from the valves, or remove the sparking plug from No. 1 cylinder and turn the engine until compression can be felt by a thumb pressed over the plughole. Now turn the engine a little more as necessary until the timing marks align as shown in **FIG 3 : 6**.

Loosen the distributor clamp nut 2 shown in **FIG 3 : 1**. Connect a 12-volt test lamp between the LT terminal on the side of the distributor and earth. Turn the distributor if necessary to ensure that the contact points are fully closed. Now switch on the ignition and turn the distributor slowly until the test lamp just lights, which indicates that the points are just opening. Without moving the distributor from this position, tighten the clamp securely.

Stroboscopic timing :

This method can be used to accurately set the ignition timing if the appropriate equipment is to hand, or the work can be carried out at a service station. Set the ignition by the test lamp method first. Connect the timing light to the ignition circuit of No. 1 cylinder. Run the engine at normal idling speed and direct the timing light on to the timing pointer. Turn the distributor until the timing marks are aligned, then tighten the distributor clamp securely. With electronic ignition do not use the coil terminals for the test lamps.

Dwell angle :

If suitable equipment is available, check that the dwell angle, contacts closed, is between 52 and 58 deg.

3 : 8 Sparking plugs

Inspect and clean sparking plugs regularly. Before removing sparking plugs, ensure that their recesses are clean and dry so that nothing can fall into the cylinder. Plug gaskets can be re-used, providing that they are not less than half their original thickness. Have sparking plugs cleaned out on an abrasive-blasting machine and tested

under pressure with the electrode gaps correctly set at between .020 to .024 inch (.5 to .6 mm) for conventional distributors or .024 to .028 inch (.6 to .7mm) for electronic. The gaps must always be set by adjusting the earth electrodes. **Do not try to bend the centre electrode.** Renew plugs at about 10,000 mile (16,000 km) intervals or before if badly worn.

Before refitting the plugs, clean the threads with a wire brush. Clean the threads in the cylinder head if the plugs cannot be screwed in by hand. Failing a proper tap for this purpose, use an old sparking plug with cross-cuts down the threads. Plugs should be tightened with a proper plug spanner, as other types of spanner may slip off during tightening and crack the plug insulation. Do not overtighten the plugs.

Inspection of the deposits on the plug electrodes can be helpful when tuning. Normally, from mixed periods of high and low speed driving, deposits should be powdery and range in colour from brown to greyish tan. There will also be slight wear of the electrodes. Long periods of constant speed driving or low speed city driving will give white or yellowish deposits. Dry, black fluffy deposits are due to incomplete combustion and indicate running with a rich mixture, excessive idling and, possibly, defective ignition. Overheating plugs have a white blistered look about the centre electrode and the side electrode may be badly eroded. This may be caused by poor cooling, a weak mixture, incorrect ignition timing or sustained high speeds with heavy loads.

Black, wet deposits result from oil in the combustion chamber from worn pistons, rings, valve stems or guides. Sparking plugs which run hotter may alleviate the problem, but the cure is an engine overhaul.

3 : 9 Fault diagnosis

(a) Engine will not fire

1 Battery discharged
2 Contact points dirty, pitted or wrongly adjusted
3 Distributor cap dirty, cracked or tracking
4 Contact inside distributor cap not touching rotor
5 Faulty cable or loose connection in low-tension circuit
6 Distributor rotor arm cracked or dirty
7 Faulty coil
8 Broken contact breaker spring
9 Contact points stuck open

(b) Engine misfires

1 Check 2, 3, 4 and 7 in (a)
2 Weak contact breaker spring
3 High-tension plug or coil lead defective
4 Sparking plugs loose
5 Sparking plug insulation cracked
6 Sparking plug gaps incorrectly set
7 Ignition timing incorrect
8 Faulty capacitor

(c) Poor acceleration

1 Ignition retarded
2 Centrifugal weights seized
3 Centrifugal springs weak, broken or disconnected
4 Distributor clamp loose
5 Incorrect contact points gap
6 Worn plugs

CHAPTER 4

THE COOLING SYSTEM

4:1 Description

The cooling system is of the pressurised sealed type. Coolant circulation is assisted by a water pump driven by a belt, a thermostat preventing full circulation until normal engine operating temperature is reached, thus ensuring a rapid warm-up and good heater operation.

Air flow through the radiator is assisted by an electric fan unit controlled by a temperature switch mounted in the radiator.

An expansion tank containing a quantity of coolant is connected to the radiator by means of a hose. At high operating temperatures, when the coolant in the sealed system expands, excess coolant passes through a valve into the expansion tank. When the system cools, the valve allows coolant from the expansion tank to flow back into the radiator. With this system, no coolant loss should occur during normal operations.

4:2 Routine maintenance

Apart from an occasional check on the condition of the hoses and hose clips and a visual check on coolant level in the expansion tank, very little maintenance should be necessary. There should also be no need for regular topping up of the coolant. If regular topping up is required,

the system should be examined for leaks before adding coolant.

Check the level of coolant in the expansion tank and top up as required. The level should be $2\frac{1}{2}$ to $2\frac{3}{4}$ inch (6 to 7 cm) above the MIN mark on the tank, as shown in **FIG 4:1**, when the engine is cold. The level will be higher when the engine is hot. If antifreeze is being used, top up with antifreeze mixture to prevent dilution of the coolant.

Every two years the system should be drained, flushed and refilled with a new coolant solution in the manner described later.

Drive belt tension should be checked at approximately 6000 mile intervals.

Draining:

Set the heater controls to the full heat position and remove the cap from the expansion tank. Remove the filler cap from the radiator. Open the tap at the bottom of the radiator and remove the drain plug from the right-hand side of the cylinder block. Allow the coolant to drain, collecting it in a clean container if it is to be re-used. Release the expansion tank mounting strap and hold the tank up so that its contents run into the radiator.

FIG 4:1 The cooling system expansion tank

Flushing:

Use a hose to run clean water in through the radiator filler until it runs clean through the drain plugs. Refit the drain plug and close the radiator tap, fill the system with water and run the engine long enough to open the thermostat for complete circulation. This will be when the top hose feels warm to the touch. Stop the engine and drain the system again before the sediment has time to settle. Allow the engine to cool, then repeat the flushing operation. Do not add cold water to the cooling system when the engine is warm, otherwise there is the danger of cracking the cylinder block. Repeat the flushing operation, refit the drain plug and close the drain tap then refill the system with coolant solution.

Filling:

Make sure the heater control is in the hot position and that both drain points are closed. Slowly fill the system

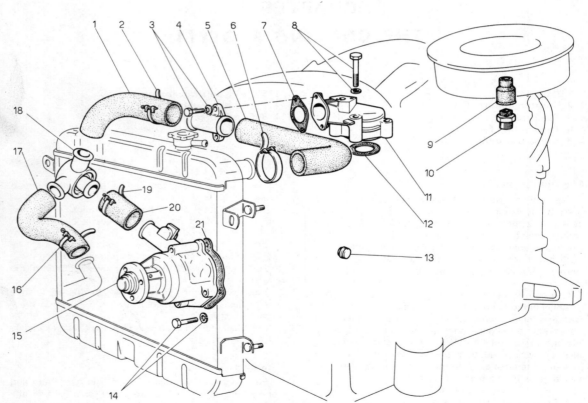

FIG 4:2 The cooling system components

Key to Fig 4:2 1 Cylinder head to thermostat hose   2 Hose clamp   3 Screw and flat washer   4 Connector   5 Connector to radiator hose   6 Hose clamp   7 Outlet gasket   8 Screw and flat washer   9 Sender unit cap   10 Temperature gauge sender unit   11 Cylinder head water outlet   12 Gasket   13 Drain plug   14 Screw and lockwasher   15 Water pump   16 Hose clamp   17 Radiator to thermostat hose   18 Thermostat   19 Hose clamp   20 Thermostat to water pump hose   21 Gasket

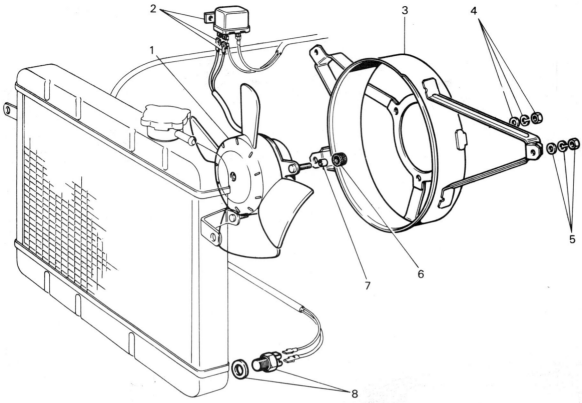

FIG 4:3   The electric cooling fan components

Key to Fig 4:3   1 Motor and fan   2 Relay and power cables   3 Shroud   4, 5 Nuts, lockwashers and flat washers
6 Rubber bush   7 Spacer   8 Temperature switch and gasket

through the filler on the radiator. When the radiator is full, run the engine for a few minutes to disperse any air and top up the radiator again. Fit the radiator cap. Fill the expansion tank to the correct level and run the engine until it has reached its normal operating temperature, which will be when the electric cooling fan starts to operate. Leave the engine to cool right down then top up the expansion tank as required.

4:3 The radiator

The radiator, water pump and coolant hoses are shown in **FIG 4:2**.

Removal:

Detach the electrical connections from the temperature sender units at the bottom of the radiator and from the cooling fan motor relay. Remove the fixing nuts and washers and detach the fan and housing from the rear of the radiator, as shown in **FIG 4:3**.

Drain the system as described in **Section 4:2**. Disconnect the top and bottom hoses from the fittings on the radiator and disconnect the expansion tank hose from the radiator filler neck. Take out the fixing screws and carefully lift the radiator from the car.

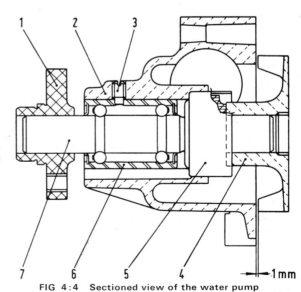

FIG 4:4   Sectioned view of the water pump

Key to Fig 4:4   1 Pulley hub   2 Pump body   3 Bearing setscrew   4 Impeller   5 Packing   6 Bearing   7 Pump shaft

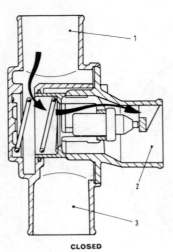 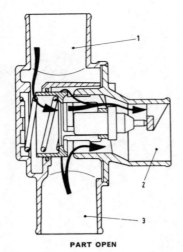 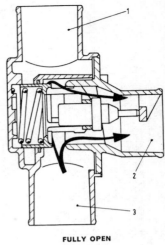

| CLOSED | PART OPEN | FULLY OPEN |

FIG 4:5 The operation of the controlled bypass thermostat

Key to Fig 4:5   1 Water inlet from engine   2 Water outlet to pump   3 Water inlet from radiator

Refitting:

Carefully refit the radiator to the car and evenly tighten the fixing screws. Reattach the top and bottom hoses and the expansion tank hose. Refit the electric fan assembly to the rear of the radiator then reconnect the electrical terminals to the sender unit and relay. On completion, refill the cooling system as described in **Section 4:2**.

4:4 The cooling fan

An electric cooling fan is fitted to assist the air flow through the radiator when the system reaches a certain temperature. Power for the fan is supplied from the relay and it is switched on and off by a temperature sender unit mounted at the bottom of the radiator. Fan removal and refitting is described in **Section 4:3**.

If the fan operates with the engine cold, the temperature sender unit is faulty or there is a shortcircuit in the fan wiring. If the fan does not operate at all, check that the fuse which protects the circuit has not burnt out. To test the motor, connect jumper leads from the battery terminals to the motor terminals. If the motor runs when connected up in this manner, check the wiring between the motor and the temperature sender unit. If the wiring and connections are all in order, the temperature sender unit must be faulty and should be renewed.

4:5 The water pump (see FIG 4:4)

Removal:

Drain the cooling system as described in **Section 4:2**. Slacken the drive belt and remove it from the water pump pulley as described in **Section 4:6**. Disconnect the hose from the water pump, then remove the fixing bolts and lift off the pump and gasket. As special press tool equipment is needed to dismantle and reassemble the water pump, the work should be carried out by a service station. The water pump bearing is factory-lubricated and sealed, no additional lubrication being required.

Refitting:

Clean the contact faces of the water pump and cylinder block to remove all traces of old gasket, taking care not to damage the surfaces. Refit the water pump, using a new gasket. Refit and correctly tension the drive belt, then attach the hose to the water pump unit. Refill the cooling system as described in **Section 4:2**.

4:6 Drive belt tensioning

The method of checking and adjusting the water pump and alternator drive belt tension is as follows. Press at the centre of the longest belt run with moderate thumb pressure and if the tension is correct the belt will deflect by approximately $\frac{1}{2}$ inch. To adjust the belt tension, loosen the alternator mounting bolts and swing the alternator towards or away from the engine as required, then tighten the mounting bolts and recheck the tension.

The belt can be removed by slackening the mountings, moving the alternator, as far as possible, towards the engine and releasing the belt from the pulleys. Note that, on models fitted with air-conditioning equipment, the air-conditioning pump drive belt must be removed before the fan belt can be removed.

When air-conditioning equipment is fitted, the drive belt should be checked in the same manner as that for the alternator and water pump units. If the belt tension is incorrect, slacken the bolts securing the pump to its mounting bracket then move the pump towards or away from the engine as required before tightening the mounting bolts and rechecking the tension.

A tight drive belt will cause undue wear on the pulleys and component bearings. A slack belt will cause slip and, possibly, lower output from the driven components.

4:7 The thermostat

A controlled bypass thermostat is fitted to the cooling system and operates as shown in **FIG 4:5**. A faulty thermostat may open at a temperature below the correct figure, preventing the engine from warming up quickly and reducing the heater output. Conversely, if the valve opens at a higher temperature than that specified, engine overheating may result.

Removal:

Drain the cooling system as described in **Section 4:2**. Disconnect the three hoses and lift off the thermostat as shown in **FIG 4:2**.

Testing:

Clean the thermostat and immerse it in a container of cold water together with a 0 to 100°C thermometer. Heat the water, keeping it stirred and check that the valve opens at approximately 85°C. The valve should be fully open at 92°C, at which temperature the thermostat valve stroke should be .29 inch (7.5 mm). If the thermostat operates satisfactorily it may be refitted, if not it must be renewed.

Refitting:

Refit the three hoses to the thermostat unit, making sure the connections are tight. Refill the cooling system as described in **Section 4:2**.

4:8 Frost precautions

When antifreeze is to be used the system should first be drained and flushed as described in **Section 4:2**. Ethylene-glycol type antifreeze should be added to the system in the correct proportion as recommended by the manufacturer, to give protection from freezing in the lowest temperatures in which the vehicle is to be operated. After the second winter, drain and flush the system and refill with fresh solution. When adding antifreeze, mix it with a suitable quantity of water before pouring it into the system. Always add the correct antifreeze mixture to the expansion tank.

4:9 Fault diagnosis

(a) Internal coolant leakage

1 Cracked cylinder wall
2 Loose cylinder head bolts
3 Cracked cylinder head
4 Faulty head gasket

(b) Poor circulation

1 Radiator matrix blocked
2 Engine coolant passages restricted
3 Low coolant level
4 Defective thermostat
5 Perished or collapsed radiator hose

(c) Corrosion

1 Impurities in the coolant
2 Too infrequent draining and flushing

(d) Overheating

1 Check (b)
2 Sludge in crankcase
3 Faulty ignition timing
4 Low oil level in sump
5 Tight engine
6 Choked exhaust system
7 Binding brakes
8 Slipping clutch
9 Incorrect valve timing
10 Retarded ignition
11 Mixture too weak
12 Faulty electric cooling fan

NOTES

CHAPTER 5

THE CLUTCH

5 : 1 Description
5 : 2 Adjusting the clutch
5 : 3 Removing the clutch cable

5 : 4 Removing and dismantling clutch
5 : 5 Assembling and refitting clutch
5 : 6 Fault diagnosis

5 : 1 Description

The clutch is a single dry plate unit of diaphragm spring type The main components are the driven plate, pressure plate assembly and release bearings.

The driven plate consists of a resilient steel disc attached to a hub which slides on the splined clutch shaft. The friction linings are riveted to both sides of the disc.

The pressure plate assembly consists of the pressure plate, diaphragm spring and housing. The release bearing is a ballbearing of special construction with an elongated outer ring that presses directly against the diaphragm spring when the clutch pedal is operated. The bearing is mounted on a guide sleeve in the gearbox bellhousing.

Clutch operation is by a sheathed cable and lever linkage.

When the clutch is fully engaged, the driven plate is clamped between the pressure plate and the engine flywheel and transmits torque to the gearbox through the splined input shaft. When the clutch pedal is depressed, the pressure plate is withdrawn from the driven plate by cable pressure, the driven plate then ceasing to transmit torque.

5 : 2 Adjusting the clutch

Correct clutch cable adjustment is essential. Insufficient free play will cause the release bearing to press against the diaphragm when the clutch is engaged, causing clutch slip and excessive bearing and driven plate wear. Excessive free play will prevent proper disengagement of the clutch, resulting in clutch drag and consequent difficult gear changing.

The clutch cable adjuster is located beneath the car as shown in **FIG 5 : 1**.

Free play at the clutch pedal pad should be $\frac{1}{2}$ to 1 inch (12.5 to 25 mm) on 1600 models, or exactly 1 inch (25 mm) on 1800 models.

To adjust the free play, loosen the locknut and turn the adjuster nut in the appropriate direction, tightening the locknut firmly on completion to secure the adjustment.

On the 1600 and 2000 models produced after April 1977 the release sleeve remains in contact with the diaphragm spring. No adjustment of pedal free travel is required and plate wear is taken up by the return springs. After taking up the free travel, the movement of the pedal, between fully engaged to fully released, should be 130 mm.

Lubrication:

The clutch operating mechanism should be lubricated by the application of a good quality grease to the ball pivots shown in **FIG 5 : 2**.

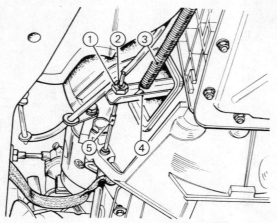

FIG 5:1 Clutch cable adjuster mechanism

Key to Fig 5:1   1 Adjustment nut   2 Locknut
3 Lever return spring   4 Release lever   5 Cable

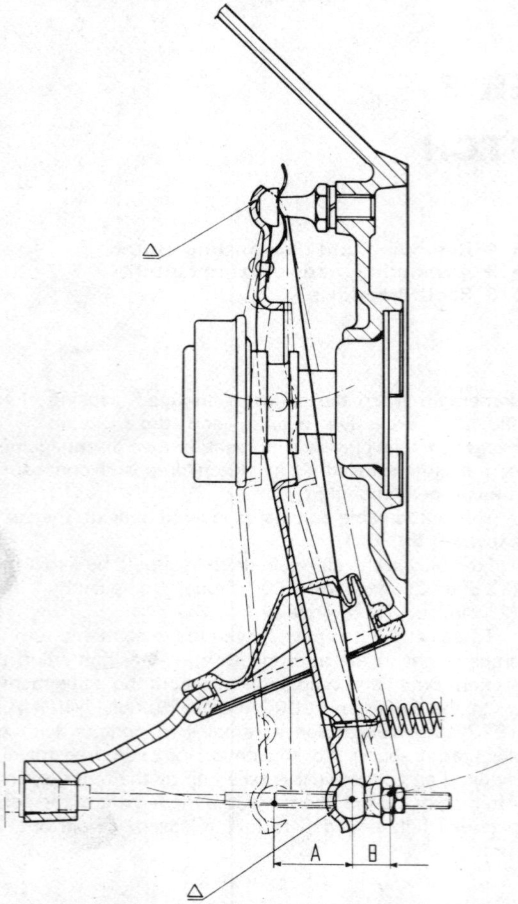

FIG 5:2 Clutch release mechanism lubrication points

Key to Fig 5:2   A = Declutching travel   B = Displacement
due to wear
A (1600) = 1.3 inch (33 mm); B (1600) = .59 inch (15 mm)
A (1800) = 1.18 inch (30 mm); B (1800) = .67 inch (17 mm)

5:3 Removing the clutch cable

FIG 5:3 shows the clutch release mechanism components. Remove the locknut and the adjuster nut from the release lever end of the cable, then release the other end of the cable from the pedal connection. Remove the cable from the car. Examine the rubber components 4 and 21 and renew them if they are worn or damaged.

Refitting:

Fit the clutch cable to the car in the reverse order of removal, adjusting the pedal free play as described in **Section 5:2** on completion.

5:4 Removing and dismantling clutch

Support the engine and remove the gearbox as described in **Chapter 6**.

Mark the clutch cover and the flywheel with a small daub of paint so that on reassembly the clutch will be in the same relative position to retain the original balance of the assembly.

Loosen the bolts holding the clutch assembly to the engine flywheel alternately and evenly to avoid distortion, then lift off the clutch assembly. Remove the driven plate, taking care not to get grease or oil on the friction linings. The release bearing assembly can be removed from the clutch housing on the gearbox.

Servicing:

Thoroughly clean all parts in a suitable solvent, with the exception of the driven plate friction linings and the release bearing. The release bearing must not be cleaned with solvent as this would wash the internal lubricant from the bearing, so simply wipe it clean with a cloth.

The clutch cover, spring and pressure plate assembly is an integral unit and must not be dismantled. If any part is defective the assembly must be renewed complete.

Inspect the surface of the flywheel where the driven plate makes contact. Small surface cracks or scratches are unimportant, but if there are any deep scratches the flywheel should be machined smooth or renewed. Check the pressure plate for scoring or damage and that the operating surface is flat and true. Check the diaphragm spring for cracks and other damage and the release bearing for roughness when it is pressed and turned by hand. Any worn or damaged parts must be renewed.

Check the driven plate for loose rivets and broken or very loose torsional springs. The friction linings should be well proud of the rivets and have a light colour, with a polished glaze through which the grain of the material is clearly visible. A dark, glazed deposit indicates oil on the facings and, as this condition cannot be rectified, a new or relined unit will be required. Any signs of oil in the clutch will call for examination of the crankshaft rear oil seal, as described in **Chapter 1**. Check the disc for run out at the outer circumference, preferably using a dial gauge as shown in **FIG 5:4**. Excessive warping can usually be cured by sliding the disc on to the gearbox splined shaft and twisting the disc as necessary by hand until it is true. If this method does not succeed, however, the disc should be renewed. A warped driven disc will cause clutch judder and wear out very quickly in service.

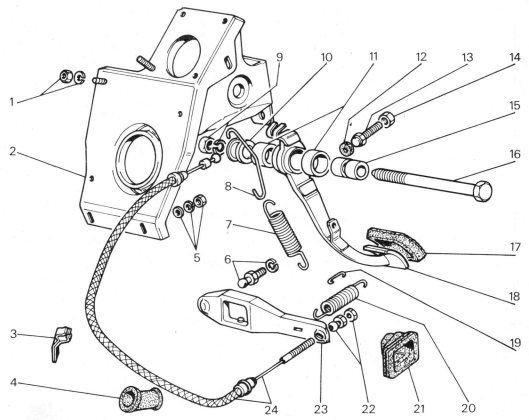

FIG 5:3 Clutch release mechanism components

Key to Fig 5:3   1 Nut   2 Support   3 Cable clip   4 Boot   5 Nut, flat washer and lockwasher   6 Ball joint head and lockwasher   7 Pedal return spring   8 Spring hook   9 Nut and lockwasher   10 Spacer   11 Bushings   12 Rubber pad   13 Screw   14 Nut   15 Spacer   16 Brake and clutch pedal pivot screw   17 Pedal rubber   18 Clutch pedal   19 Return spring hook   20 Return spring   21 Dust boot   22 Cable adjuster nut and locknut   23 Release lever   24 Clutch cable

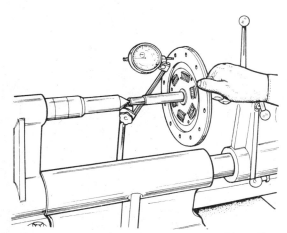

FIG 5:4   Using a dial gauge to check clutch driven plate runout

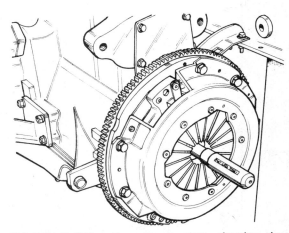

FIG 5:5   Refitting the pressure plate, showing the alignment tool through the centre of the clutch

FIG 132

49

It is not recommended that owners' attempt to reline the clutch driven plate themselves, as the linings must be riveted and trued on the disc and the whole checked under a press. For this reason, the driven plate should be relined at a service station or an exchange unit obtained and fitted. Check the driven plate hub for a smooth, sliding fit on the splined shaft, removing any burrs on the shaft or in the hub with a fine stone.

5:5 Assembling and refitting clutch

This operation is basically the reverse of the removal operation, noting the following points. The use of the special Fiat tool or a spare gearbox input shaft is essential for clutch alignment.

Locate the clutch driven disc in position, then fit the pressure plate assembly in position and insert the special tool or the spare shaft through the whole clutch assembly and into the pilot bearing in the flywheel, as shown in **FIG 5:5**. This aligns the unit so that the gearbox input shaft can be fitted correctly. With the tool in place, fit and tighten the clutch mounting bolts alternately and evenly. Remove the alignment tool, then refit the gearbox as described in **Chapter 6**. On completion, adjust the clutch operating cable as described in **Section 5:2**.

5:6 Fault diagnosis

(a) Drag or spin

1 Oil or grease on driven plate linings
2 Clutch cable binding

3 Distorted driven plate
4 Warped or damaged pressure plate
5 Broken driven plate linings
6 Excessive clutch free play

(b) Fierceness or snatch

1 Check 1, 2, 3 and 4 (a)
2 Worn driven plate linings

(c) Slip

1 Check 1 in (a) and 2 (b)
2 Weak diaphragm spring
3 Seized clutch cable
4 Insufficient clutch cable free play

(d) Judder

1 Check 1, 3 and 4 in (a)
2 Contact area of friction linings unevenly worn
3 Bent or worn splined shaft
4 Badly worn splines in driven plate hub
5 Faulty engine or gearbox mountings

(e) Tick or knock

1 Badly worn driven plate hub splines
2 Worn release bearing
3 Bent or worn splined shaft
4 Loose flywheel

CHAPTER 6

MANUAL TRANSMISSION

6:1 Description

Either a four-speed or five-speed gearbox may be fitted according to model type. All forward speeds have synchromesh engagement but reverse gear is engaged by sliding an idler gear into mesh between the gears on the main and countershafts. Synchromesh engagement is not required on reverse as this is only engaged with the car stationary.

The five-speed gearbox is a modification of the four-speed unit and has an extra gear and synchromesh unit mounted in the rear cover, so servicing procedures for both types of gearbox are very similar. Later five-speed gearboxes are a little different, having been used in the Fiat 131, but removal and refitting procedures are similar.

A sectioned view of the four-speed gearbox is given in **FIG 6:1**, of a five-speed gearbox in **FIG 6:2**. The input shaft is splined to the driven plate of the clutch and revolves with it. The input shaft rotates in a bearing mounted in the casing. Integral with the input shaft is a helical-cut gear. This gear meshes with the front gear on the countershaft gear cluster so that the countershaft is always driven by the input shaft. The remaining gears on the countershaft are in constant mesh with those on the main shaft so that these two are always revolving when the input shaft is driven. The mainshaft gears are free to rotate about the mainshaft without transmitting drive to it. The mainshaft rotates in bearings in the casing and rear cover and the front end spigot is supported in a needle roller bearing in the input shaft. The gear selector mechanism moves the outer sleeves of the synchromesh units. As the sleeve moves it presses the conical surfaces of the baulk rings so that drive is transmitted, by friction only, between the rotating gear and the mainshaft. All the parts are then brought to the same speed and further movement of the synchromesh sleeve allows it to slide over the dog teeth of the baulk ring and on to those of the gear, making the drive positive. Drive is then transmitted along the mainshaft and propeller shaft to the rear axle. For top gear, the input and mainshafts are connected together to make the drive direct through the gearbox. Reverse gear is engaged by sliding a straight-toothed idle gear into mesh between the gear on the countershaft and the gear on the mainshaft. The rest of the gears have helical-cut teeth and are in constant mesh.

FIGS 6:3 to **6:10** show the various components of the two types of gearbox.

6:2 Maintenance

The gearbox oil level should be checked at intervals of 6000 miles (10,000 km). Remove the filler plug from the

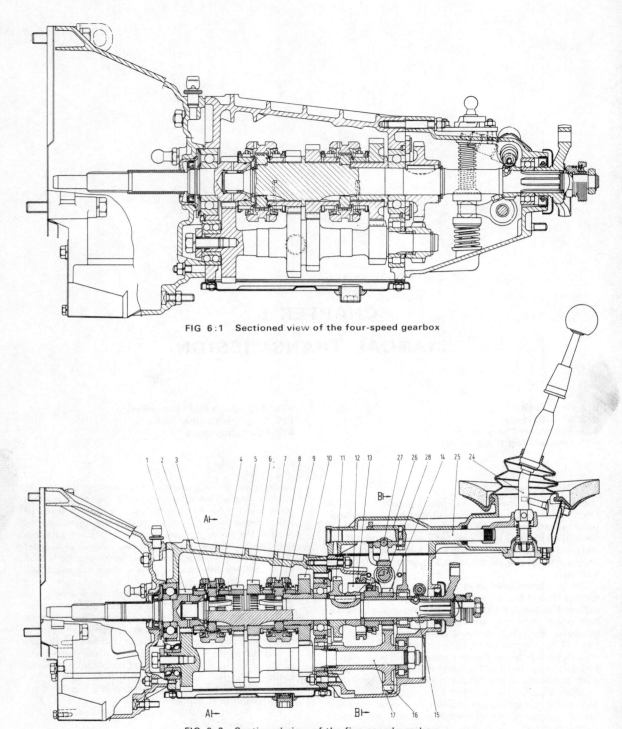

FIG 6:1 Sectioned view of the four-speed gearbox

FIG 6:2 Sectioned view of the five-speed gearbox

Key to Fig 6:2   1 Input shaft   2 Synchroniser ring   3 3rd and 4th sliding sleeve   4 Synchroniser ring   5 3rd gear
6 2nd gear   7 Synchroniser ring   8 1st and 2nd sliding sleeve   9 Synchroniser ring   10 1st gear   11 Reverse gear
12 Hub   13 5th sliding sleeve   14 5th gear and synchroniser   15 Mainshaft   16 5th and reverse gears   17 Countershaft
24 Gearlever   25 Rod   26 Lug   27 Gear selector and engagement lever   28 Shaft

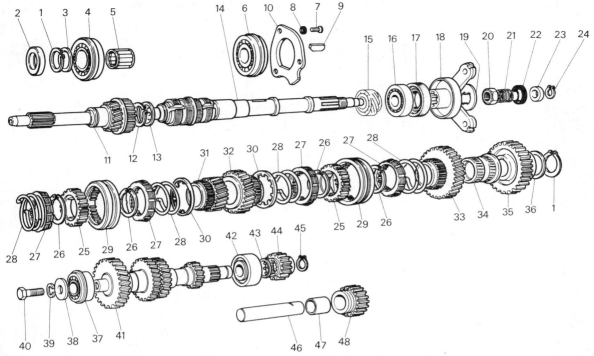

FIG 6:3 The gears and shafts for the four-speed gearbox

Key to Fig 6:3 1 Snap ring   2 Seal   3 Spring washer   4 Front ballbearing   5 Roller cage   6 Mainshaft intermediate ballbearing   7 Screw   8 Lockwasher   9 Key   10 Bearing retainer   11 Input shaft   12 Snap ring   13 Spring washer   14 Mainshaft   15 Speedometer drive gear   16 Mainshaft rear ballbearing   17 Seal   18 Sleeve   19 Lock plate   20 Nut   21 Spring   22 Seal   23 Ring   24 Snap ring   25 Hub   26 Snap ring   27 Synchroniser   28 Spring   29 Sleeve   30 Disc   31 3rd gear   32 2nd gear   33 1st gear   34 Bush   35 Reverse driven gear   36 Spring washer   37 Counter-shaft front ball bearing   38 Flat washer   39 Lockwasher   40 Screw   41 Countershaft   42 Countershaft rear roller bearing   43 Spring washer   44 Reverse drive gear   45 Snap ring   46 Reverse idler gear shaft   47 Bush   48 Reverse idler gear

side of the gearbox and check that the oil is up to the lower level of the filler hole. Top up if necessary using SAE 90 oil (not EP type) containing anti-wear additives. Allow any surplus oil to drain out of the filler hole before installing the filler plugs.

At intervals of 18,000 miles (30,000 km) drain out the oil into a suitable container by removing the gearbox drain plug and, on five-speed models, the extension housing drain plug at the rear right of the housing. Refill to the correct level with fresh lubricant. At the same time use a grease gun to lubricate the front propeller shaft joint through the grease nipple provided.

6:3 Gearbox removal

The gearbox is removed from beneath the car so if the work cannot be carried out from a pit or garage hoist, it will be necessary to raise the car off the ground. **Make sure that all supports are firmly based and strong enough to take the weight of the car.**

Disconnect the battery earth cable. Remove the air cleaner assembly, then disconnect the accelerator relay spindle from the carburetter. Disconnect the front

section of the exhaust pipe from the exhaust manifold flange.

On five-speed units, work from the car interior to remove the gearlever as follows. Remove the upper and lower dust boots on the transmission tunnel. Push the gearlever downward and use a screwdriver to remove the snap ring from its seat on the lever. Slip the gearlever out of the ball-end lever.

On four-speed units, work from the car interior to remove the gearlever as follows. Remove the knob from the gearlever, then remove the dust boot and disconnect the shift rod from the gearlever.

Drive the car over a pit or raise and suitably support it on stands.

Refer to **FIGS 6:11** and **6:12**. Remove the propeller shaft protection bracket 8. Disconnect the handbrake linkage from control lever 1 and from the propeller shaft centre cushion block. Disconnect the front propeller shaft yoke 9 from the flexible joint 3. Removal of the flexible joint is facilitated by the use of tool A.70025.

Disconnect the exhaust pipe bracket 13 from the main transmission case and from the exhaust pipe front section. Disconnect the electric wires from the reversing

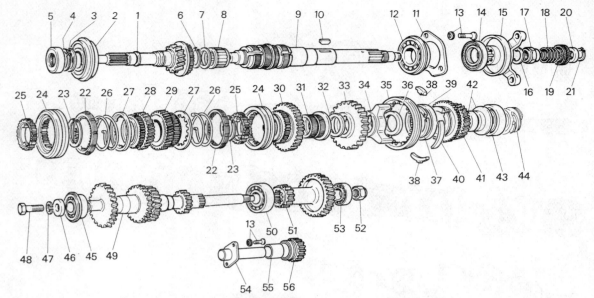

FIG 6:4   The gears and shafts for the five-speed gearbox

Key to Fig 6:4   1 Input shaft   2 Front ballbearing   3 Spring washer   4 Snap ring   5 Seal   6 Snap ring   7 Spring washer   8 Roller cage   9 Mainshaft   10 Key   11 Bearing retainer   12 Mainshaft intermediate ballbearing   13 Screw and lockwasher   14 Seal   15 Sleeve   16 Lockwasher   17 Nut   18 Spring   19 Seal   20 Ring   21 Snap ring   22 1st, 2nd, 3rd and 4th synchronisers   23 Snap ring   24 1st, 2nd, 3rd and 4th sleeves   25 Hub   26 Spring   27 Disc   28 3rd gear   29 2nd gear   30 1st gear   31 Bush   32 Lockwashers   33 Reverse gear   34 Hub   35 5th sleeve   36 Flat washer   37 Snap ring   38 Insert   39 5th synchroniser   40 Spring   41 5th gear   42 Bush   43 Rear roller bearing   44 Speedometer drive gear   45 Front ballbearing   46 Flat washer   47 Lockwasher   48 Screw   49 Countershaft   50 Roller bearing   51 Reverse and 5th gear   52 Nut   53 Rear ballbearing   54 Reverse gear shaft   55 Bush   56 Reverse gear

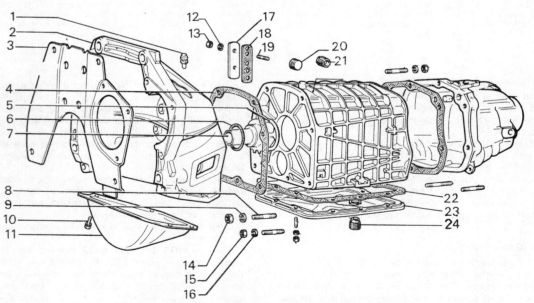

FIG 6:5   The casing and covers on the four-speed gearbox

Key to Fig 6:5   1 Breather   2 Housing   3 Cover   4 Gasket   5 Circlip   6 Ring seal   7 Cover   8 Stud   9 Spring washer   10 Bolt   11 Cover   12 Spring washer   13, 14, 15 Nuts   16 Spring washer   17 Cover plate   18 Gasket   19 Stud   20, 21 Plugs   22 Gasket   23 Cover plate   24 Drain plug

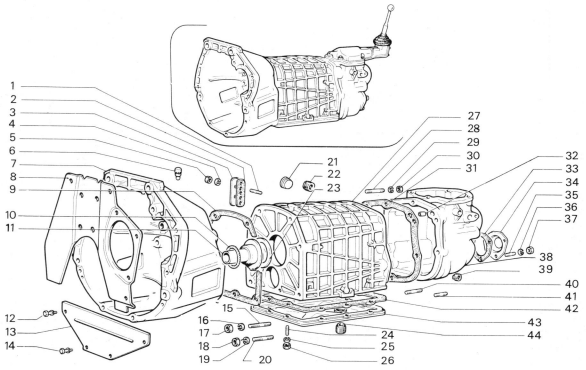

FIG 6:6   The casing and covers on the five-speed gearbox

Key to Fig 6:6   1 Stud   2 Gasket   3 Cover   4 Spring washer   5 Nut   6 Breather plug   7 Housing   8 Cover
9, 10 Gaskets   11 Cover   12 Bolt and spring washer   13 Cover   14 Bolt   15 Stud   16 Spring washer   17, 18 Nuts
19 Spring washer   20 Stud   21 Screw plug   22 Screw cover   23 Circlip   24 Stud   25 Spring washer   26 Nut
27 Housing   28 Stud   29 Spring washer   30 Nut   31 Gasket   32 Setpin   33 Gasket   34 Cover   35 Stud
36 Spring washer   37 Nut   38 Cover   39 Screw cap   40, 41 Studs   42 Gasket   43 Cover plate   44 Screw cap

light switch 10. Loosen the attachment nuts on the engine mount insulators as described in **Chapter 1**. Remove the transmission rear mount 11 from the body. Unscrew the fastening ring and remove the speedometer cable from its support on the transmission. Disconnect the clutch cable 14 from the release lever. Remove the flywheel cover from the bellhousing. Using a suitable swivel wrench, such as tool A.50095, remove the starter motor.

Attach engine support cross rail A.70526 or similar tool so that the engine rear end can be tilted down as far as possible. Securely support the transmission with a jack placed beneath the main housing.

Remove the attaching screws to separate the transmission from the engine crankcase. Carefully move the transmission rearwards, tilting it as necessary to slide the input shaft out of the clutch assembly. Lower the jack and remove the transmission from beneath the car. **Do not allow the weight of the gearbox to hang on the splined input shaft while it is in the clutch unit, or severe damage to the clutch driven plate and hub may occur.**

Refitting:

The gearbox is installed in the reverse order of removal. Make sure that all attachments are tightened to the correct torque loads. Set the correct clutch free-play and check that the lubricant level in the gearbox is correct. Check that the gears engage smoothly and freely. Before installing the gearbox, be sure that the breather is clear, as a blocked breather will allow pressure to rise inside the casing as the unit heats up which can force oil past the internal seals.

6:4 Dismantling the gearbox

Thoroughly clean the exterior of the unit to remove all road dirt and grease. Drain the lubricant from the gearbox. Invert the gearbox and remove the bottom cover, then remove the clutch release mechanism parts. Detach the crossmember from the gearbox, and if not already done, remove the speedometer drive adaptor by taking off the nut that secures it in place.

Remove the seven attachment nuts shown in **FIG 6:13** that secures the clutch housing to the casing and withdraw the clutch housing off its studs. Remove the front oil seal from the clutch housing centre cover. Wash the parts to remove any dirt and press a new oil seal back in position so that its lips face towards the gearbox. Lightly lubricate the lips of the oil seal with grease ready for reassembly.

FIG 132   55

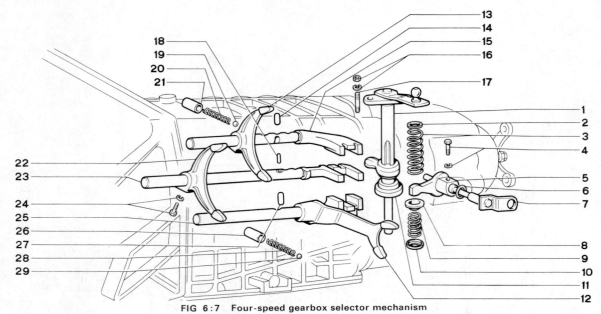

FIG 6:7 Four-speed gearbox selector mechanism

Key to Fig 6:7 1 Gear engagement control shaft 2 Seal 3 1st and 2nd stiffening spring 4 Screw and spring washer 5 Gear selector lever 6 Seal 7 Gear selector lever shaft 8 Upper cup 9 Reverse stiffening spring 10 Lower cup 11 Gear engagement control sleeve 12 Reverse fork 13 1st and 2nd fork 14 1st and 2nd roller 15 1st and 2nd fork rod 16 Nut and spring washer 17 Stud 18 3rd and 4th roller 19 1st and 2nd detent ball 20 Spring 21 Bush 22 3rd and 4th fork 23 3rd and 4th fork rod 24 Screw and spring washer 25 Reverse fork rod 26 Bush 27 Reverse roller 28 Spring 29 Reverse detent ball

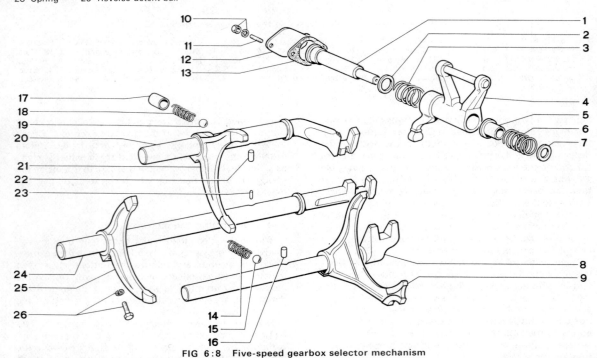

FIG 6:8 Five-speed gearbox selector mechanism

Key to Fig 6:8 1 Shaft 2 1st and 2nd shoulder washer 3 1st and 2nd stiffening spring 4 Lever 5 Bush 6 5th and reverse stiffening spring 7 5th and reverse shoulder washer 8 5th and reverse fork rod 9 5th and reverse fork 10 Nut and spring washer 11 Stud 12 Cover 13 Gasket 14 Spring 15 5th and reverse detent ball 16 5th and reverse roller 17 Bushing 18 Spring 19 1st and 2nd detent ball 20 1st and 2nd fork rod 21 1st and 2nd fork 22 1st and 2nd roller 23 3rd and 4th roller 24 3rd and 4th fork rod 25 3rd and 4th fork 26 Screw and spring washer

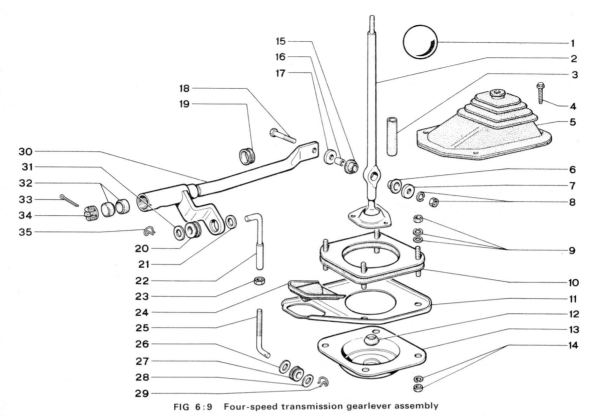

FIG 6:9   Four-speed transmission gearlever assembly

Key to Fig 6:9   1 Knob   **2** Gearlever   **3** Tube   **4** Screw   **5** Dust boot   **6** Bush   **7** Flat washer   **8** Nut and spring washer   **9** Nut, spring washer and flat washer   **10** Rubber pad   **11** Plate   **12** Ball socket   **13** Support   **14** Nut and spring washer   **15** Bushing   **16** Spacer   **17** Flat washer   **18** Screw   **19, 20** Grommets   **21** Flat washer   **22** Gear selector adjustable sleeve   **23** Tie rod locknut   **24** Rubber boot   **25** Tie rod   **26** Flat washer   **27** Grommet   **28** Flat washer   **29** Retainer   **30** Tie rod   **31** Flat washer   **32** Sockets   **33** Cotterpin   **34** Plug   **35** Spring retainer

Use a pair of circlip pliers to remove the circlip that secures the ring collar and ring seal to the end of the mainshaft, then withdraw the collar and seal. Make a thin painted line across the drive flange and the end of the mainshaft so that the drive flange will be installed in the same relative position. Remove the attachment bolt from one selector fork so that the fork can be slid independently along its shaft. Engage two gears simultaneously so that the gearbox is locked and cannot rotate. Free the tabs on the lockwasher and unscrew the nut that secures the drive flange to the mainshaft. Use a suitable puller to withdraw the drive flange from the mainshaft. Note that it may be necessary to use the universal puller to withdraw the ring collar from the shaft before the nut is accessible. Remove the nuts that secure the rear cover to the main casing and draw the rear cover back off its studs so that it can be removed.

Draw the speedometer drive gear off the mainshaft, taking care not to lose the ball that secures it. Remove the coverplate and its gasket from over the detent springs, shown in **FIG 6:14**, then remove the balls and springs. Note that the spring for the reverse detent is of heavier construction and therefore care should be taken to store

the parts in order and not intermix them. Remove the reverse gear selector shaft with its selector fork and the reverse gear idler wheel. These parts are shown assembled in **FIG 6:15**.

Remove the circlip that secures the reverse drive gear to the countershaft and withdraw the gear. Similarly remove the circlip that secures the reverse gear to the mainshaft, withdraw the gear and remove the drive key from the shaft.

With two gears still simultaneously engaged, remove the bolt and washers from the front of the countershaft, as shown in **FIG 6:16**, and withdraw the double ball-bearings. Remove the ballbearing from the rear end of the countershaft and lift the countershaft assembly out of the casing.

Free the bolts that secure the selector forks to the shafts and move them all back to the neutral positions. Draw out the selector shaft for third/fourth followed by the shaft for first/second. **Carefully collect the safety rollers as the shafts are withdrawn, noting how they are fitted for reassembly.**

Take out the three screws that secure the retainer plate for the central mainshaft bearing to the casing and remove

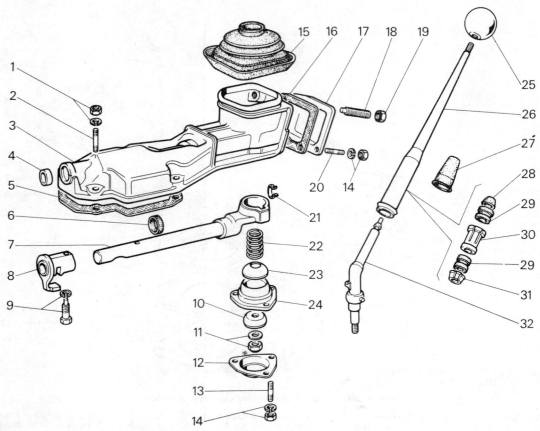

FIG 6:10   Five-speed transmission gearlever assembly

Key to Fig 6:10   1 Nut and lockwasher   2 Stud   3 Support   4 Plug   5 Gasket   6 Seal   7 Rod   8 Lug   9 Screw and lockwasher   10 Inner cup   11 Nut and flat washer   12 Lower socket   13 Stud   14 Nut and lockwasher   15 Dust boot   16 Gasket   17 Cover   18 Reverse stop pin   19 Nut   20 Stud   21 Retainer   22 Reverse spring   23 Cap   24 Upper cup   25 Knob   26 Gearlever   27 Boot   28 Pad   29 Bush   30 Spacer   31 Spring ring   32 Ball end lever

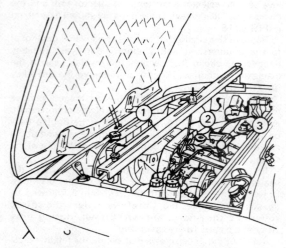

FIG 6:11   Installing the engine support tool

the retaining plate. Remove the ballbearing from the casing. Withdraw the input shaft assembly from the front of the casing. This action will release the two end plugs and 23 needle rollers that comprise the bearing between input and mainshaft. **Carefully collect all the needle rollers from the casing.** The mainshaft assembly can now be lifted out of the casing.

The bearing can be removed from the input shaft using a press and suitable tool after removal of the securing circlips.

The mainshaft parts can be dismantled after removal of the circlips. Care should be taken not to intermix the baulk rings as they will have mated in with the gear and synchromesh unit. Remove the synchromesh units complete without dismantling them. Before dismantling the synchromesh units, wrap them in cloth to catch all the parts then press the outer sleeve off the inner hub.

6:5 Inspection and reassembly

Wash all the parts in a suitable solvent such as fuel, paraffin or trichlorethylene and dry them with compressed

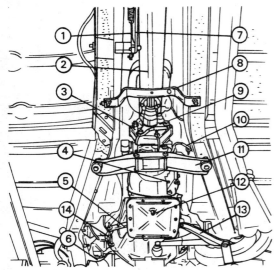

FIG 6:12 Items to be disconnected for gearbox removal

Key to Fig 6:12   1 Handbrake return spring plate
2 Front propeller shaft 3 Flexible joint 4 Rear oil drain plug
5 Clutch release lever   6 Earth lead   7 Handbrake rod
8 Protection bracket   9 Flexible joint sliding yoke
10 Reversing light leads   11 Gearbox rear mount and
insulator   12 Main oil drain plug   13 Exhaust pipe support
brackets   14 Clutch cable

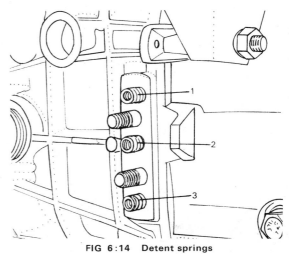

FIG 6:14   Detent springs
Key to Fig 6:14   1 Reverse gear spring   2 3rd/4th gear
spring   3 1st/2nd gear spring

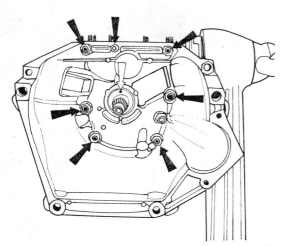

**FIG 6:13 The clutch housing attachment nuts. The
white arrow points to the oil drain hole**

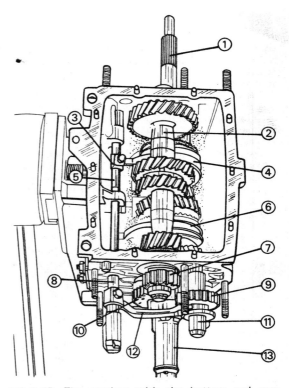

**FIG 6:15 The gearbox with the bottom and rear
covers removed**

Key to Fig 6:15   1 Input shaft   2 Countershaft
3 Selector fork for 3rd/4th gear   4 Selector sleeve for
3rd/4th gear   5 3rd/4th fork rod   6 Selector sleeve for
1st/2nd gear   7 Driven cog for reverse gear   8 Selector rod
for reverse gear   9 Reverse gear idler   10 Driving cog for
reverse gear   11 Reverse pinion   12 Selector fork of reverse
gear   13 Mainshaft

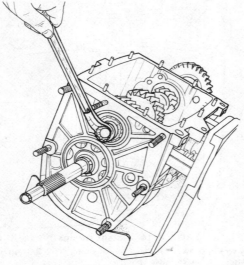

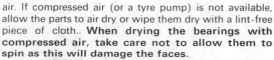

FIG 6:16 Removing the bolt from the countershaft

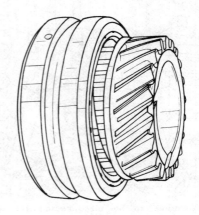

air. If compressed air (or a tyre pump) is not available, allow the parts to air dry or wipe them dry with a lint-free piece of cloth. **When drying the bearings with compressed air, take care not to allow them to spin as this will damage the faces.**

Discard all old gaskets and seals and use new ones on reassembly. If the old gaskets or seals must be used again, wipe them clean but do not wash or moisten them with any harsh solvent. Old sealing compound should be softened with trichlorethylene or carbon tetrachloride then scraped off with a piece of wood or perspex.

Check all the mating faces of the castings and covers for nicks, burrs or other damage. Light damage can be cleaned off by careful use of a scraper, fine file or oilstone. At the same time check all the castings for cracks, or damaged studs or threads.

Oil the bearings with thin oil and spin them to check for roughness in operation. Roughness can be caused by small specks of dirt, so wash the bearings again if they feel rough. Check the faces of the races for damage such as fret marks, scores, pitting or wear. If the condition of a bearing is at all in doubt it should be renewed.

Examine all the gears for broken or worn teeth, including the baulk ring teeth. If a tooth is found broken or damaged, pay particular attention to the teeth of the mating gear. Renew any damaged parts.

Check the shaft for fret marks, wear, or other damage, and check that all splines are unworn and undamaged. Bushes must rotate freely on the shafts and hubs must slide freely on the splines. The mainshaft should be supported between centres and checked for runout with a dial indicator. If the runout on the countershaft or mainshaft exceeds .001 inch (.025 mm) a new shaft should be fitted. Check all clearances and renew parts as required to bring clearances within limits. All bushes should have a clearance of .002 to .004 inch (.05 to .10 mm) on the shafts, with a maximum permissible clearance of .006 inch (.15 mm). The fitting clearance between the groove

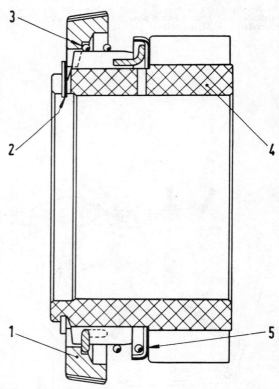

FIG 6:17 A synchromesh unit assembled (upper) and in cross-section (lower)

Key to Fig 6:17   1 Baulk ring   2 Circlip   3 Spring
4 Gear   5 Cup ring

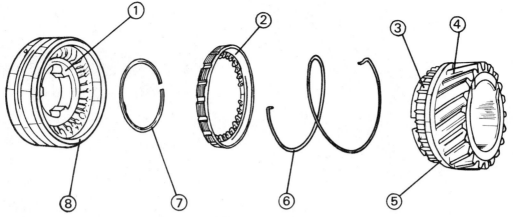

FIG 6:18   The components of a synchromesh unit

Key to Fig 6:18   1 Hub   2 Baulk ring   3 Blocker ring   4 Gear   5 Cup ring   6 Spring   7 Circlip   8 Sliding sleeve

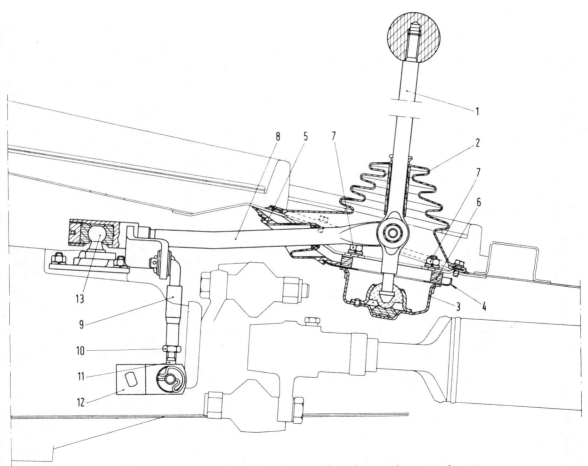

FIG 6:19   Sectioned view of the four-speed gearbox gearlever attachments

Key to Fig 6:19   1 Gearlever   2 Rubber cover   3 Support bracket   4 Cup   5 Cowl   6 Rubber buffer   7 Attachment nuts   8 Selector rod   9 Adjustable link   10 Locknut   11 Selector rod   12 Selector lever   13 Ball socket

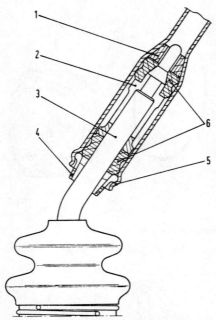

FIG 6:20 Section through the five-speed gear lever joint

Key to Fig 6:20 1 Shoulder block 2 Split collet spacer 3 Stub lever 4 Spring ring 5 Lever jacket 6 Rubber bushes

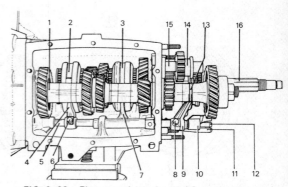

FIG 6:22 Five-speed gearbox with cover removed

Key to Fig 6:22 1 Countershaft 2 3rd and 4th sliding sleeve 3 1st and 2nd sliding sleeve 4 3rd and 4th selector fork 5 3rd and 4th selector fork rod 6 Screw, fork to 3rd and 4th rod 7 1st and 2nd selector fork 8 Screw, fork to 5th and reverse rod 9 5th and reverse selector fork 10 5th and reverse rod 11 1st and 2nd rod 12 3rd and 4th rod 13 5th and reverse gear on countershaft 14 Reverse idler gear 15 Reverse shaft 16 Mainshaft

flanks of the gear sliding sleeves should be .0027 to .0063 inch (.07 to .16 mm) with a maximum allowable clearance of .0079 inch (.2 mm).

As a safety precaution, new circlips should always be used on reassembly. Avoid spreading the circlips excessively and wherever possible use a suitable hollow drift to drive them back into position. Parts must be assembled scrupulously clean and they should be lubricated with SAE 90 oil as they are fitted.

The components and assembly of the synchromesh unit is shown in **FIGS 6:17** and **6:18**.

The gearbox is reassembled in the reverse order of dismantling. All attachments, nuts and bolts should be tightened to the correct torque loadings.

6:6 The selector mechanism

The components of the four-speed gearbox mechanism are shown in **FIG 6:9**. A sectioned view of the assembly is shown in **FIG 6:19**. The only adjustment possible is at the locknut 10 and this should be used to ensure that the selector 12 is in the neutral position when the gearlever is central in the lateral plane. Faults in the selector mechanism may be caused by slack attachments or worn rubber bushes, giving a sloppy feel to the gearlever.

The gearlever components for the five-speed gearbox are shown in **FIG 6:10**. There are no adjustments to be made as the linkage is direct. To ensure that vibration and noise from the gearbox is not transmitted into the car, the gearlever is in two parts with rubber bushes between them. Defective rubber bushes will give a poor feel to the gearlever and may also cause rattles. A sectioned view of the attachment is shown in **FIG 6:20**. Free the upper lever from the lower and free the spring ring 4 from the lever jacket, so that the upper portion can be removed for access to the rubber bushes and spacer.

An internal view of the rear cover showing the levers and springs assembled is shown in **FIG 6:21**, and the position of the selector forks and gears in **FIG 6:22**.

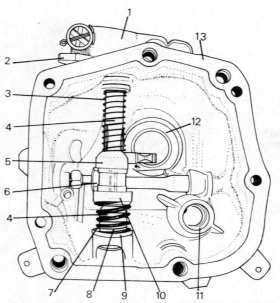

FIG 6:21 Selector linkage installed in the rear cover

Key to Fig 6:21 1 Connecting linkage for gearbox selector system 2 Outer selector lever 3 Thrust spring, imparting thrust when 1st/2nd gears are engaged 4 Selector shaft 5 Inner selector lever 6 Shaft with intermediate lever 7, 8 Thrust springs imparting thrust when reverse gear is engaged 9 Lower cup 10 Upper cup 11 Reverse idler shaft support 12 Seal 13 Rear cover

6:7 Fault diagnosis

(a) Jumping out of gear

1 Weak, broken or incorrectly fitted detent spring
2 Detent ball broken or omitted on reassembly
3 Badly worn detent groove in selector shaft
4 Worn baulk rings or synchromesh units
5 Selector fork loose on shaft
6 Worn selector forks

(b) Noisy gearbox

1 Insufficient or incorrect lubricant
2 Excessive end floats and clearances
3 Worn or damaged bearings
4 Worn or damaged gear teeth

(c) Oil leaks

1 Blocked breather
2 Too high lubricant level
3 Defective oil seals
4 Defective gaskets or loose attachments
5 Damaged joint faces

(d) Difficult gearchanging

1 Excessively worn clutch
2 Incorrectly adjusted clutch
3 Defective input shaft spigot bearing in crankshaft end
4 Worn synchromesh cones
5 Stiff gearlever mounting

NOTES

CHAPTER 7

AUTOMATIC TRANSMISSION

7:1 Description

Automatic transmission is supplied as optional extra to take the place of the usual clutch and gearbox. The automatic transmission (see **FIG 7:1**) consists of a torque converter and hydraulically controlled automatic epicyclic gearbox with three forward speeds and one reverse. In all gears the drive is through the torque converter which results in maximum flexibility, especially in top gear. The gears are selected automatically as the hydraulic control system engages clutches and/or applies brake bands in various combinations. The hydraulic control system and the torque converter assembly are supplied with pressure oil from an oil pump mounted within the transmission case. A manually controlled mechanical parking pawl is incorporated so that the transmission output shaft can be locked when the vehicle is stationary.

The torque converter consists of an impeller connected through a drive plate to the engine crankshaft, a turbine which is splined to the transmission input shaft and a stator connected to the unit by a one-way clutch. The impeller, driven by the engine, transmits torque by means of the transmission fluid to the turbine which drives the automatic gearbox. The stator redirects the flow of fluid as it leaves the turbine so that it re-enters the impeller at the most effective angle.

When the engine is idling, the converter impeller is being driven slowly and the energy of the fluid leaving it is low, so little torque is imparted to the turbine. For this reason, with the engine idling and drive engaged, the vehicle will have little or no tendency to move from rest. As the throttle is opened impeller speed increases and the process of torque multiplication begins. As the turbine picks up speed and the slip between it and the impeller reduces, the torque multiplication reduces progressively until, when their speeds become substantially equal, the unit acts as a fluid coupling. In this condition, the stator is no longer required to redirect the fluid flow and the roller clutch permits it to rotate with the impeller and turbine.

7:2 Maintenance

Every 3000 miles (5000 km) the fluid in the automatic transmission should be checked. The car should be taken for a run of at least five miles to ensure that the automatic transmission is at normal operating temperature. Apply the handbrake, start the engine and allow it to idle in P (Park). Leave the engine idling while the fluid level is checked. Remove the automatic transmission dipstick, wipe it clean on a non-fluffy cloth and recase it fully. Remove the dipstick and check the level of fluid against

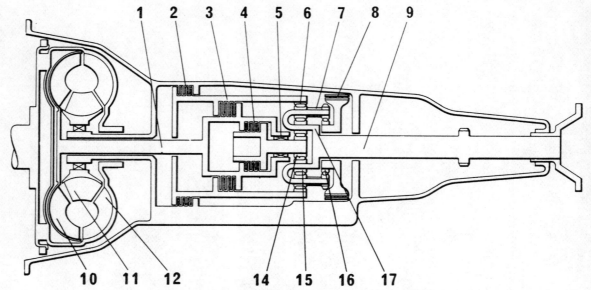

FIG 7:1   Schematic diagram of the automatic transmission

Key to Fig 7:1   1 Input shaft   2 Reverse clutch   3 Intermediate clutch   4 High clutch   5 One-way clutch   6 Ring gear   7 Long pinion gear   8 Brake band   9 Output shaft   10 Turbine   11 Stator   12 Impeller   14 Front sun gear   15 Short pinion gear   16 Rear sun gear   17 Pinion carrier

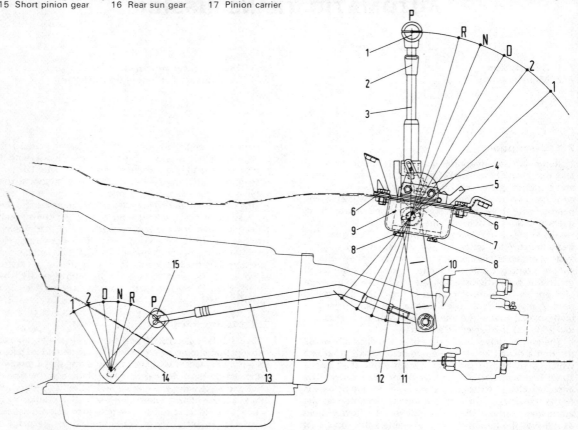

FIG 7:2   Side view of the automatic transmission selector mechanism   For key see Fig 7:3

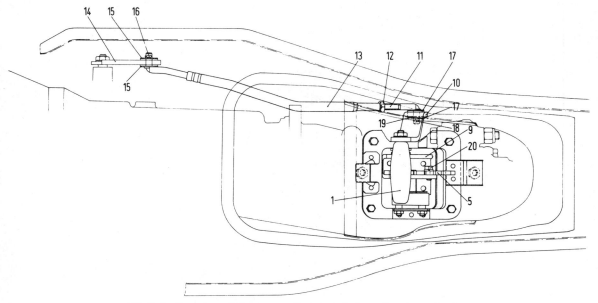

FIG 7:3   Top view of the automatic transmission selector mechanism

Key to Figs 7:2 and 7:3   1 Handle   2 Release catch   3 Selector lever   4 Starter inhibitor switch   5 Gear selector
6 Screw   7 Support   8 Screw   9 Bracket   10 Relay lever   11 Tie rod adjustable end   12 Locknut   13 Tie rod
14 Cross-shaft actuating lever   15 Flat washer   16 Cotterpin   17 Flat washer   18 Cotterpin   19 Bush   20 Gear
selector screw

the marks. Top up through the dipstick tube if necessary to bring the fluid level to the upper mark on the dipstick. **Do not overfill.** Use Fiat GI/A oil or DEXRON Automatic Transmission Fluid. **Never use anything but the recommended fluid in the automatic transmission.**

Every 25,000 miles (40,000 km) or every second year, the automatic transmission fluid should be changed. Remove the drain plug from beneath the automatic transmission and allow the fluid to drain into a suitable container. Refit the drain plug and refill the transmission with the correct grade of fluid. 4.4 pints (2.5 litres) of new fluid will be required to refill the transmission after draining. Check the fluid level again when the transmission is at normal operating temperature and top up if necessary as described previously.

7:3 Gear selector linkages

A manual selector, located on the floor in the centre of the driver's compartment, offers a choice of six positions by moving a T-handled lever in a quadrant. These positions, illuminated at night, are marked P–R–N–D–2–1 and give the following services:

P or Park:

In this position the engine may be started and run without any drive being transmitted to the road wheels. At the same time the mechanical lock is applied and the car cannot be moved in either direction. P must never be selected while the car is in motion.

R or Reverse:

The car should always be brought completely to a halt before reverse is selected.

N or Neutral:

Similar in application to P, but the lock is not applied.

D or Drive:

This position is used for all normal running. When D is selected from rest the car will move off in first gear and the transmission will change automatically to second and third gears, and down again, at speeds appropriate to road speeds and throttle positions.

2 or Second:

As for D, but there will be no upward change into top gears. If selected while running in top gear, an immediate change down to second will be made, thus providing engine braking or the possibility of improved acceleration.

1 or First:

In this position the transmission is locked in low gear.

Selector lever release catch:

A spring loaded grip on the selector lever is incorporated to engage or release a catch mechanism in the selector quadrant to prevent accidental selection of certain positions. The grip has to be raised for the following position changes—P–R, R–P, N–R, D–N and 2–1.

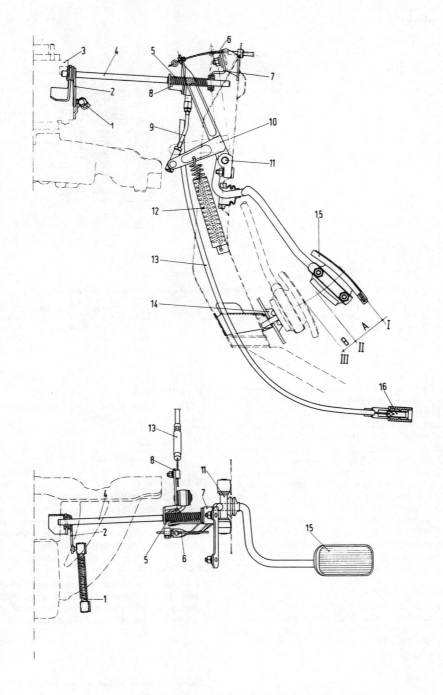

FIG 7:4 Accelerator pedal and downshift valve control linkage

Key to Fig 7:4   1 Accelerator control rod   2 Actuating lever   3 Carburetter   4 Control shaft   5 Return spring   6 Manual accelerator cable   7 Accelerator control shaft bracket   8 Relay lever   9 Control rod   10 Control arm   11 Pivot pin   12 Return spring   13 Kick-down control cable sheath   14 Accelerator pedal stop   15 Accelerator pedal   16 Kick-down valve   A Accelerator pedal travel from position I to position II   B Accelerator pedal travel from position II to position III

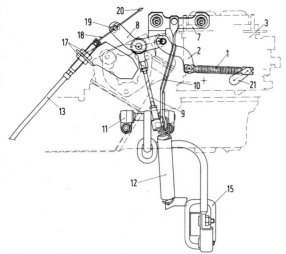

FIG 7:5 The accelerator linkage at the carburetter

For key see Fig 7:6

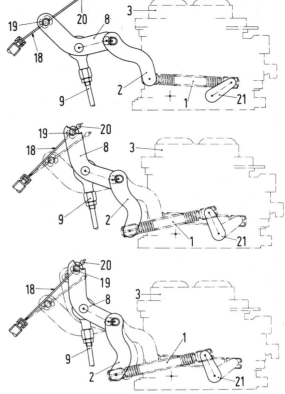

FIG 7:6 The three accelerator linkage checking positions

Key to Figs 7:5 and 7:6   1 Telescoping link
2 Actuating arm   3 Carburetter   7 Throttle control shaft
support bracket   8 Bellcrank   9 Adjustable rod
10 Accelerator control lever   11 Pivot pin   12 Return spring
13 Kick-down cable sheath   15 Accelerator pedal   17 Cable
sheath adjustment nuts   18 Kick-down valve control cable
19 Cable pin   20 Cable terminal   21 Accelerator control
lever

Also included in the base of the selector quadrant is a starter inhibitor switch, the purpose of which is to ensure that the starter can be operated only when the selector lever is in the P or N positions.

Selector linkage adjustment:

Linkage adjustment is not likely to be needed unless difficulty is encountered in gear selection, or if the transmission has been removed and refitted for servicing purposes. If adjustment is necessary, carry out the work as follows, referring to **FIGS 7:2** and **7:3**.

Make sure that the car is standing on level ground and fully apply the handbrake. Disconnect the tie rod 13 from relay lever 10 and set this in position P by moving the selector lever in the car fully forward. From beneath the car, set lever 14 in position P (fully back). To check that lever 14 is correctly in the P position, release the handbrake and check that the car is locked against movement by the parking pawl in the transmission. Turn the threaded end 11 to adjust the length of rod 13 until it fits smoothly in relay lever 10 without any binding. Lock nut 12 and reconnect rod 13 to the relay lever 10. Hold the lever locking catch up and move the selector lever through all six gear positions, checking that a definite click can be felt as each position is selected.

Check the selector lever 3 for correct positioning in gear selector gate 5. To do this, lift catch 2 and move the selector to position 1. When the catch is released with the selector lever in position 1, the selector lever should not move at all. If necessary, readjust rod 13 to achieve this condition. Check also that the reversing light comes on in position R.

Accelerator linkage adjustment:

This adjustment is necessary to ensure that the transmission makes upward and downward changes at the correct points according to accelerator pedal travel. For the purposes of obtaining the correct adjustment of this control the travel of the accelerator pedal may be

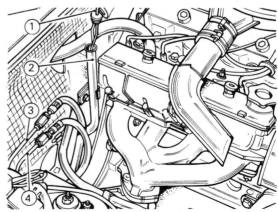

FIG 7:7 Items to be detached before automatic transmission removal

Key to Fig 7:7   1 Dipstick   2 Oil filler tube
3, 4 Transmission oil lines

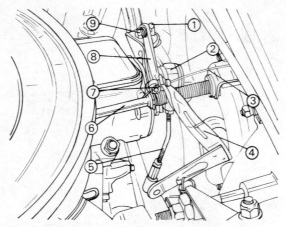

FIG 7:8   Disconnecting the accelerator control linkage

Key to Fig 7:8   1 Kick-down control cable   **2** Ball joint head   **3** Accelerator hand control cable   **4** Accelerator control lever   **5** Adjustable control rod   **6** Control shaft   **7** Cable clamp   **8** Idler lever   **9** Cable clamp

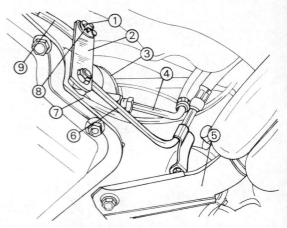

FIG 7:10   The gear selector and parking valve linkage

Key to Fig 7:10   1 Clip   **2** Cross-shaft control lever   **3** Vacuum line   **4** Oil line   **5** Front exhaust pipe support bracket   **6** Oil line   **7** Kick-down cable sheath   **8** Flat washer   **9** Link

considered as divided into two parts. These are designated A and B as shown in **FIG 7:4**. Part A is from the pedal at rest position I to full throttle II, part B is from full throttle to the pedal stop 14 in position III. This latter part of the travel is accomplished by means of a telescoping link which overcomes the action of a built-in spring.

Travel B (kick-down travel) is adjusted first, followed by adjustment of travel A (accelerator travel). Refer to **FIGS 7:4**, **7:5** and **7:6** when making adjustment.

Travel B:

Disconnect the end of the telescoping link 1 at throttle control lever 21. Bring the cable pin 19 into contact with cable terminal 20. Pull pin 19 so that cable 18 moves the full length of its travel, corresponding to the travel of kick-down valve 16 in the transmission. Press the accelerator pedal fully down against its stop 14 when the minimum clearance between the control arm 10 and the bracket 7 should be .157 inch (4.0 mm).

Working on the adjustable end of link 1, push it in to fully compress its built-in spring. Under these conditions, it should be possible to insert the end of link 1 to the throttle shaft lever 21 with the spring fully compressed. If not, loosen the locknut and nut 17 and the upper end of the cable 13 until the correct fitting of link 1 is obtained. Take care not to overtighten the kick-down valve cable 18 to avoid excessive wear of the cable sheath 13.

Travel A:

Disconnect the end of the telescoping link 1 at the throttle control lever 21. Bring cable pin 19 into contact with cable terminal 20. Move the throttle control lever 21 to the wide open position.

The travel of the kick-down valve cable 18 should be between .275 and .354 inch (7 to 9 mm) and it should be possible to re-insert the end of link 1 on lever 21 without compressing the link spring. If these conditions are not obtained, adjust the accelerator control rod 9 as necessary.

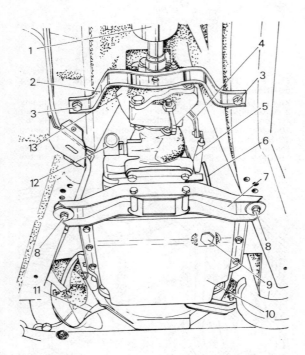

FIG 7:9   The automatic transmission viewed from beneath the car

Key to Fig 7:9   1 Front propeller shaft   **2** Protection bracket   **3** Screws   **4** Idler lever   **5** Rod   **6** Vacuum line   **7** Rear mount and insulator   **8** Screws   **9** Oil drain plug   **10** Oil sump   **11** Earth lead   **12** Speedometer drive gear support   **13** Flexible joint

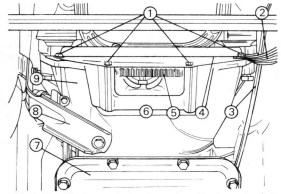

FIG 7:11   The transmission to engine attachment points

Key to Fig 7:11   1 Flywheel cover screws   2 Earth lead
3 Speedometer cable   4 Flywheel cover   5 Flywheel
6 Torque converter   7 Oil sump   8 Front exhaust pipe
support bracket   9 Transmission front housing

If the valve cable travel is more than 9 mm, shorten the
control rod, lengthen it if the travel is less than 7 mm.

Check that when the manual throttle knob is fully home
there is a gap of .12 to .16 inch (3 to 4 mm) between the
stop on the end of the cable 6 and the throttle control
lever.

**Note that it is essential that when the accelerator
pedal is against its stop 14 the kick-down valve 16
has completed its travel.**

7:4   Transmission removal

Remove the drain plug from beneath the transmission
and allow the fluid to drain into a suitable container.
Disconnect the battery negative terminals.

Refer to **FIGS 7:7** and **7:8**. Remove the oil filler tube
and dipstick and disconnect the delivery and return lines
from the heat exchanger. Remove the kick-down control
cable clamp.

Disconnect and remove the vacuum line from the
carburetter and modulator. Refer to **FIGS 7:9, 7:10** and
7:11. Remove the flywheel cover and disconnect the
front exhaust pipe support bracket. Remove the cross-
shaft control lever safety clip and unhook the longitudinal
rod. Detach the speedometer drive gear support and
sheath. Remove the front propeller shaft protection
bracket. Disconnect the propeller shaft from the transmission, then remove the transmission rear mount
attachment screws.

Working through the opening of the flywheel cover,
remove the three screws which secure the torque
converter to the flywheel (see **FIG 7:12**), rotating the
flywheel as necessary for access.

Remove the starter motor. Detach the kick-down cable
bracket and unhook the cable. Detach the oil return line
support bracket. Remove the upper flywheel cover
attachment screw.

Place a suitable jack beneath the car to support the
transmission, then remove the screws securing the
transmission front housing to the engine and slide out
the transmission and converter assembly. Keep the rear
end of the transmission tilted downwards during removal
to prevent the torque converter from falling out.

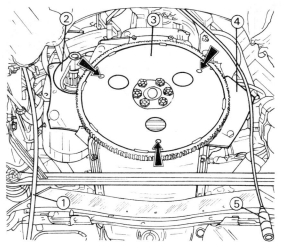

**FIG 7:12   The torque converter to flywheel attachment
points (arrowed)**

Key to Fig 7:12   1 Speedometer cable   2 Starter motor
3 Flywheel   4 Upper flywheel cover   5 Kick-down valve

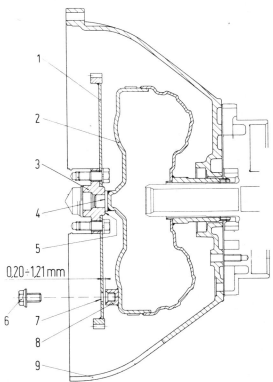

0,20÷1,21 mm

FIG 7:13   Checking torque converter installation

Key to Fig 7:13   1 Flywheel   2 Torque converter
3 Flywheel attachment flange   4, 5 Contact surfaces
between converter and flywheel   6 Converter to flywheel
screw   7 Attachment point of converter to flywheel
8 Attachment boss   9 Front transmission housing

Refitting:

This is a reversal of the removal procedure, noting the following points. As the converter is balanced by the manufacturers it can be installed to the flywheel in any position.

When the transmission housing has been attached to the engine crankcase, refer to **FIG 7:13** and push the converter 2 against the flywheel attachment flange 3. In this position, use a feeler gauge to check that a gap of .008 to .048 inch (0.20 to 1.21 mm) exists between each one of the converter attachment bosses 8 and the corresponding attachment point 7 on the flywheel 1. If the measured clearance is beyond these limits, it will be necessary to renew the engine flywheel.

On completion, check the selector and accelerator linkage adjustments as described in **Section 7:3**. Refill the transmission with fluid, the total capacity after overhaul being 10 pints (5.6 litres). Add fluid until the level is at the lower mark on the dipstick, then drive the car until the transmission is at normal operating temperature before finally correcting the level as described in **Section 7:2**.

CHAPTER 8

THE PROPELLER SHAFT, REAR AXLE
AND REAR SUSPENSION

8:1 Description

Power is transmitted from the transmission output shaft to the differential unit pinion shaft by a two-piece propeller shaft, the rear part of this shaft being fitted with universal joints to accommodate suspension movement. An intermediate ballbearing is mounted to the floor assembly by a flexible rubber mounting. Power is transmitted from the differential assembly to the rear wheels by drive shafts splined into the differential side gears.

Rear suspension is by means of coil springs and telescopic hydraulic dampers. The rear axle is positively located by means of two longitudinal and two inclined struts.

The items of maintenance and overhaul which can be carried out by a reasonably competent owner/mechanic are given in this chapter, but it is not advised that any further operations be attempted. Special tools and equipment are essential to overhaul the drive shafts and differential components and set the necessary preloads, so, for these reasons, the components mentioned should be dismantled and serviced only by a Fiat agent having the necessary equipment and trained fitters.

8:2 Routine maintenance

At 6000 miles (10,000 km) intervals the lubricant level in the differential unit must be checked. With the car standing on level ground and the axle cold, wipe dirt from around the filler plug at the rear of the differential unit and remove the plug. The oil level is correct if it reaches to the lower edge of the filler hole. If the level is low, top up with SAE.90 EP oil. Allow the surplus to drain out before refitting the filler plug. At the same time check the breather on top of the casing to see that it is clean and clear.

At intervals of 18,000 miles (30,000 km) remove the drain plug from beneath the differential and allow the oil to drain out. Draining will be easier if it is carried out after a run when the oil is hot. Fit the drain plug, remove the filler plug and slowly fill the axle to the correct level with new oil. Lubricate the front propeller shaft sliding joint with lithium-base grease, applying the grease gun at the nipple provided.

8:3 The propeller shaft

Removal:

Refer to **FIG 8:1** and disconnect the handbrake linkage by removing cotterpin 2 and disengaging return spring plate 3 and lever rod 6.

The flexible rubber coupling is shown in **FIG 8:2**. Mark with paint dots the appropriate lugs of the drive flanges, then fit the tool A.70025 around the couplings as

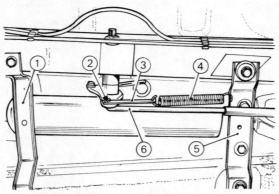

FIG 8:1 Disconnecting the handbrake linkage

Key to Fig 8:1 1 Front protection bracket 2 Cotterpin
3 Spring plate 4. Return spring 5 Centre bearing
crossmember 6 Lever rod

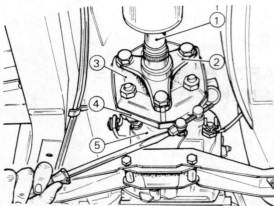

FIG 8:2 Removing the flexible joint with the special tool

Key to Fig 8:2 1 Front propeller shaft 2 Sliding yoke
3 Flexible joint 4 Compressor A.70025 5 Insulator

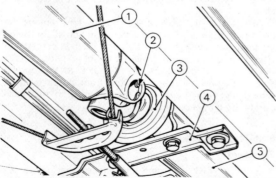

FIG 8:3 Disconnecting the propeller shaft centre bearing assembly

Key to Fig 8:3 1 Rear propeller shaft 2 Snap ring
3 Ballbearing 4 Centre bearing crossmember 5 Front
propeller shaft

shown in the illustration and tighten the clamp on the tool. Remove the nuts and bolts which secure the coupling to the transmission drive flange. The special tool must be used to compress the coupling otherwise it will be found practically impossible to remove the bolts. New couplings may be supplied with a steel strap around them and this should be left in place until the coupling is installed, as it takes the place of the special tool. Do not forget to remove the tool or strap after installation.

Remove the bolts and washers that secure the central bearing mounts to the frame as shown in **FIG 8:3**.

Paint aligning marks across the flanges of the rear propeller shaft universal joint flange and the differential pinion flange so that they can be correctly realigned when refitting. Remove the nuts and bolts that secure the universal joint to the pinion flange (see **FIG 8:4**). Detach the propeller shaft front protection bracket from the body and remove the propeller shaft assembly from beneath the car.

Servicing:

The propeller shaft components are shown in **FIG 8:5**. When the propeller shaft has been removed, check the condition of the centring ring and the seal behind it on the gearbox output shaft. If worn or damaged, they can be pulled off after removal of the retaining circlip.

Front coupling and sliding joint:

If the flexible coupling shows any sign of damage or perishing it should be renewed. The sliding coupling should slide freely along the shaft but there should be no rotational play. If rotational play is detected, new parts must be fitted.

Universal joints:

Repair kits for servicing universal joints are available and if the joint is worn or defective all the parts supplied in the kit should be used. Do not renew individual parts of the joint.

Remove the four circlips that secure the bearing cups in place, using suitable circlip pliers. If difficulty is found in removing the circlips, clean the area and bore thoroughly to remove dirt and corrosion then lightly tap the bearing cup inwards to relieve the pressure on the circlips.

Lay the arms on to two blocks of wood so that the arms only are supported. Tap gently downwards on the other portion of the shaft so that the spider, being supported on the arms, forces the upper bearing out of the upper arm. When the bearing cup has been driven out sufficiently, grip it with the fingers or pliers and pull it completely out. Turn the shaft over and remove the opposite bearing cup in a similar manner. The shaft can then be turned through 90 deg. so that the other pair of arms is supported and remaining pair of bearing cups removed in a similar manner. Manoeuvre the spider out of the arms.

If the bores in the arms are worn oval then the shaft parts must be renewed. Check that the bearing cups are a light drive fit through the bores.

Check that the seals on the spider arms are securely in place and undamaged. If the seals are damaged, remove them and install new ones. Lightly smear the bottom of the seal with jointing compound and drive it firmly back into position with a suitable hollow drift.

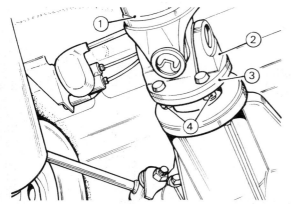

FIG 8:4 The rear propeller shaft to differential flange attachment

Key to Fig 8:4 1 Rear propeller shaft 2 Universal joint yoke 3 Drive pinion flange 4 Attachment screws and nuts

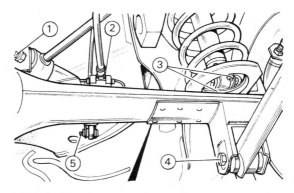

FIG 8:6 The damper and reaction strut mounting points

Key to Fig 8:6 1 Upper reaction strut attaching screw 2 Brake fluid line connector 3 Damper lower mounting nuts 4 Lower reaction strut attaching screw 5 Brake regulator link attaching screw

Each bearing cup must be filled with needle rollers held in place by grease. The correct number of needle rollers precisely fills the cup, leaving no gaps or surplus needles.

Fit the spider back into place and carefully press one cup back into position, between the padded jaws of a vice. Take great care that the spider enters the bearing cup correctly, without displacing any needle rollers, and that the recesses in the spider are well packed with grease. Install the opposite bearing cup in a similar manner. The vice will only press the cups back in flush with the arms. Use either a mandrel of a diameter just smaller than the bearing cups as a spacer between cup and vice jaw, or else use a soft-nosed drift of the correct diameter to drive

the cups back into place. Secure the cups with new circlips, making sure that the circlips are fully and squarely seated in their recesses.

Install the remaining pair of bearing cups in a similar manner. When all four bearing cups are in place, make sure that the joint moves freely without binding. If the joint is stiff, tap on the arms of the yokes so that the bearing cups free and move back again to the circlips.

Centre bearing:

Remove the crossmember from the rubber mounting assembly. Check that the rubber mounting for the bearing is in good condition and that the rubber is neither splitting

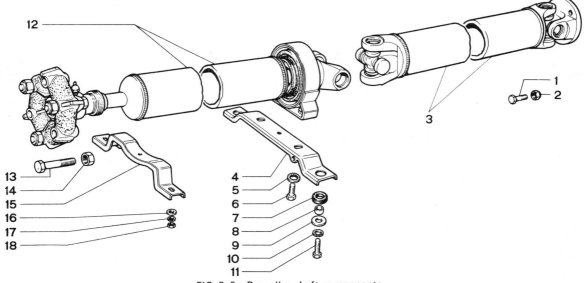

FIG 8:5 Propeller shaft components

Key to Fig 8:5 1, 2 Screw and nut 3 Rear propeller shaft 4 Crossmember 5 Lockwasher 6 Screw 7 Insulator 8 Spacer 9 Flat washer 10 Lockwasher 11 Screw 12 Front propeller shaft 13, 14 Screw and nut 15 Front protection bracket 16 Flat washer 17 Lockwasher 18 Nut

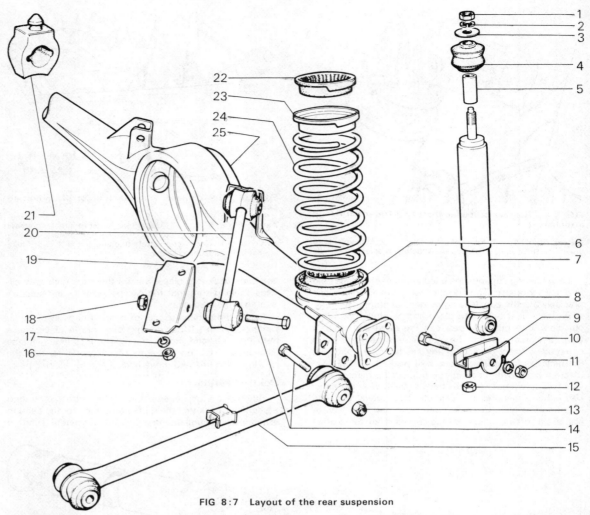

FIG 8:7 Layout of the rear suspension

Key to Fig 8:7   1 Damper upper attachment nut   2 Lockwasher   3 Cup   4 Insulator   5 Spacer   6 Coil spring lower insulator   7 Damper   8 Screw   9 Lower support   10 Lockwasher   11, 12, 13 Nuts   14 Strut screws   15 Lower strut   16 Nut   17 Lockwasher   18 Nut   19 Upper strut mounting   20 Upper strut   21 Rubber buffer   22, 23 Coil spring upper insulators   24 Coil spring   25 Axle housing

or perishing. The bearing itself must rotate freely without noise or binding. If the parts are defective, take off the nut and remove the yoke from the rear shaft assembly, using a suitable puller. It is essential to mark the shaft and yoke so that they are reassembled without disturbing the balance of the shaft. Pull the centre bearing assembly off the front shaft. Remove the circlip that secures the bearing in the rubber mount and press the bearing out.

The parts are reassembled in the reverse order of removal after renewing defective components.

8:4 Rear axle

Removal:

Raise the rear of the car onto chassis stands and remove the rear road wheels. Drain the oil from the differential unit. Disconnect the handbrake cable from the brake caliper at each rear wheel.

Disconnect the propeller shaft from the pinion shaft flange as described in **Section 8:3**. Disconnect the brake caliper hoses from the pipes and the three-way connector from the axle housing, plugging the open ends of the brake lines to prevent fluid loss.

Disconnect the brake regulator control link, then support the rear axle with a suitable jack. Disconnect the damper lower mounts and the longitudinal and transverse reaction struts as shown in **FIG 8:6**. Lower the axle and remove the assembly from beneath the car.

Refitting:

The axle is installed in the reverse order of removal. Set the suspension static heights, as described in the next

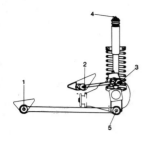
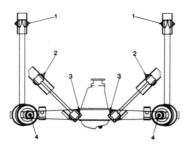
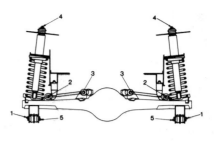

FIG 8:8   Rear suspension mounting points

Key to Fig 8:8   1 Lower struts to body attachment screws   2 Upper struts to body support attachment screws   3 Upper struts to axle housing attachment screws   4 Damper upper attachment studs   5 Lower struts to axle housing attachment screws

section, before fully tightening the nuts that secure the bolts of the flexible bushes. On completion, bleed the braking system and check the handbrake adjustment as described in **Chapter 11**.

8:5 Rear suspension

The layout of the rear suspension components is shown in **FIG 8:7**. The diagrams in **FIG 8:8** show the rear suspension mounting points.

Coil spring and damper removal:

From inside the luggage compartment disconnect the upper end of the damper from the body floor. This is done by unscrewing the hexagon nut while holding the squared end of the damper stud to prevent its rotation.

Raise the rear end of the car and support it on stands, then support the axle casing with a jack.

Disconnect the upper struts 20 from the body, brake lines and brake regulator torsion bar from the axle housing and the damper lower fixings.

Lower the axle on the jack and remove the coil springs and dampers.

Check the rubber bushes for wear or deterioration, renewing faulty parts as necessary. Defective damper units can be overhauled at a Fiat service station.

Refitting:

Refitting is a reversal of the removal operation, but it is essential to set the suspension to the correct static height in the following manner before tightening the upper and lower strut mountings.

Working on the bench, mount the upper struts to their supports making sure that the angle formed by the strut axis with the plane of the support is 12 deg., as shown in **FIG 8:9**. Maintain the correct angle while tightening the nut to 32.5 lb ft (4.5 kgm). Attach the upper struts supports to the studs provided on the body and tighten the nuts to 40 lb ft (5.5 kgm).

Position the coil springs on to their seats on the axle housing. Raise the axle housing until it is possible to fit the lower damper attachment screws to the anchors on the axle housing, then connect the upper struts to the axle housing and the lower struts to the body. Do not tighten any of the attachment nuts yet. Now raise the

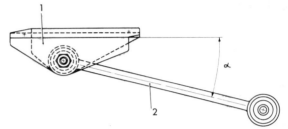

FIG 8:9   Setting the upper suspension strut to the correct angle of 12 deg. before installation

Key to Fig 8:9   1 Mounting   2 Upper strut

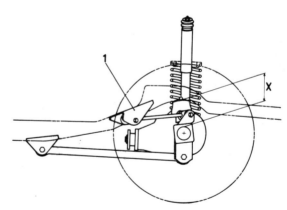

FIG 8:10   Setting the suspension to the correct static height before tightening the strut mountings

Key to Fig 8:10   1 Upper strut support   X = 4.63 inch (117.5 mm)

axle housing until distance **X** (see **FIG 8:10**) is 4.63 inch (117.5 mm). In this position, tighten the lower damper attachment nuts to 14.5 lb ft (2 kgm) and the strut attachment nuts to 32.5 lb ft (4.5 kgm).

On completion, bleed the braking system and check the handbrake adjustment as described in **Chapter 11**.

8:6 Fault diagnosis

(a) Noisy axle

1 Incorrect or insufficient lubricant
2 Worn bearings
3 Worn gears
4 Damaged or broken gear teeth
5 Incorrect adjustments in differential
6 General wear

(b) Excessive backlash

1 Worn gears or bearings
2 Worn drive shaft splines
3 Worn universal joints
4 Defective flexible couplings
5 Loose wheel attachments

(c) Oil leaks

1 Defective oil seals
2 Defective gasket or distorted casing
3 Blocked breather
4 Overfilled rear axle

(d) Vibration

1 Propeller shaft out of balance
2 Defective centre bearing or flexible coupling
3 Worn universal joints

(e) Rattles

1 Worn universal joints
2 Worn suspension rubber bushings
3 Loose or worn damper mountings

(f) Knock

1 Check (a)
2 Badly worn splines on drive shafts
3 Worn universal joints

CHAPTER 9

FRONT SUSPENSION AND HUBS

9:1 Description

A general view of the complete steering and front suspension is shown in **FIG 9:1** and a sectioned view of one suspension assembly in **FIG 9:2**.

Unequal length wishbones are used, pivoting vertically about their inner ends. The steering knuckle assembly is fitted to the outboard ends of the wishbones by means of ball joints which accommodate lateral steering and vertical suspension movement. Coil springs are fitted between the upper wishbone and the frame of the car. A telescopic damper is fitted concentrically inside each coil spring to control the suspension movements and to damp out oscillations. On 132 GL/GLS models the dampers are progressive-rate type and an anti-roll bar also is fitted.

The road wheel is fitted to a hub which revolves about the stub axle of the steering knuckle on two opposed tapered bearings.

9:2 Maintenance

At intervals of 3000 miles (5000 km) check the suspension for faults or defects. The steering linkage should be checked at the same time. Examine the dust covers over all ball joints for splits, chaffing or other damage. Faulty dust covers must be renewed as soon as possible, otherwise road dirt will enter the joint and cause excessive wear. Check for excessive play in the steering linkage and suspension components.

At 18,000 miles (30,000 km) intervals, remove the hubs so that the bearings can be examined, packed with clean fresh grease and adjusted after installation. These operations are dealt with in the next sections.

9:3 The front hubs

FIG 9:3 shows the components of the front hub assembly.

Jack-up the front of the car so that the road wheels are clear of the ground. Spin the wheels and check that they rotate freely without bearing noise, taking care not to confuse noise from the brake with that from a defective bearing. Grasp the tyre at the top and bottom of the wheel and attempt to rock the top of the wheel in and out while noting the play. Repeat the test with the tyre gripped at each side of the wheel. Excessive play will dictate overhaul of the wheel bearings.

Removal:

Slacken the road wheel attachments and raise the front of the car onto stands. Remove the road wheels. Remove

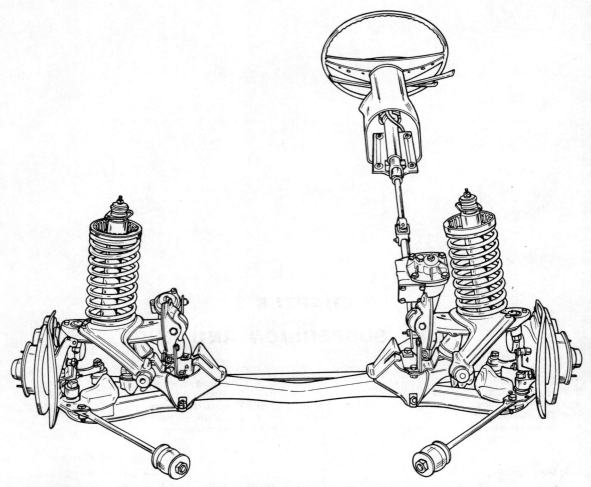

FIG 9:1   The steering and front suspension assembly

the brake caliper and wire it to the suspension to avoid straining the hose.

Carefully lever or pull the grease cap from the hub. Free the lockwasher and remove the hub nut. Discard both washer and nut as new components must be used when reassembling the bearings.

Use a suitable puller to remove the hub assembly from the stub axle, collecting the inner race of the outer bearing as it comes free. Remove the oil seal from the hub and remove the inner race of the inner bearing.

Cleaning and examination:

Wipe the old grease from the hub and bearings, then thoroughly degrease the parts in petrol, paraffin or a similar solvent. Wash the bearing races separately by rotating them in a bowl of clean solvent. The brake disc must be thoroughly washed with solvent to remove all traces of grease or dirt.

Examine the operating face of the stub axle on which the oil seal operates for scoring or nicks. Light damage can be smoothed with fine grade emerycloth. Check the stub axle for hair line cracks or other damage.

Check the outer races of the bearings for fretting, scoring or wear. If damage is found, both outer races must be driven out with a suitable copper drift, working evenly round the races to prevent jamming, then both bearings renewed.

Lubricate the inner races with light oil. Press each inner race firmly back into its outer and rotate the bearing to check for any roughness in operation. Dirt can be a cause of roughness, so wash the bearing again thoroughly before repeating the test. If an airline is used to dry the bearings, do not allow them to spin in the air blast as this chips the faces. If a bearing is defective, both bearings must be completely renewed, including the outer races in the hub.

Reassembly:

If the outer races of the hubs have been driven out they should be driven back evenly and fully using a suitable drift.

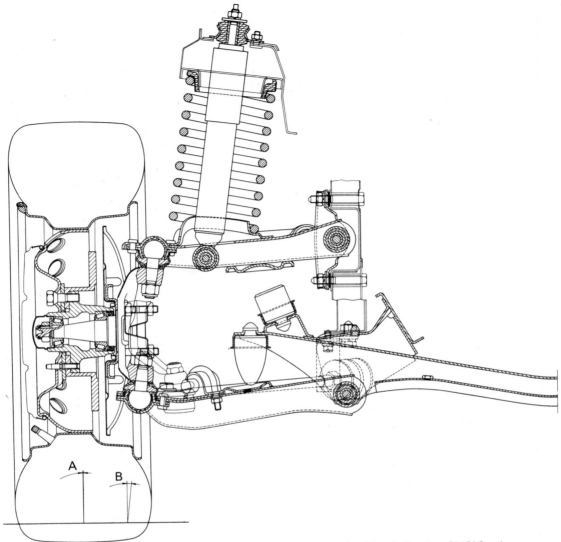

FIG 9:2 Sectioned view of the front suspension. The anti-roll bar is fitted to GL/GLS only

Key to Fig 9:2   **A** Camber angle = 0° 30′ ± 30′   **B** Knuckle pillar inclination = 6° ± 20′

The wheel bearing must be lubricated with lithium-based grease. Evenly pack the inside of the hub with fresh grease and liberally pack the inner race of the inner bearing with grease, working it well into the rollers. Install the inner race of the inner bearing into the hub and press a new oil seal into the hub to retain the race in position.

Slide the hub assembly back onto the stub axle, taking care not to damage the grease seal. Pack the inner race of the outer bearing with grease and fit it back into place, followed by the new washer and new nut. Adjust the wheel bearings and install the grease cap, filling the cap with .9 oz (25 g) of grease. Refit the brake caliper, bleeding the brakes where the flexible hose was disconnected, then pump the brake pedal hard several times to take up the adjustment in the brakes. Refit the road wheel and lower the car to the ground.

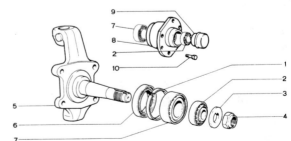

FIG 9:3 The components of the wheel hub assembly

Key to Fig 9:3   1 Spacer   2 Outer bearing   3 Flat washer   4 Nut   5 Steering knuckle   6 Seal   7 Inner bearing   8 Wheel hub   9 Grease cap   10 Wheel stud

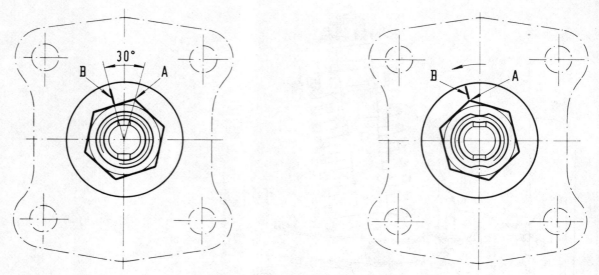

FIG 9:4   Hub bearing adjustment

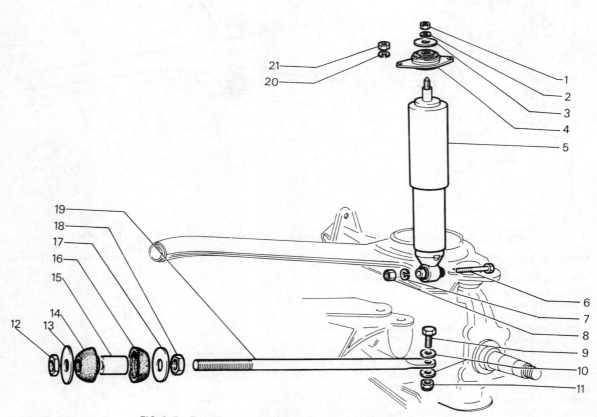

FIG 9:5   Front suspension damper and reaction strut mountings

Key to Fig 9:5   1 Damper upper stud nut   2 Lockwasher   3 Cup   4 Support plate and insulator   5 Damper   6 Damper lower attachment screw   7 Lockwasher   8 Nut   9 Screw   10 Spacers   11 Self-locking nut   12 Nut   13 Flat washer 14 Front insulator   15 Spacer   16 Rear insulator   17 Flat washer   18 Nut   19 Reaction strut   20 Lockwasher   21 Nut

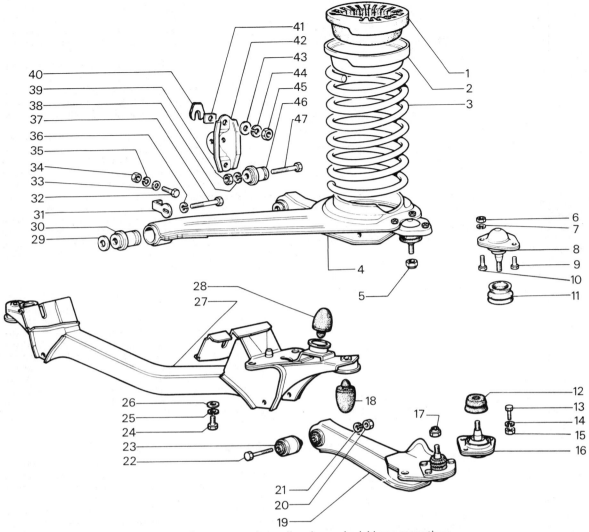

FIG 9:6 Front suspension coil spring and wishbone mountings

Key to Fig 9:6 1, 2 Coil spring upper insulators 3 Coil spring 4 Upper wishbone 5 Self-locking nut 6 Nut 7 Lockwasher 8 Upper ball joint 9, 10 Screws 11 Upper ball joint insulator 12 Lower ball joint insulator 13 Screw 14 Lockwasher 15 Nut 16 Lower ball joint 17 Self-locking nut 18 Lower wishbone rebound rubber 19 Lower control arm 20 Nuts 21 Lockwasher 22 Screw 23 Rubber bush 24 Screw 25 Lockwasher 26 Flat washer 27 Crossmember 28 Upper wishbone rebound rubber 29 Plate 30 Rubber bush 31 Safety plate 32 Screw 33 Flat washer 34 Nut 35, 36 Lockwashers 37 Screw 38 Lockwasher 39 Nut 40, 41 Adjustment shims 42 Upper wishbone support 43 Flat washer 44 Lockwasher 45 Nut 46 Rubber bush 47 Screw

Adjustment:

Tighten the hub nut to a torque of 15 lb ft (2 kgm) whilst spinning the hub in order to settle the bearings. Slacken back the nut then tighten it again to a torque of 5 lb ft (.7 kgm). Make a mark on the washer at the midpoint of a convenient flat, as shown in **FIG 9:4**. Hold the washer and slacken back the nut until the corner of the nut is opposite the reference mark as shown in the figure. Lock the nut by staking the edge down into the groove of the stub axle with a suitable drift. A special crimping tool is made for this purpose but careful use of a hammer and drift will be as effective.

9:4 The dampers

Removal:

The damper mountings are shown in **FIG 9:5**. From inside the engine compartment, remove the nut and washers that secure the damper to the upper mounting bracket, holding the centre stud with a second spanner to prevent rotation. Remove the two nuts which secure the

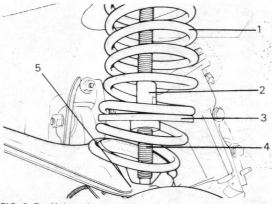

FIG 9:7 Using the special tool to compress the road spring

Key to Fig 9:7 1 Coil spring 2 Threaded bush of spring compressor A.74112 3 Bottom ring of special tool 4 Tie rod of special tool 5 Upper wishbone

bracket to the body. From underneath the car remove the bolt that secures the damper to the upper wishbone. Withdraw the damper and bracket assembly upwards out through the aperture in the body.

If the damper is faulty it should be taken to a Fiat service station for overhaul.

Refitting the damper is a reversal of the removal procedure.

9:5 Reaction struts

The reaction struts control the castor angle of the suspension units so the amount of thread protruding at the frame end should always be measured so that the struts can be set back to the same dimension on reassembly. When the struts have been refitted the suspension geometry should be checked by a service station.

The reaction strut mountings are shown in **FIG 9:5**. To free the reaction strut from the lower wishbone, remove the nut and bolt that secures the eye to the suspension. Normally the struts can then be pulled clear of the wishbone without disturbing the adjustment. If it is necessary to remove the strut completely, take off the nut and withdraw it from the bracket on the frame. Check the condition of the rubber insulators and renew them if they are defective before refitting the reaction strut.

9:6 The road springs (see FIG 9:6)

It is essential to use the correct special tool for removal or installation of the road springs. The spring is compressed when installed and if it is accidentally released serious injury can result to the operator.

Removal:

Jack-up the car and support on stands, then remove the road wheel. Remove the damper as described previously.

Insert the threaded portion of the special tool A.74112 through the body aperture for the damper upper mounting and position the top flange of the tool against one of the studs that secures the damper attachment bracket.

Fit the bottom ring of the special tool into the lower windings of the coil spring and screw the threaded rod into the disc, as shown in **FIG 9:7**. Crank the handle so that the disc moves up the threaded rod and compresses the road spring.

Remove the brake caliper as described in **Chapter 11**, tying it out of the way so that the brake hose is not strained. Remove the splitpin and nut from the steering arm ball joint shown in **FIG 9:8**. Use a suitable ball joint extractor to remove the ball joint and detach the tie rod from the steering arm.

Remove the two nuts to release the upper control arm support, then detach the upper control arm. Be sure to keep a note of the number of shims fitted between the control arm and the body. These shims must be refitted in their original positions to maintain the original wheel camber. Disengage the reaction strut from the lower control arm by removing the nut, screw and spacers. Support the suspension and remove the lower control arm to crossmember screw. The control arms and steering knuckle assembly can now be removed from the car. Crank the handle to release the spring compressor, then remove the tool and detach the road spring.

Refitting:

Refit the spring and reassemble the suspension unit in a reverse order of dismantling, using the special tool to compress the spring up into place. Be sure to fit the adjustment shims in their original positions behind the upper control arm support plate. Do not fully tighten the suspension component fixing bolts and nuts until the road wheel has been refitted and the car lowered. Then, with the car loaded with four passengers, tighten all the fixings to the correct torque loadings as given in **Technical Data**.

9:7 Suspension ball joints

Worn, stiff or damaged ball joints should be renewed as soon as possible. It is possible, though not recommended, to renew them with the suspension and wishbones installed on the car. In this case, two jacks and a solid metal bar will be required to support the upper wishbone against the pressure of the road spring, and the drilling operations described later will be more difficult. It is recommended that the method of ball joint renewal given in this section be followed wherever possible.

Compress the coil spring and remove the two wishbones and steering knuckle assembly as described in **Section 9:6**. Take off the nut that holds the appropriate ball joint to the steering knuckle then use a suitable tool, such as tool A.47058, as shown in **FIG 9:9**.

The ball joints fitted as original equipment are riveted to the wishbone assemblies, service replacement ball joints being fitted with special nuts and bolts. If an original ball joint is being removed, use an oversized drill to partially drill into the heads of the rivets that secure the ball joint. **Do not attempt to drill through the rivet and stop as soon as the head is weakened.** Knock off the head with a cold chisel and drive out the stem of the rivet with a suitable punch. Discard the old ball joint. The new ball joint is bolted back into place with the special bolts supplied in the kit. **Do not attempt to rivet the new ball joint into place and do not use bolts**

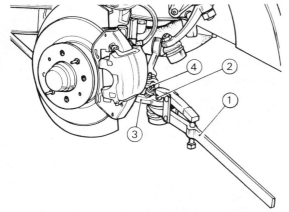

FIG 9:8   Disconnecting the steering arm ball joint

Key to Fig 9:8   1 Tool A.47035   2 Ball joint   3 Steering arm   4 Tie rod

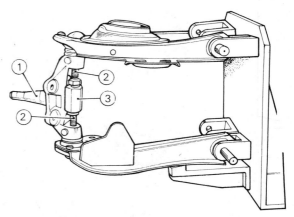

FIG 9:9   Removing control arm ball joints

Key to Fig 9:9   1 Steering knuckle   2 Ball joints   3 Tool A.47058

other than those supplied. Make sure the bolts are fitted with their heads pointing in the direction shown in **FIG 9:6**.

Take the opportunity to examine the flexible rubber bushes in the inboard end of the wishbones. If the bushes are worn or perished they must be removed with the aid of a press and suitable mandrels and new bushes pressed back into place. If a lubricant is required when installing the bushes, use only water or soft soap.

The parts are installed in the reverse order of removal, properly loading the car before tightening the suspension component fixings as described in **Section 9:6**. It is advisable to have the steering geometry checked by an agent, on completion.

9:8 The crossmember

The front engine mountings are attached to the crossmember so it will be necessary to support the engine with the special tool A.70526, as described in the engine and transmission removal procedures in **Chapters 1** and **6**, so that the front engine mountings can be freed.

Raise the front of the car and support on stands. Remove the bolts securing the crossmember to the frame and take the assembly out from beneath the car, as shown in **FIG 9:10**.

The crossmember is installed in the reverse order of removal, noting that it is most advisable to have the steering geometry checked by an agent when the work is completed.

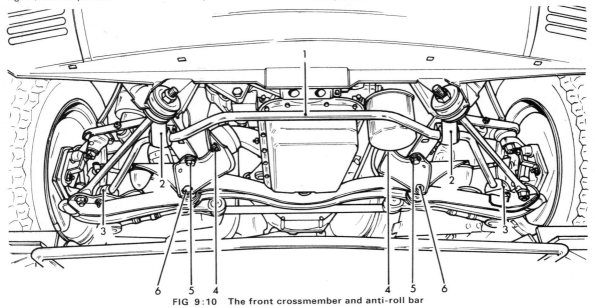

FIG 9:10   The front crossmember and anti-roll bar

Key to Fig 9:10   1 Anti-roll bar   2 Anti-roll bar to body mountings   3 Anti-roll bar to lower wishbone mountings   4 Engine mounting nuts   5 Crossmember to body bolts   6 Lower control arm attachment bolts

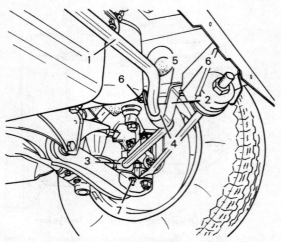

FIG 9:11 Lefthand front suspension assembly

Key to Fig 9:11   1 Anti-roll bar   2 Anti-roll bar front mounting (to body)   3 Anti-roll bar side mounting (to lower wishbone)   4 Rubber pad   5 Inner plate   6 Bolts   7 Nut

9:9 The anti-roll bar

To remove the anti-roll bar, see **FIGS 9:10** and **9:11**, first remove the front lower guard plates, normally secured by eight bolts. Remove the two front and the two side anti-roll bar mountings and rubber pads as shown.

Check the ends of the anti-roll bar for misalignment, which must not exceed ± .06 inch (1.5 mm). Very slight distortion can be corrected, otherwise fit a new unit

Using new rubber mounts if the old ones are damaged, fit the anti-roll bar after the remainder of the front suspension has been assembled.

9:10 Fault diagnosis

(a) Wheel wobble (see also Chapter 10)

1 Worn hub bearings
2 Weak front springs
3 Uneven tyre wear
4 Worn suspension bushes

(b) Car pulls to one side

1 Unequal tyre pressures
2 Incorrect suspension geometry
3 Defective suspension bushes or damaged parts
4 Weak spring on one side
5 Fault in steering system

(c) Bottoming of suspension

1 Rebound rubbers damaged or missing
2 Broken or weak front coil spring
3 Defective damper

(d) Excessive body roll

1 Check 2 and 3 in (c)

(e) Rattles

1 Check 2 and 4 in (a); 2 and 3 in (c)
2 Defective damper mounting bushes
3 Defective wishbone mounting bushes

CHAPTER 10

THE STEERING GEAR

10:1 Description

Steering gear of the worm and roller type is standard equipment on 1600 and 1800 models, and servicing operations for this type of unit are included in this chapter.

A hydraulic recirculating ball-type power assisted steering system is fitted to the 2000 model and offered as an optional extra on the later 1600 model. The hydraulic system is pressurised by a fluid pump driven from the crankshaft sprocket by a toothed belt. Movement of the steering wheel actuates the control valve which transfers power to the steering arm. The hydraulic damper on the idler arm is replaced by a support bearing. The only service procedures are topping up and bleeding the hydraulic system. If any other faults occur the unit involved must be replaced.

Ball joints are used throughout the steering linkage to ensure positive and free movement with the minimum of play. The ball joints are integral with the track rod ends or intermediate track rod and if a ball joint is defective the complete component must be renewed.

10:2 Routine maintenance

The steering gear is filled with SAE.90 EP oil, through the filler plug, and there should be no need for topping up during normal use. If the oil level is found to drop it will probably be due to leakage in the unit which should be removed for overhaul.

At intervals of 6000 miles (10,000 km) check through the linkage for play or defective ball joint covers. Have an assistant turn the steering wheel slightly from side to side while watching the linkage. Ball joint covers which show signs of failure must be renewed before they split and allow dirt to enter. All models are fitted with sealed ball joints which do not require routine lubrication.

10:3 Steering column

The components of the early type steering column are shown in **FIG 10:1**. 132 GLS cars are fitted with an adjustable column, regulated by a handwheel projecting through the column cowling. Instructions for removing the steering wheel on these later installations are given in **Section 10:7**.

Removal:

Take out the two screws from behind the steering wheel spokes and detach the centre trim. Hold the steering wheel and use a socket or box spanner to remove the nut that secures the steering wheel to the column. Make light alignment marks across the steering wheel hub and the end of the steering shaft to ensure correct refitting. Rock the wheel slightly from side to side and tap firmly at the base of the spokes with the flat of the hand. If this treatment does not free the steering wheel

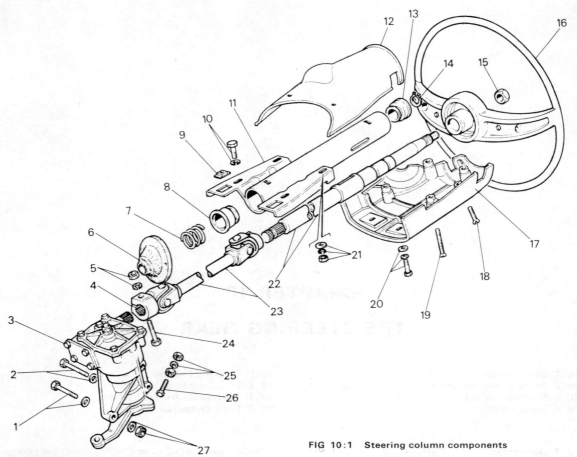

FIG 10:1 Steering column components

Key to Fig 10:1   1, 2 Screws and flat washers   3 Steering gear housing   4 Lower universal joint yoke   5 Nut and lockwasher   6 Rubber boot   7 Spring   8 Lower bearing   9 Lockplate   10 Screw and lockwasher   11 Upper steering shaft support bracket and tube   12 Upper shield   13 Upper bearing   14 Snap ring   15 Steering wheel nut   16 Steering wheel   17 Lower shield   18, 19 Screws   20 Screw, lockwasher and flat washer   21 Flat washer, lockwasher and nut   22 Upper steering shaft   23 Lower steering shaft   24 Screw   25 Nuts and flat washer   26 Wheel lock angle adjustment screw   27 Nut and flat washer

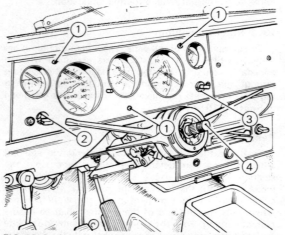

FIG 10:2 Instrument panel and light switch attachments

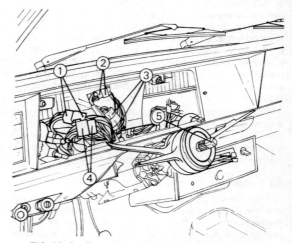

FIG 10:3 Detaching the electrical connectors

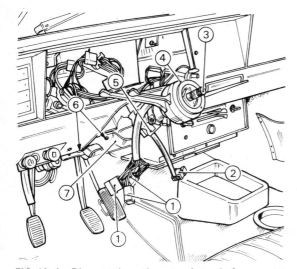

FIG 10 : 4   Dismounting the steering shaft support bracket

Key to Fig 10 : 4   1 Turn signal and windscreen wiper wire connector   2 Ignition switch and anti-theft device wire connector   3 Upper steering shaft   4 Turn signal switch   5 Anti-theft device   6 Support bracket screws   7 Upper steering shaft support bracket

from the splines, a special extractor will be needed to pull it off.

Disconnect the battery earth lead to prevent accidental shortcircuits when disconnecting electrical components. Refer to **FIG 10 : 2**. Remove the instrument panel attaching screws 1 and the lighting switch bezel nuts 2 and 3. Remove the front trim pad and pull the instrument panel out of its housing. Disconnect the electric leads and the speedometer cable from the rear of the instrument panel, then remove the panel entirely. Detach the electrical connectors 1, 2, 3 and 4 shown in **FIG 10 : 3**.

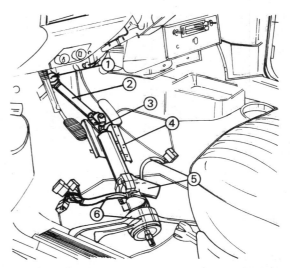

FIG 10 : 5   Removing the steering column assembly from the car

Key to Fig 10 : 5   1 Lower universal joint yoke screw   2 Lower steering shaft   3 Upper universal joint yoke screw   4 Upper steering shaft support bracket   5 Ignition switch and anti-theft device   6 Turn signal and windscreen wiper switches

On later cars these are combined in one multi-connector.

Refer to **FIG 10 : 4** and remove the screws securing the upper steering shaft support bracket to the body. Lower the steering column assembly to the floor of the car and remove the screws securing the lower steering shaft to the universal joint yoke as shown in **FIG 10 : 5**. The steering column assembly can then be removed from the car. Examine all components, especially the upper and lower universal joints (see **FIG 10 : 6**), and renew any components that are worn or damaged.

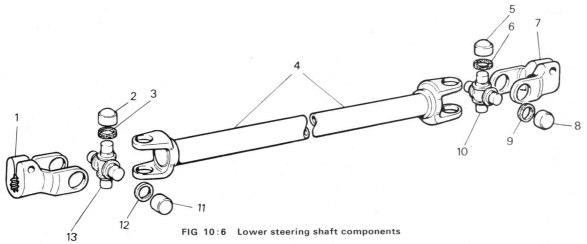

FIG 10 : 6   Lower steering shaft components

Key to Fig 10 : 6   1 Lower universal joint yoke   2 Spider bearing   3 Seal   4 Lower steering shaft   5 Spider bearing   6 Seal   7 Upper universal joint yoke   8 Spider bearing   9 Seal   10 Upper universal joint spider   11 Spider bearing   12 Seal   13 Lower universal joint spider

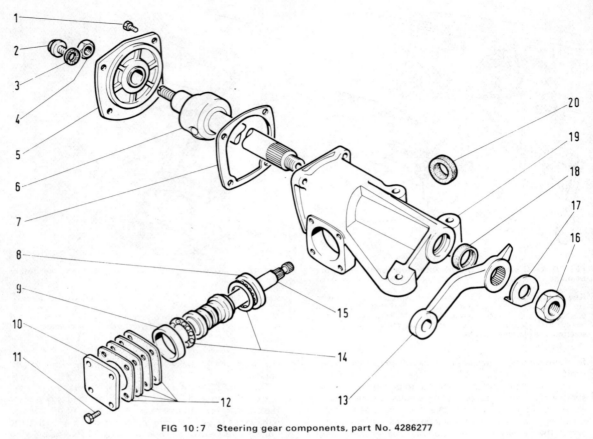

FIG 10:7 Steering gear components, part No. 4286277

Key to Fig 10:7   1 Screw   2 Plug   3 Seal   4 Nut   5 Steering gear housing cover   6 Cross-shaft   7 Gasket
8, 9 Bearing outer races   10 Worm thrust cover   11 Screw   12 Adjustment shims   13 Pitman arm   14 Worm shaft
ballbearings   15 Worm shaft   16 Pitman arm nut   17 Lockwasher   18 Seal   19 Steering gear housing   20 Seal

Refitting :

The steering column is refitted in the reverse order of
removal, noting the following points. If the position of the
steering linkage has been disturbed with the steering
column removed, set the linkage Pitman arm to the mid-
travel position before connecting the steering shaft at the
lower universal joint yoke and make sure that the steering
wheel spokes are horizontal when the steering wheel is
installed. Tighten the universal joint yoke nut to 18 lb ft
(2.5 kgm), then fit but do not fully tighten the upper
steering shaft support bracket fixings. Fit the steering
wheel and tighten the attaching nut to 36 lb ft (5 kgm).
Turn the steering wheel both ways from lock to lock, to
ensure that the support bracket is properly seated, then
tighten the support bracket attaching screws to 7 lb ft
(1 kgm).

10:4 Steering gear

One of two alternative types of steering gear may be
fitted, the two types being designated part No. 4225666
and No. 4286277 respectively. The servicing procedures
given in this section apply to steering gear type No.
4225666, but the instructions will apply to both types
as design and construction is very similar. **FIGS 10:7**
and **10:8** show the essential differences between the two
types of steering gear.

Removal :

From inside the car, disconnect the lower steering
column universal joint at the joint yoke and remove the
bolt.

Jack-up the front of the car and safely support on
stands.

Remove the road wheel on the side nearest the steering
gear. Refer to **FIG 10:9** which shows the steering gear
installation. Remove pin and unscrew the nut on the
intermediate link ball joint, which connects the link to the
Pitman arm. Use a suitable tool (see **FIG 9:8**) to
disconnect the ball joint from the Pitman arm. Unscrew
the nuts on the through-bolts securing the steering gear
housing to the body and slide out the bolts. Move the
steering gear housing far enough forward to clear the
worm shaft from the rubber boot, then pull out the steering
gear assembly.

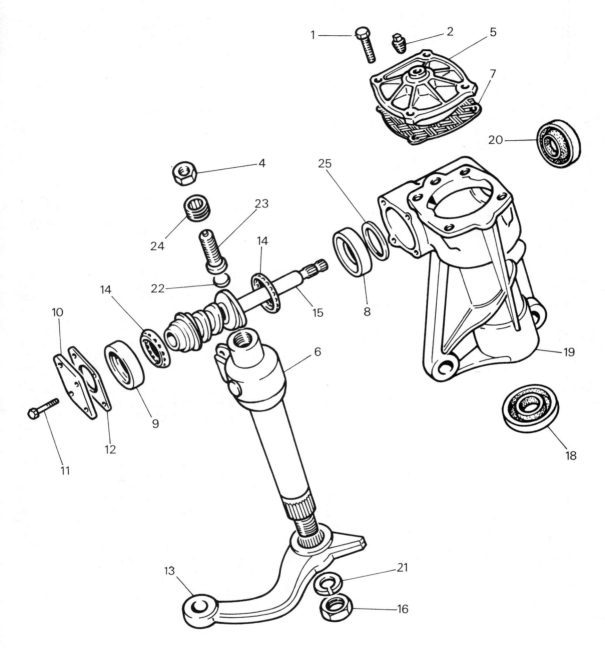

FIG 10:8 Steering gear components, part No. 4225666

Key to Fig 10:8   1 Screw   2 Plug   4 Nut   5 Steering gear housing cover   6 Cross-shaft   7 Gasket   8, 9 Bearing outer races   10 Worm thrust cover   11 Screw   12 Adjustment shims   13 Pitman arm   14 Worm shaft ballbearings   15 Worm shaft   16 Pitman arm nut   18 Seal   19 Steering gear housing   20 Seal   21 Lockwasher   22 Adjustment screw disc   23 Cross-shaft adjustment screw   24 Ring nut   25 Adjustment shim

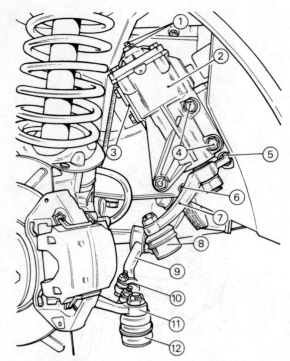

FIG 10:9 The steering gear mountings and attachments

Key to Fig 10:9   1 Cross-shaft adjustment screw and nut
2 Steering gear housing   3 Side cover   4 Screws
5 Right steering lock adjustment screw and nut   6 Left
steering lock adjustment screw and nut   7 Pitman arm
8 Intermediate link ball joint   9 Left tie rod   10 Tie rod
adjustment sleeve clamp   11 Left steering arm   12 Left
tie rod ball joint

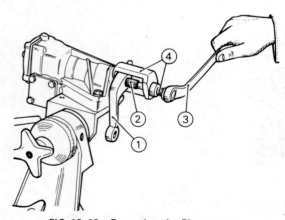

FIG 10:10   Removing the Pitman arm

Key to Fig 10:10   1 Pitman arm   2 Cross-shaft
3 Spanner   4 Puller

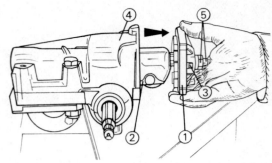

FIG 10:11   Removing the cover and cross-shaft

Key to Fig 10:11   1 Cover   2 Cross-shaft   3 Cover plug
4 Steering gear housing   5 Cross-shaft adjustment screw
and nut

Refitting:

The steering gear is refitted in the reverse order of
removal. Make sure that the Pitman arm is in the mid-
travel position and the steering wheel spokes horizontal
when the steering gear is refitted to the car.

Dismantling:

**Never attempt to remove the Pitman arm from
its shaft by hammering.** If the arm is hammered in any
way, shocks will be transmitted up the spindle and will
either indent the worm or damage the sector teeth.
Remove the Pitman arm with a suitable puller, such as
tool A. 47043 (steering gear No. 4225666) or A.47071
(steering gear No. 4286277), as shown in **FIG 10:10**.
Remove the nut and washer that secures the Pitman arm
to the spindle then make aligning marks across the arm
and end of the spindle before pulling the arm off.

Remove the filler plug and drain out the oil from the
unit. Temporarily refit the filler plug and wash down the
outside with petrol or paraffin to remove road dirt.

Remove the four screws attaching the cover to the
housing, then slide out the cover and cross-shaft as
shown in **FIG 10:11**.

Refer to **FIG 10:8**. Remove the four bolts 11 that
secure the cover 10 and remove the cover with the shim
pack 12. Gently tap on the upper end of the worm shaft 15
until the outer ballbearing race 9 and ballbearing 14 can
be removed from the housing. Withdraw the worm shaft
completely and collect the rear ballbearing 14. A special
extractor is made for removing the outer race of the rear
bearing but if care is taken it can be driven out with a
suitable drift. Carefully collect and store the shims 25
behind the rear outer race 8.

It is advisable to remove and discard the ring seals 18
and 20 as well as the gasket 7, and fit new ones on
reassembly.

Cleaning and examination:

Wash all the parts in a suitable solvent. Absolute
cleanliness is essential. The ring seals and gasket, if
being re-used, should not be allowed to come into contact
with solvents.

Examine the worm shaft for damage, wear or indenta-
tions on the worm itself. Check the worm shaft for

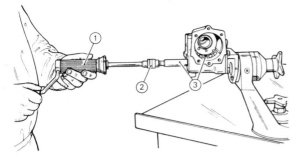

FIG 10:12   Checking the worm shaft turning torque

Key to Fig 10:12   1 Dynamometer A.95697   2 Socket
A.95697/7   3 Worm shaft

straightness. If the shaft is bent, do not attempt to
straighten it but install a new shaft complete. Similarly
renew the shaft if the worm is defective or damaged.

Check all the bearings for damage, rough operation,
displaced needles or balls, or any other defects.

Examine the main housing for hairline cracks or
damaged mating faces. The faces can be carefully
cleaned up using an oil stone, fine file, or emerycloth
spread over plate glass, if they are slightly distorted or
have nicks and burrs. Deep damage or excessive
distortion requires renewal of the components.

Check the cross-shaft for signs of wear or seizing
where the bearings seat and check that the steering sector
is in good condition and revolving freely about its pin.

Renew any damaged or defective components.

Assembly and adjustments:

Lightly lubricate the parts with SAE.90 EP oil as
they are fitted back into place. A torque spanner is
required for accurately adjusting the steering box.

Install the worm shaft rear ballbearing cup to the
steering gear housing. Mount the rear ballbearing over
the worm shaft and slide the assembly into the housing.
Install the front ballbearing and cup, the adjustment
shims and the thrust cover. Tighten the attachment
screws to 14.5 lb ft (2 kgm). Now check the worm shaft
rolling torque by turning the shaft with the torque spanner
or, if available, the special dynamometer tool A.95697
(see **FIG 10:12**). The turning torque should be 4.3 lb
inch (5 kgcm). If the torque is less than specified, reduce
the thickness of adjustment shims; conversely increase
the thickness of adjustment shims if the torque exceeds
the limit.

Install the cross-shaft and fit the cover with gasket. To
fit the cover to the housing it will be necessary to turn the
cross-shaft adjustment screw until the cover contacts the
housing. Secure the cover with the attaching screws.
Starting from the mid-travel position, move the Pitman
arm both ways and check that by rotating the worm shaft
(not the Pitman arm) through an angle of 30 degs. at
least both ways, the play between roller and worm is nil.
If any play is found, it must be eliminated by carefully
turning the adjusting screws. Tighten the adjusting
screw locknuts without changing the adjustment.

Check the worm shaft turning torque again, using the
torque spanner or dynamometer as before. The turning
torque should be 7.8 to 10.4 lb inch (9 to 12 kgcm),

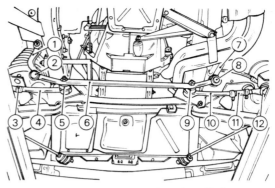

FIG 10:13   Steering linkage installation

Key to Fig 10:13   1 Pitman arm   2 Ball joint
3 Adjustment sleeve   4 Left tie rod   5 Ball joint   6 Centre
link   7 Idler arm   8, 9 Ball joints   10 Right tie rod
11 Adjustment sleeve   12 Ball joint

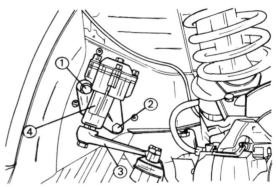

FIG 10:14   Removing the idler arm assembly

Key to Fig 10:14   1, 2 Attachment screws   3 Idler arm
4 Idler arm support and damper assembly

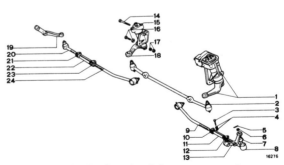

FIG 10:15   Steering linkage components

Key to Fig 10:15   1 Steering gear housing   2 Centre link
3 Screw   4 Nut and lockwasher   5 Cotterpin   6 Nut
7 Boot   8 Ball joint   9 Left tie rod   10, 12 Clamps
11 Left tie rod adjusting sleeve   13 Left steering knuckle
arm   14 Screw   15 Hydraulic damper   16 Screw and flat
washer   17 Nut and flat washer   18 Idler arm   19 Right
steering knuckle arm   20 Ball joint   21, 23 Clamps
22 Right tie rod adjusting sleeve   24 Right tie rod

starting from the Pitman arm mid-travel position and through an angle of approximately 30 deg. of the worm shaft in both directions. From this 30 deg. angle to a point almost at the full lock position, the turning torque should be 6 lb inch (7 kgcm) or less. If the turning torque is incorrect, loosen the locknut and make further adjustments to the adjuster screw until the correct figure is obtained. Tighten the locknut on completion and recheck the turning torque.

The adjustment of the play between worm and roller must be carried out with the Pitman arm in the mid-travel position, which corresponds to the straight-ahead position of the road wheels. The mid-travel position can be determined by halving the number of worm shaft turns required to move the Pitman arm from lock to lock.

When the steering gear is assembled and correctly adjusted, fill the unit with .25 litre (just under $\frac{1}{2}$ pint) of suitable SAE.90 EP oil and install the filler plug.

10:5 Steering linkage

FIG 10:13 shows the steering linkage installation.

Removal:

Remove the cotterpins and nuts attaching the tie rod ball joints to the steering knuckle arms and the Pitman arm and idler arm. Use a suitable tool to extract the ball joints. Remove the steering linkage from beneath the car and disconnect the two side tie rods from the centre link.

Check the ball joints for wear or damage and renew components as necessary. Any fault in the centre link demands that the centre link be renewed entirely. However, if a side tie rod is affected, only the damaged adjustable end need be renewed. When removing a tie rod end, count the number of turns taken when unscrewing in order that the new components can be refitted in the same position, to maintain as closely as possible the original wheel alignment. Note that one end on a tie rod has a lefthand thread and the other a righthand thread. The ends are locked onto the tie rod sleeve by clamps. The slots in the sleeves and those in the clamps must be in the same plane.

Refitting:

Refit the steering linkage in the reverse order of removal. To secure the ball joint tapers, press them together and secure them with a nut tightened to a torque of 43 lb ft (6 kgm). Lock each nut with a new cotterpin.

Idler arm assembly:

To remove the idler arm assembly from the body, disconnect the centre link ball joints from the idler arm as described previously, then remove screws 1 and 2 in **FIG 10:14**.

If excessive steering wheel vibration which is not attributable to unbalanced road wheels, or the car tends to straighten up too quickly after making a turn, the idler arm assembly complete with internal hydraulic damper should be renewed. It is not possible to repair the unit.

Refit the unit to the car in the reverse order of removal, tightening the mounting nuts to 25 lb ft (3.5 kgm) and the ball joint securing nut to 43 lb ft (6 kgm). Lock the ball joint nuts with new cotterpins.

After servicing any part of the steering linkage the front wheel toe-in setting should be checked as described in the next section.

10:6 Toe-in setting

The front wheel tracking should be set so that the wheels toe-in .20 ± .08 inch (5 ± 2 mm) with the car unloaded, or .12 ± .08 inch (3 ± 2 mm) when the car is loaded with four persons. Adjustment is carried out by slackening the tie rod clamps (see **FIG 10:15**) on both sides of the car, then rotating the sleeves equal amounts until the angles are correct. It is not recommended that owners attempt this work themselves, as great accuracy is essential. Instead, the work should be entrusted to a Fiat service station or a wheel and tyre specialist having optical setting equipment, the complete procedure taking only a short time under these conditions.

10:7 Adjustable steering wheel

Removal:

Pull off the centre horn control cap, remove the two spring retainers and unscrew the wheel retaining nut.

The instrument panel is removed after unscrewing the two switch ring nuts, 2 and 3 in **FIG 10:2** and the screws 1.

The cowling is removed by taking out the retaining screws from the lower section and unscrewing the handwheel. Take out the nuts securing the upper section of the steering column support to the body and remove the steering wheel assembly.

10:8 Fault diagnosis

(a) Wheel wobble

1 Unbalanced wheels and tyres
2 Slack steering connections
3 Incorrect steering goemetry
4 Excessive play in steering gear
5 Faulty suspension
6 Worn or loose hub bearings

(b) Wander

1 Check 2, 3 and 4 (a)
2 Uneven tyre pressures
3 Ineffective dampers
4 Uneven tyre wear

(c) Heavy steering

1 Check 3 (a)
2 Very low tyre pressures
3 Lack of lubrication
4 Wheels out of track
5 Steering gear adjustment too tight
6 Tight or damaged bearings

(d) Lost motion

1 Loose steering wheel connections
2 Worn steering gear
3 Worn steering ball joints
4 Worn steering knuckle joints
5 Worn steering gear bearings
6 Steering gear out of adjustment

CHAPTER 11

THE BRAKING SYSTEM

11 : 1 Description

Hydraulically operated brakes are fitted at all four wheels, the handbrake operating on the rear wheels only by means of a cable operated linkage. On cars produced before April 1977 disc brakes were fitted to all four wheels. Since that date self-adjusting drum brakes have been fitted to the rear wheels of all models. A brake regulating valve, operated mechanically by the pitch of the body on the suspension, reduces the effect of braking on the rear wheels according to the degree of retardation, to minimise the possibility of the rear wheels locking under heavy braking. A vacuum servo unit is connected directly between the brake pedal and the master cylinder and, by using the depression in the engine inlet manifold, assists the pressure applied by the driver on the brake pedal.

All models are fitted with a tandem braking system. A special master cylinder is fitted so that the rear and front brakes are hydraulically independent. The master cylinder is so designed that a failure in one half of the system will still allow the other half to operate, though with increased pedal stroke, so that the car can be safely stopped. As well as increased pedal stroke the overall efficiency of the braking system will be reduced as only two brakes will be operating.

11 : 2 Routine maintenance

Normal servicing of the hydraulic system is confined to checking the level of the brake fluid in the reservoirs at regular intervals and topping up with the approved grade of fluid as necessary. **Use only FIAT DOT 3 Blue Label Fluid in the braking system.** The fluid level must never be allowed to fall below that which would allow air to enter the hydraulic lines or braking will become spongy and inefficient. The system will then have to be bled.

The capacity of the master cylinder is sufficient to supply enough fluid to all cylinders at a single stroke, regardless of wear. As the rear brakes are self-adjusting, there is no indication of pad or lining wear at either the foot or handbrake. Wear can only be determined by measurement of the friction material. This should be checked every 3000 miles (5000 km) and the pads or shoes renewed when the thickness is down to .06 inch (1.5 mm) or there is indication that this figure will be reached before the next service.

Checks on the condition and serviceability of the brake pipes and hoses, the adjustment and condition of handbrake cables and the setting of the brake regulator should be carried out at 12,000 mile (20,000 km) intervals.

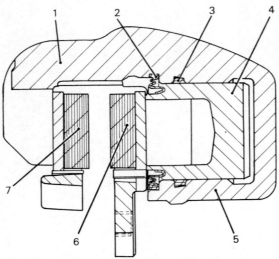

FIG 11:1 Section through a front brake caliper

Key to Fig 11:1   1 Caliper body   2 Piston protection
cap 3 Seal 4 Piston 5 Cylinder 6 Moving friction pad
7 Fixed friction pad

11:3 The disc brakes

FIG 11:1 shows a section through a front disc brake
caliper. These are of the non-compensating pattern and
comprise a simple hollow piston 4 within the cylinder 5 of
the caliper body 1, sealed against fluid leakage by the
seal 3, and against the ingress of dirt by rubber boot 2.
Forward motion of the piston is communicated to one
brake pad 6, while the reaction to the pressure on the
brake disc pulls the caliper body and the opposing pad 7
into contact with the opposite face of the disc, the two
pads gripping the disc firmly between them.

On rear brake calipers, an additional feature is the
compensating piston and mechanical linkage for handbrake operation, as shown in **FIG 11:2**. This comprises a

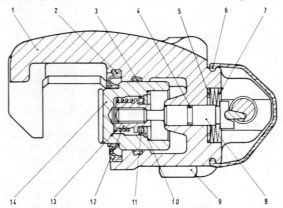

FIG 11:2 Section through a rear brake caliper

Key to Fig 11:2   1 Brake caliper   2 Brake piston boot
3 Piston seal   4 Spindle seal   5 Thrust washer
6 Handbrake lever cover   7 Belleville washers
8 Automatic adjuster spindle   9 Handbrake acutating lever
10 Shim   11 Ballbearing   12 Automatic adjuster nut
13 Nut spring   14 Brake piston

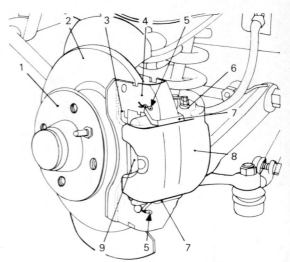

FIG 11:3 The front caliper installed

Key to Fig 11:3   1 Hub   2 Brake disc   3 Friction pad
locking spring   4 Caliper support bracket   5 Cotterpins
6 Bleed screw   7 Caliper locking blocks   8 Caliper body
9 Friction pad

nut 12 rotating within the piston on a ball thrust bearing
11 engaged with the thread on the butt of the handbrake
plunger 8. The spring tightly coiled around the nut and
anchored at one end to the hydraulic piston, permits
rotation in one direction to unscrew the nut on the butt
while preventing counter-rotation in the other. Each time
the handbrake is applied by operation of the cam lever 9,
the full mechanical thrust of the butt-and-nut combination
is applied through the piston wall to the brake pad. On
the return stroke, the piston is gripped by the seal 3, and
apart from a slight movement to free the pads from the
disc, further withdrawal of the plunger 8 only serves to
rotate the nut, fractionally extending the length of the
combination to give a reduced travel on the cam lever for
the next brake application.

11:4 Servicing the front brakes

The front brake installation is shown in **FIG 11:3**, the
components of the brake unit being shown in **FIG 11:4**.

Removal:

If the brake unit is being removed for pad renewal or for
servicing of the suspension system, the flexible hose can
remain attached to the caliper. Under these conditions,
the caliper should be suitably supported to avoid strain
on the flexible hose. If the caliper is being removed for
internal servicing, plug the outlet in the fluid reservoir
with a pointed piece of hardwood and disconnect the
flexible hose from the caliper. Alternatively, plug the end
of the flexible hose when it is removed to avoid fluid
loss.

The brake unit may be cleaned using a solution of hot
water and Fiat LDC detergent or with methylated spirits.
**Use no other solvent to clean the caliper assembly
or the rubber seals will be damaged.** Use a small
brush to clean out crevices then dry with compressed air.

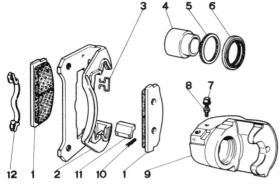

FIG 11:4   The front brake caliper components

Key to Fig 11:4   1 Pad and lining   2 Caliper support
bracket   3 Spring   4 Piston   5 Seal   6 Piston dust boot
7 Dust cap   8 Bleed screw   9 Caliper body   10 Cotterpin
11 Locking block   12 Pad retaining spring

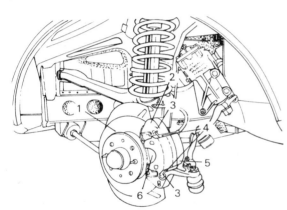

FIG 11:5   Front left brake assembly

For key see Fig 11:9

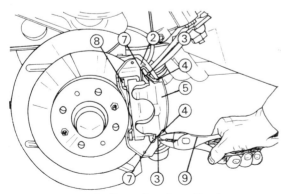

FIG 11:6   Removing the cotterpins

For key see Fig 11:9

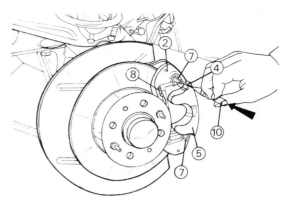

FIG 11:7   Removing the retainer blocks

For key see Fig 11:9

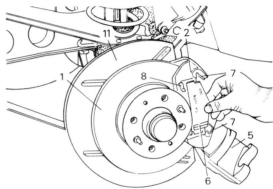

FIG 11:8   Removing the brake pads

For key see Fig 11:9

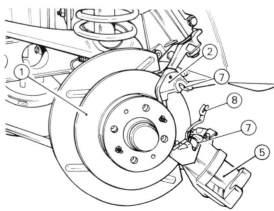

FIG 11:9   Removing the pad springs

Key to Figs 11:5, 11:6, 11:7, 11:8 and 11:9   1 Brake
disc   2 Brake caliper support bracket   3 Cotterpin
4 Retainer block   5 Brake caliper   6 Friction pad
7 Lock spring   8 Pad retaining springs   9 Pliers   10 Punch
11 Brake disc splash shield

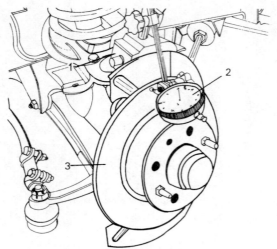

FIG 11:10 Measuring disc brake runout

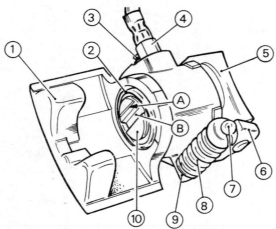

FIG 11:11 Rear wheel brake caliper

Key to Fig 11:11 1 Caliper body 2 Dust boot 3 Bleed screw 4 Fluid inlet connection 5 Dust boot 6 Handbrake control lever 7 Handbrake cable stop pawl 8 Spring 9 Handbrake cable anchor 10 Piston A Index notch on piston B Groove on piston for engaging brake shoe boss

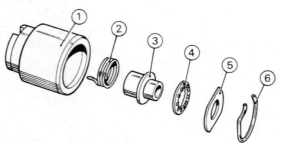

FIG 11:12 Components of the rear brake self-adjusting device

Key to Fig 11:12 1 Piston 2 Spring 3 Self-adjusting device 4 Ballbearing 5 Shim 6 Circlip

Apply the handbrake, raise and safely support the front of the car, then remove the road wheels (see **FIG 11:5**). Remove the cotterpins from the caliper retaining blocks as shown in **FIG 11:6**. Use a suitable punch to drive the caliper to bracket retainer blocks from the caliper as shown in **FIG 11:7**. Remove the brake pads from the caliper assembly as shown in **FIG 11:8**, marking them for refitting in their original positions if they are not to be renewed. Remove the pad springs as shown in **FIG 11:9**.

If the pads are fit for further service it is essential that they are installed back into their original positions and not interchanged. Pads must be renewed when the thickness of the linings has worn down to .06 inch (1.5 mm). Pads must also be renewed if they are contaminated with grease or oil, or are cracked or deformed. If any one friction pad is worn or faulty, all four pads on that axle (front or rear) should be renewed. Do not renew pads singly or on one side only, as uneven braking will result.

Fit new brake pads and reassemble the caliper in the reverse order of dismantling. The extra thickness of the new pads will cause the caliper piston to be pushed back into its bore. This will cause the fluid level in the brake master cylinder reservoir to rise and it may be necessary to syphon off a little of the fluid to prevent overflow. On completion, pump the brake pedal hard several times to adjust the brakes. If this is not done the brakes may not work the first time they are used on the road. Check the level of fluid in the reservoir and correct if necessary.

Brake disc:

Check the runout of the brake disc with a dial gauge as shown in **FIG 11:10**, making sure that the hub end float is correct as described in **Chapter 9**. The runout, measured at a point approximately .08 inch (2 mm) from the disc edge, must not exceed .004 inch (.10 mm). If the runout is excessive, first check that there are no specks of dirt between the mating faces of the hub and the disc, then try rotating the disc 180 deg. relative to the hub to see whether this will reduce the runout. If the runout is still excessive, or if the disc is deeply scored, renew the disc or have it machined down at a Fiat service station.

Wipe the disc with a suitable solvent such as methylated spirit to remove any grease or finger marks before reinstalling the caliper. Deposits on the disc can be cleaned off by softening with solvent and scrubbing off gently with worn emerycloth.

Servicing the caliper:

Remove the caliper as described previously. Use compressed air at the inlet port to force the piston out of its bore. Carefully remove and discard the dust cap and piston seal. Wash the remaining parts in commercial alcohol, methylated spirits or clean approved brake fluid. **Use no other cleaner or solvent on brake components.** Inspect all parts for wear or damage and the piston and cylinder bore for scoring or pitting. Renew any parts found worn, damaged or corroded, making sure that the correct replacement part is obtained and fitted.

Use new rubber parts throughout, fitted with the fingers only to avoid damage to the sealing lips. Dip all internal parts in clean brake fluid during assembly. Fit the piston seal, making sure that it is fully and squarely seated. Press the piston fully and squarely back into the

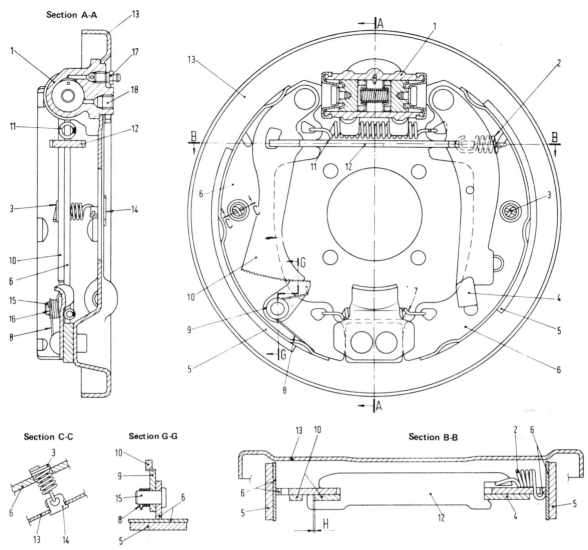

Section A-A

Section C-C   **Section G-G**   **Section B-B**

FIG 11 : 13   Rear drum brake layout. Lefthand unit shown

Key to Fig 11 : 13   1 Wheel cylinder   2 Spring   3 Shoe retaining spring   4 Link   5 Lining   6 Shoe   7 Lower return spring   8 Spring   9 Ratchet stop   10 Self-adjusting link   11 Upper return spring   12 Shoe control link   13 Backplate   14 Clip   15 Pin   16 Washer   17 Bleed screw   18 Brake pipe connection

Clearance **H** equals 1 to 1.2 mm (.04 to .05 inch)

bore, taking great care not to allow it to tilt and jam in the bore. Install the dust cover around the piston and into its bore in the caliper. Bleed the brakes if the flexible hose was disconnected.

11 : 5 Servicing the rear brakes

Disc brakes:

The procedure for dismantling the rear disc brakes is similar to that already described for the front brake assemblies, with the additional step of removing the front

part of the splash shield and disconnecting the handbrake cable from the lever arm and anchorage if necessary. When working on rear brake calipers, engage first or reverse gear, chock the front wheels against rotation and fully release the handbrake.

The piston is unscrewed from the caliper using a screwdriver in the slot in the end of the piston, as shown in **FIG 11 : 11**. **FIG 11 : 12** shows the components of the brake clearance self-adjusting device. If any part of this device is worn or damaged, the entire caliper must be renewed, as no parts are available for service.

FIG 132

99

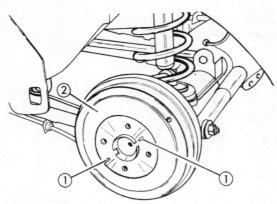

FIG 11 : 14   Brake drum removal. For key see Fig 11 : 15

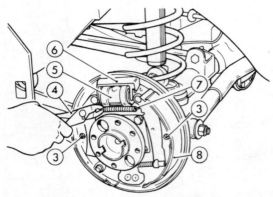

FIG 11 : 15   Removing upper return spring

Key to Figs 11 : 14 and 11 : 15   1 Retaining studs   2 Brake drum   3 Shoe retaining spring   4 Pliers   5 Wheel cylinder   6 Retaining tool   7 Upper return spring   8 Brake shoe

When reassembling the piston to the caliper, screw in the piston so that index notch A in **FIG 11 : 11** points towards the bleed screw. Always renew the piston dust boot and inner seal. Lubricate all internal parts with clean brake fluid during reassembly.

Carry out the remaining servicing operations and reassemble the caliper in the manner previously described for front brake units. On completion, fill and bleed the hydraulic system, then pump the brake pedal hard to take up the adjustment of the brake.

Self-adjusting drum brakes :

The layout of a rear drum brake unit including self-adjustment mechanism components is shown in **FIG 11 : 13**. As brake linings 5 wear in normal use, the free play between brake drum and shoes 6 increases so that self-adjuster link 10 with ratchet teeth will be forced by spring 2, through reaction rod 12, to move as necessary through tooth stop 9 and therefore assume a new position which will eliminate the free play. Whenever the brake pedal is operated, free play in the mechanism is taken up by this means.

When the brake pedal is released, return springs 7 and 11 will return the brake shoes through a shorter distance than before, because self-adjusting lever 10, in contact with toothed stop 9, will prevent further movement until free play between linings and drum increases due to wear.

Removing brake shoes :

Apply the handbrake and slacken the rear wheel bolts. Chock the front wheels firmly against rotation, then raise and safely support the rear of the car on floor stands. Remove the rear road wheels and fully release the handbrake.

Remove the two studs 1 (see **FIG 11 : 14**) and remove brake drum 2. If the brake drum cannot be pulled off by hand, use a suitable puller tool. Do not attempt to drive the drum from position as this may result in damage.

Refer to **FIG 11 : 15**. Install tool A72257 to the wheel cylinder to retain the pistons, as shown at 6. If such a tool is not available, wind a length of soft wire around the cylinder for this purpose. Use a suitable pair of curved pliers to unhook upper return spring 7 from brake shoes 8. Use tool A72264, or make up a similar tool with a slotted end from an old screwdriver, to remove the shoe retaining springs (see **FIG 11 : 16**). Push spring 3 (see **FIG 1 : 15**) into backplate with the special tool, then turn the spring to disconnect from clip 1 (see **FIG 11 : 16**). Use a suitable pair of pliers to unhook lower return spring 12 from the brake shoes (see **FIG 11 : 17**). Disconnect handbrake cable 11 from the link, then remove the brake shoes, taking care not to contaminate the friction linings with grease or dirt.

To remove the self-adjusting mechanism, refer to **FIG 11 : 18**, and lever spring retainer 4 from pin 3. Remove spring 1 and ratchet stop 5. To remove adjusting lever 6, remove the clip securing the lever to the back of shoe 7.

Clean all dirt and grease from the inside of the brake assembly. Clean the inside surfaces of the brake drum, using a suitable solvent to remove all traces of grease. If the inside surface of the drum, against which the friction linings operate, is scored or out of round, the drum can be refaced at a Fiat service station. However, if resurfacing would require the removal of too much metal, a new drum will be required.

Refitting :

This is a reversal of the removal procedure, set the automatic adjustment mechanism so that sufficient clearance exists between the brake shoes and drum to allow the drum to be refitted. On completion, pump the brake pedal hard several times to correctly adjust the brakes.

Servicing a wheel cylinder :

Remove the rear brake shoes as described previously. Refer to **FIG 11 : 16** and disconnect brake pipe 4 from the wheel cylinder. Plug the end of the pipe to prevent fluid leaks and the entry of dirt. Remove the two bolts 2 to detach the wheel cylinder from the brake backplate. Remove the piston retaining tool or the soft wire fitted previously.

A section through the wheel cylinder assembly is shown at 1 in **FIG 11 : 13**. Remove the dust boots from each end of the cylinder then remove the pistons, seals and spring.

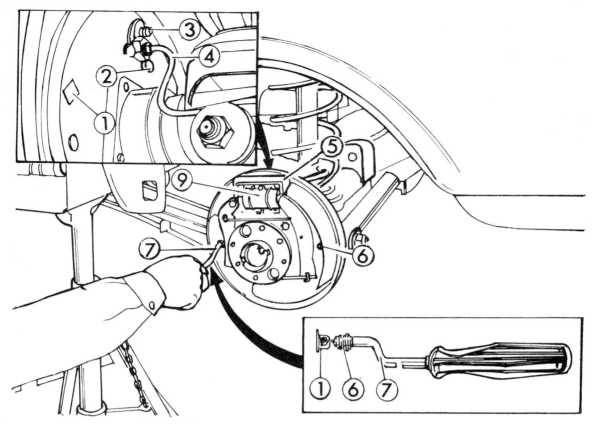

FIG 11 : 16   Removing shoe retaining springs. For key see Fig 11 : 17

Discard the rubber parts, then wash the remaining parts in commercial alcohol, methylated spirits or clean approved brake fluid only. Inspect the piston and cylinder bore surface for scoring or pitting, which would dictate the renewal of the cylinder complete.

. Reassemble the wheel cylinder using new seals and dust boots, installing the seals with the fingers only to avoid damage. Dip the pistons and seals in clean approved brake fluid before installing. Refit the wheel cylinder to the backplate and connect the brake pipe, then install the brake shoes as described previously. On completion, bleed the brakes as described in **Section 11 : 8**.

11 : 6 The brake regulator

The rear wheel brake regulator comprises a piston within a cylinder operated by a torsion bar. Movement of the piston varies the flow of hydraulic fluid to the rear brake cylinders according to the degree of braking effort applied to the car by application of the footbrake.

FIG 11 : 19 shows the brake regulator components, **FIG 11 : 20** the operation of the regulator. Weight-transference to the front wheels during braking results in the rear of the chassis lifting away from the rear axle. This is translated as a downward pull by the rear axle case on the link coupled to the long cranked end of the torsion bar. At the opposite end, the short crank which has been

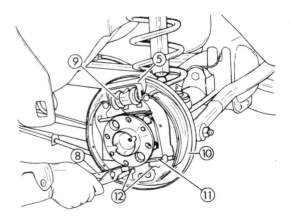

FIG 11 : 17   Removing lower return spring and hand-brake cable

Key to Figs 11 : 16 and 11 : 17   1 Clip   2 Bolts   3 Bleed screw   4 Brake pipe   5 Retaining tool   6 Retaining spring   7 Special tool   8 Pliers   9 Wheel cylinder   10 Backplate   11 Handbrake cable   12 Lower return spring

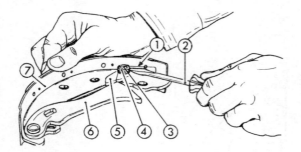

FIG 11:18　Removing self-adjusting mechanism

Key to Fig 11:18　　　1 Spring　　2 Screwdriver　　3 Pin
4 Spring retainer　5 Ratchet stop　6 Adjusting lever　7 Brake
shoe

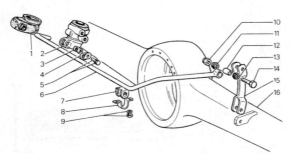

FIG 11:19　Brake regulator assembly components

Key to Fig 11:19　　1 Dust boot　2 Brake regulator　3 Pin
4 Lockplate　　5 Screw and lockwasher　　　6 Torsion bar
7 Rubber insulator　　　8 Retainer　　9 Nut and lockwasher
10 Nut　　11 Rubber bush　　12 Spacer　　13 Rubber bush
14 Screw　15 Link　16 Rear axle housing

bearing on the end of the regulator piston moves away
from it and the piston now moves with it under the
pressure of the fluid from the master cylinder.

Up to this moment, the piston has been positioned by
the torsion bar crank so that there is a free flow around its
head and the piston seal is clear of the transfer slots in the
piston. Under these conditions, any brake pressure applied
is transmitted equally to all four brake cylinders.

As the piston moves outwards the grooves are gradually
closed, thus reducing the pressure to the rear brake units
until, under maximum braking conditions, fluid entry to
the rear brake circuit is completely cut off. Any further
increase in pressure from master cylinder now cannot be
applied to the rear brake cylinders but only to the front.
The rear brakes are still held partially on since the fluid
already trapped in the lines cannot return.

As retardation decreases, the body returns to an even
keel and the torsion bar re-exerts pressure on the piston
to re-open the transfer route to the rear brake circuit.

Dismantling the regulator:

Chock the front wheels and raise the rear of the car onto
stands, allowing the rear suspension to hang free. Plug
the outlets to the rear fluid reservoir and disconnect the

two hydraulic lines to the brake regulator. Disconnect the
upper end of the link from the torsion bar, unscrew the
hydraulic unions, then unbolt the torsion bar brackets
from the chassis. Unbolt the regulator mounting bracket
from the car and transfer the regulator and torsion bar to
the bench. Remove the dust boot and bar.

Unscrew the end plug from the regulator and remove
the internal components as shown in **FIG 11:21**. Discard
the rubber components and wash the remaining parts in
commercial alcohol, methylated spirits or clean brake
fluid only. Examine all parts for wear, damage or corrosion
and renew any faulty parts. Fit new rubber components
when reassembling the regulator. Reassemble in the
reverse order of dismantling, lubricating all internal
components with clean brake fluid.

Installing the regulator:

Refer to **FIG 11:22**. Loosely attach the brake regulator
with torsion bar and dust boot, to its support bracket by

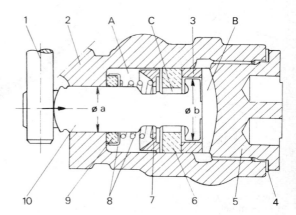

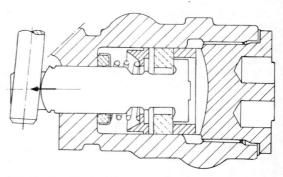

**FIG 11:20　Sectioned views of the brake regulator at
rest and in operation**

Key to Fig 11:20　　　　　1 Torsion bar　　　　2 Outer cylinder
3 Bush　4 Seal　5 Plug　6 Seal　7 Cup　8 Seal thrust
ring and spring　9 Seal　10 Piston　　A Normal pressure
chamber　　B Pressure regulating chamber　　C Grooves on
piston and fluid transfer chamber　　　　a Piston rod diameter
b Piston head diameter

FIG 11:21   Components of the rear brake regulator

Key to Fig 11:21   1 Regulator body   2 Seal   3 Cup
4 Spring   5 Cup   6 Seal   7 Piston   8 Bush   9 Seal
10 Plug

means of screws 3 and 4. Attach the torsion bar 2 to the body by its support.

Position the torsion bar end 2b so that distance X equals 5.9 ± .2 inch (150 ± 5 mm) from the rubber buffer seating area. Pull back dust boot 6 and check the contact of the regulator piston 5 with torsion bar end 2a. Pivot the regulator body on screw 4 until piston 5 is just touching torsion bar end 2a. Fully tighten first screw 4 then screw 3. Connect link 1 to the torsion bar end 2b with the screw and nut, inserting the rubber bushings and spacer. Before refitting dust boot 6, coat the contact area

between piston 5 and torsion bar end 2a and the pin 7 rotation area with FIAT SP 349 or PRF 1 grease. Reconnect the hydraulic lines to the regulator. Remove the plug in the fluid reservoir, lower the car to the ground and bleed the rear brakes.

11:7 The master cylinder

A section view of the master cylinder and brake vacuum servo unit is shown in **FIG 11:23**, the installation of the unit being shown in **FIG 11:24**.

Removal:

Either plug the outlets from the fluid reservoirs with sharpened hardwood sticks or syphon out the fluid. Disconnect the hoses connecting the reservoirs to the master cylinder. **Take great care to catch any spillage of fluid with rags, as hydraulic fluid rapidly softens and removes paint.** Disconnect the pressure lines from the master cylinder. Unscrew the nuts that secure the master cylinder to the servo and remove the unit from the car.

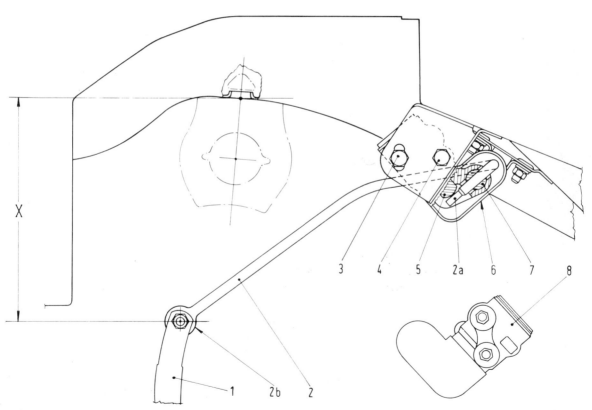

FIG 11:22   Rear brake regulator adjustment diagram

Key to Fig 11:22   1 Link connecting torsion bar to axle housing   2 Torsion bar   2a Torsion bar and contacting regulator piston
2b Torsion bar eye end   3, 4 Regulator mounting screws   5 Regulator piston   6 Dust boot   7 Regulator pin 8 Brake pressure
regulator

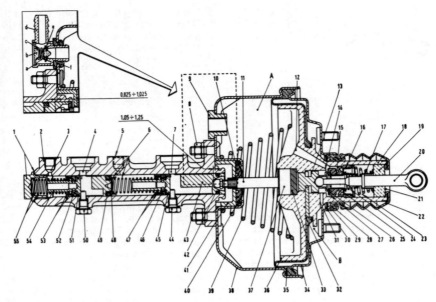

FIG 11:23 Sectioned view of the master cylinder and vacuum servo unit. Inset shows vacuum line valve on **132 GL/GLS** models and new fitting dimension for master cylinder

Key to Fig 11:23   1 Threaded plug and seal   2 Master cylinder body   3 Rear wheel brake line connector seat   4 Rear circuit reservoir line connector seat   5 Front left wheel brake line connector seat   6 Spring and cup   7 Front circuit reservoir line connector seat   8 Nut   9 Vacuum line connector seat   10 Front seal   11 Piston control rod   12 Vacuum passage   13 Piston valve   14 Vacuum passage orifice   15 Valve   16, 17 Cups   18 Control piston guide tube   19 Filter   20 Valve control rod   21 Servo air inlet   22 Dust boot   23 Piston valve return spring   24 Valve return spring   25 Cup   26 Outside air passage   27 Vacuum passage   28 Rear seal   29 Shoulder ring   30 Lockwasher   31 Vacuum and air passage control duct   32 Piston retainer   33 Reaction disc   34 Rear body   35 Diaphragm   36 Control piston   37 Working piston   38 Front body   39 Piston return spring   40 Cup   41 Guide bush   42 Seal   43 Rear floating ring carrier   44 Screw and seal   45 Spacer   46 Seal   47 Spring and cup   48 Flat washer   49 Seal   50 Screw and seal   51 Spacer   52 Seal   53 Spring and cup   54 Front floating ring carrier   55 Spring and cup   A Front chamber   B Rear chamber   a Valve   b Cup   c Spring   d Fitting   e Seal ring   f Fitting bush

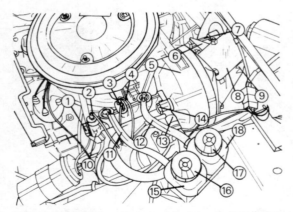

FIG 11:24 Master cylinder and brake servo installations (lefthand drive)

Key to Fig 11:24   1 Master cylinder plug   2 Fluid line to rear brakes   3 Fluid line to front right brake   4 Fluid line to front left brake   5 Vacuum servo   6 Servo actuating lever   7 Servo control rod and adjustment nuts   8 Servo support bracket   9 Servo valve control rod   10 Master cylinder body   11 Rear circuit reservoir fluid line   12 Front circuit reservoir fluid line   13 Vacuum line connector   14 Vacuum line inlet   15 Rear brake circuit reservoir   16, 17 Reservoir caps   18 Front brake circuit reservoir

Refitting:

Install the master cylinder in the reverse order of removal. When all connections have been made, fill the reservoirs with fresh fluid and bleed all four brake units.

Servicing:

Wash down the outside of the unit with methylated spirits or hot water and Fiat LDC detergent. **Use no other solvent.**

Remove the end plug and dismantle the master cylinder components into the order shown in **FIG 11:25**. Remove and discard all the old seals.

Wash all remaining parts in commercial alcohol, methylated spirits or approved brake fluid. **Use no other cleaner or solvent on the components.** Inspect all components for wear, corrosion or scoring. The cylinder bore should be completely smooth. If any faults are found, the entire master cylinder must be renewed as the floating ring carriers are not supplied for service separately.

Obtain a service kit which contains a complete set of new seals. Wet the new seals with clean approved brake fluid and fit them back into position, using only clean fingers and rotating the seals so that they seat fully and

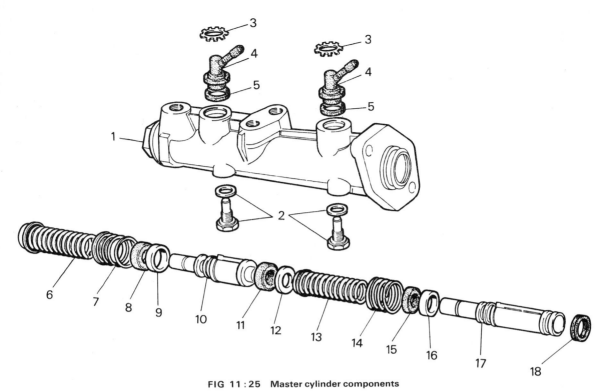

FIG 11 : 25   Master cylinder components

Key to Fig 11 : 25   1 Master cylinder body and plug   2 Screws and seals   3 Lockwashers   4 Fluid inlet connectors
5 Seals   6, 7 Springs and cups   8 Seal   9 Spacer   10 Front floating ring carrier   11 Seal   12 Flat washer   13, 14 Springs and
cups   15 Seal   16 Spacer   17 Rear floating ring carrier   18 Seal

squarely. Dip the internal parts in brake fluid and insert them back into the bore while still wet. **Take care not to bend or damage the lips of the seals as they enter the bore.** Keep each floating ring carrier pressed into the bore while fitting the stop screws. Use a new seal for each stop screw. Check that the pistons return freely after being pressed down the bore.

11 : 8 Vacuum servo unit

The vacuum servo unit operates to assist the pressure applied at the brake pedal and so reduce braking effort. The vacuum cylinder in the servo is connected to the engine inlet manifold by a hose.

Testing :

To test the servo unit, switch off the engine and pump the brake pedal several times to clear all vacuum from the unit. Hold a steady light pressure on the brake pedal and start the engine. If the servo is working properly, the brake pedal will move further down without further foot pressure, due to the build-up of vacuum in the system.

With the brakes off, run the engine to medium speed and turn off the ignition, immediately closing the throttle. This builds up a vacuum in the system. Wait one or two minutes, then try the brake action with the engine still switched off. If not vacuum assisted for two or three

operations, the servo check valve is faulty. If servo assistance is weak, the air filter in the unit may be clogged, preventing outside air from entering the unit at the proper rate.

If the vacuum servo unit is faulty or inoperative, remedial work should be carried out at a fully equipped service station.

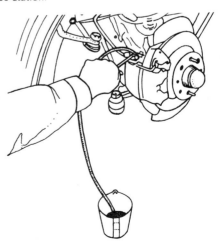

FIG 11 : 20   Bleeding the braking system

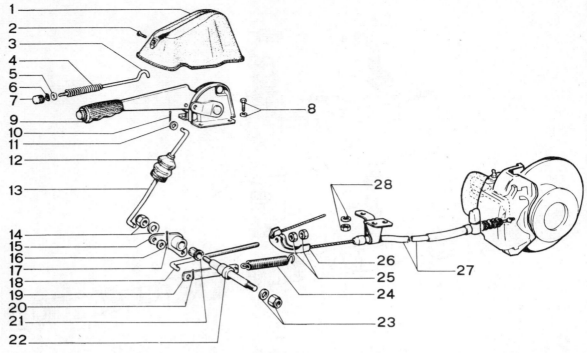

FIG 11 : 27   Handbrake linkage components

Key to Fig 11 : 27   1 Dust boot   2 Screw   3 Link   4 Spring   5 Flat washer   6 Seal   7 Push button   8 Screw and lockwasher   9 Handbrake lever   10 Cotterpin   11 Flat washer   12 Boot   13 Rod   14 Nut and flat washer   15 Lever   16 Flat washer   17 Cotterpin   18 Rod   19 Plate   20 Cotterpin   21 Rubber bush   22 Pin   23 Nut and flat washer   24 Return spring   25 Rod nuts   26 Equaliser   27 Cable   28 Nut and lockwasher

Failure of the servo unit does not impair the efficiency of the brakes, but greater pedal pressure will be needed to stop the car.

11 : 9 Bleeding the brakes

This is not routine maintenance and is only necessary if air has entered the hydraulic system due to parts being dismantled, or because the level in the master cylinder reservoir has dropped too low. The need for bleeding is indicated by a spongy feeling of the brake pedal; accompanied by poor braking performance. **Do not bleed the brakes with any friction pad or caliper removed. The brake regulator must be open.**

Bleed the rear brake furthest from the master cylinder first, followed by the second rear brake. Then bleed the front brake furthest from the master cylinder followed by the second front brake.

Remove the caps and top up the reservoirs to the correct level with approved brake fluid. Clean dirt from around the appropriate bleed screw and remove the dust cap. Fit a length of rubber or plastic tube to the screw as shown in **FIG 11 : 26** and lead the free end of the tube into a clean glass jar containing a small amount of brake fluid. The end of the tube must remain immersed in the fluid during the bleeding operation.

Unscrew the bleed screw about half a turn and have an assistant depress the brake pedal fully then allow it to

return. Fluid will be pumped into the jar. Continue pumping the pedal in this manner until no air bubbles can be seen in the fluid flowing into the jar. Always let the pedal rest for three seconds after being allowed to return, to allow the master cylinder to refill with fluid from the reservoir. When no more air bubbles can be seen, hold the pedal against the floor on a downstroke while the bleed valve is tightened. **Do not overtighten.**

During all bleeding operations, check the level of fluid in the reservoirs at frequent intervals, topping up as needed. If the level drops too low, air will enter the system and the operation will have to be restarted.

Remove the bleed tube, refit the dust cap and repeat the operation on the other calipers in turn.

On completion, top up the fluid to the correct level. Discard all used fluid. Always store brake fluid in clean, sealed containers to avoid air or moisture contamination.

11 : 10 The handbrake

Handbrake linkage components are shown in **FIG 11 : 27** and the installation in **FIG 11 : 28**. Normally, handbrake adjustment is taken up automatically by the rear brakes. If the handbrake lever travel is excessive or the handbrake operates inefficiently, check that the handbrake levers on the rear brakes are returning fully and moving freely and check that the handbrake cables and linkage are not binding or defective. **Under no**

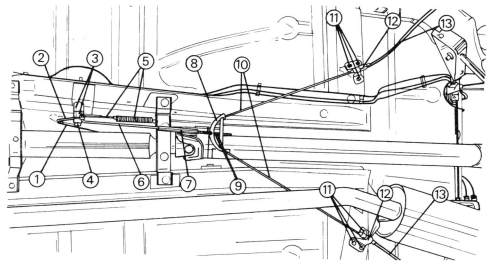

FIG 11:28 Handbrake linkage installation

key to Fig 11:28   1 Rod   2 Lever   3 Pin and lever   4 Nut   5 Plate and spring   6 Rod   7 Rod sheath   8 Equaliser
9 Adjustment nut and locknut   10 Cable   11 Cable clip nuts   12 Cable clips   13 Cable with sheath

circumstances may the linkage adjustment be **used to adjust the rear brakes.** If no faults are found, excessive handbrake lever movement will be caused by cable stretch. Raise and safely support the rear of the car so that the road wheels are clear of the ground. Pump the footbrake pedal hard several times to make sure that the rear brakes are fully adjusted.

Apply the handbrake by three notches from the fully-off position. Loosen the locknut and tighten the adjuster nut 9 until the rear wheels are locked against rotation by hand. Tighten the locknut. Apply the handbrake lever a few times and check that the rear wheels are still locked with the handbrake applied by three notches. Now release the handbrake fully and check that the rear wheels are free to rotate. If one or both rear wheels are locked against rotation with the handbrake released, or if there is any binding, check the handbrake cables for free movement. Lubricate the cable where it passes through the equaliser 8. If the wheels are not locked against rotation with the handbrake applied by three notches, or if there is any binding when the lever is released, re-adjust the linkage to obtain the correct conditions. Make sure that the adjuster locknut is fully tightened on completion.

11:11 Fault diagnosis

(a) Brake locked on

1 Swollen brake pads through oil contamination
2 Damage to hydraulic lines
3 Master cylinder compensating hole blocked

4 Master cylinder piston seized
5 Dirt in hydraulic system
6 Weak handbrake return springs
7 Bent regulator torsion bar

(b) Spongy pedal

1 Leak in the system
2 Worn master cylinder
3 Leaking caliper cylinder
4 Air in the fluid system

(c) Excessive pedal movement

1 Check 1 and 4 in (b)
2 Excessive friction pad wear
3 Very low fluid level in reservoir(s)
4 Faulty seals in caliper or master cylinder

(d) Brakes grab or pull to one side

1 Distorted disc
2 Wet or oily friction pads
3 Loose caliper
4 Disc loose on hub
5 Worn suspension or steering connections
6 Mixed linings of uneven grades
7 Uneven tyre pressures
8 Seized handbrake linkage
9 Seized caliper piston

NOTES

CHAPTER 12

THE ELECTRICAL SYSTEM

12:1 Description

All models covered by this manual have 12-volt electrical systems in which the negative battery terminal is earthed to the car bodywork.

There are wiring diagrams in **Technical Data** at the end of this manual that will enable those with electrical experience to trace and correct faults, that section also contains details and specifications for the units fitted to the models in the range.

Instructions for servicing the electrical equipment are given in this chapter, but it must be pointed out that it is not sensible to try to repair units that are seriously defective, either electrically or mechanically. Such equipment should be replaced by new or reconditioned units which can be obtained on an exchange basis.

12:2 The battery

To maintain the performance of the battery it is essential to carry out the following operations, particularly in winter when heavy current demands must be met.

Keep the top and surrounding parts of the battery clean and dry, as dampness can lead to current leakage. Clean off corrosion from the metal parts of the battery mountings with diluted ammonia and coat them with anti-sulphuric paint. Clean the terminal posts and smear them with petroleum jelly, remaking the connections properly and tightening the terminal clamps securely. High electrical resistance due to corrosion at the terminals can be responsible for lack of sufficient current to operate the starter motor.

Top up the electrolyte in the battery cells to the correct level at frequent intervals, using distilled water for this purpose. Test the condition of the cells, if necessary, with an hydrometer. **Never add neat acid to the battery. If it is necessary to prepare new electrolyte due to loss or spillage, add sulphuric acid to distilled water. It is highly dangerous to add water to acid.** It is safest to have the battery refilled with electrolyte, if necessary, by a service station.

The indications from the hydrometer readings of the specific gravity are as follows:

For climates below 27°C or 80°F		*Specific gravity*
Cell fully charged	..	1.270 to 1.290
Cell half discharged	..	1.190 to 1.210
Cell discharged ..	..	1.110 to 1.130
For climates above 27°C or 80°F		
Cell fully charged	..	1.210 to 1.230
Cell half discharged	..	1.130 to 1.150
Cell discharged ..	..	1.050 to 1.070

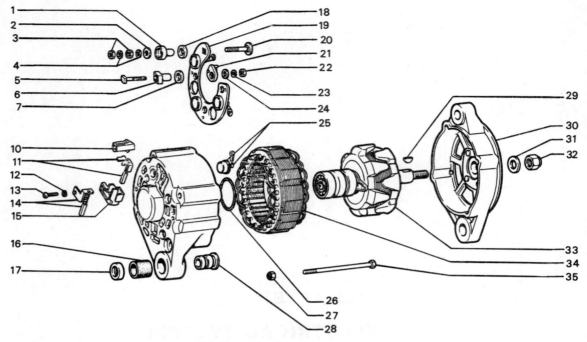

FIG 12:1   The alternator components

Key to Fig 12:1   1 Insulator   2 Washer   3 Nut   4 Locking washer   5 Bolt   6 Insulator   7 Insulator   10 Coupling
11 Carbon brush   12 Locking washer   13 Bolt   14 Carbon brush   15 Brush holder   16 Bush   17 Washer   18 Insulator
19 Plate   20 Bolt   21 Insulator   22 Nut   23 Spring washer   24 Washer   25 Rectifier   26 Sealing ring   27 Nut   28 Boss
29 Key   30 End bracket   31 Spacer   32 Nut   33 Rotor   34 Stator   35 Bolt

These figures assume an electrolyte temperature of 60°F or 16°C. If the temperature of the electrolyte exceeds this, add .002 to the readings for each 5°F or 3°C rise. Subtract .002 for any corresponding drop below 60°F or 16°C.

All cells should read approximately the same. If one differs radically from the others it may be due to an internal fault or to spillage or leakage of the electrolyte.

If the battery is in a low state of charge, take the car for a long daylight run or put the battery on a charger at 5 amp, with the vents removed, until it gasses freely. Do not use a naked light near the battery as the gas is inflammable. If the battery is to stand unused for long periods, give a refreshing charge every month. It will be ruined if it is left uncharged.

12:3 The alternator

The alternator provides current for the various items of electrical equipment and to charge the battery, the unit operating at all engine speeds. The current produced is alternate, this being rectified to direct current supply by diodes mounted in the alternator casing. Alternator drive is by belt from the crankshaft pulley. Very little maintenance is needed, apart from the occasional check on belt tension as described in **Chapter 4, Section 4:6** and on the condition and tightness of the wiring connections.

The alternator must never be run with the battery disconnected, nor must the battery cables be reversed at any time. Test connections must be carefully made, and the battery and alternator must be completely disconnected before any electric welding is carried out on any part of the car. The battery must be disconnected when it is being boost-charged from an outside source. The engine must never be started with a battery charger still connected to the battery. These warnings must be observed, otherwise extensive damage to the alternator components, particularly the diodes, will result.

The alternator is designed and constructed to give many years of trouble-free service. If, however, a fault should develop in the unit, it should be checked and serviced by a fully equipped service station or a reconditioned unit obtained and fitted. **FIG 12:1** shows the alternator components.

Alternator testing:

A simple check on alternator charging can be carried out after dark by switching on the headlamps and starting the engine. If the alternator is charging the headlamps will brighten considerably as the system voltage rises from the nominal battery voltage to the higher figure produced by the alternator. A more positive check is to connect a high resistance voltmeter, reading up to 20 volts, across the battery terminals and to note the reading when the engine is running at about 1000 rev/min. The voltage should remain steady at around 14.2 to 14.5. A higher voltage reading indicates a regulator failure, a lower reading indicates a fault in the alternator itself.

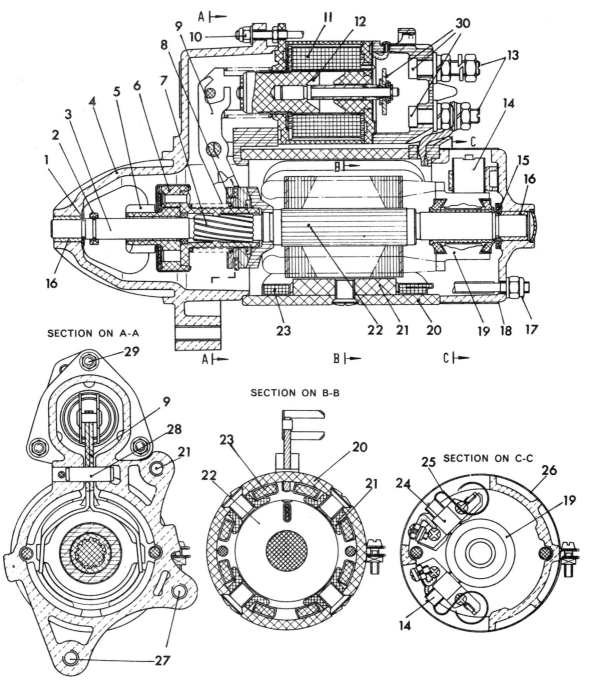

FIG 12:2 Sectioned views of the starter motor

Key to Fig 12:2   1 Washers   2 Snap ring   3 Armature shaft   4 Mounting end plate   5 Engagement drive pinion
6 Clutch   7 Splines   8 Sleeve   9 Operating lever   10 Solenoid attachment nuts   11 Solenoid winding   12 Solenoid
armature   13 Heavy current terminals   14 Brush   15 Washers   16 Bush   17 Through-bolt and nut   18 Commutator end plate
19 Commutator   20 Body housing   21 Polepiece   22 Armature winding and laminations   23 Field coil   24 Brush holder
25 Brush spring   26 Commutator end cover   27 Holes for fixing to bellhousing   28 Pivot pin   29 Solenoid attachment bolts
30 Heavy duty switch contacts

SECTION ON A-A

SECTION ON B-B

SECTION ON C-C

If the alternator is not charging, check the wiring and connections in the charging circuit. If these are in order, the alternator unit is at fault and must be checked and serviced by a Fiat agent.

Alternator removal:

Disconnect the battery then disconnect the cables to the alternator. Slacken the alternator mounting bolts, swing the unit towards the engine to slacken the drive belt, then remove the belt. Unbolt and remove the alternator. On models fitted with air-conditioning equipment, the air-conditioner drive belt must be removed first.

Refitting is a reversal of the removal procedure, adjusting the belt tension as described in **Chapter 4, Section 4:6**.

Alternator maintenance:

Check the tension of the alternator drive belt as described in **Chapter 4, Section 4:6**. The connections should be kept tight and clean and the outside of the unit should be kept free of oil and dirt particularly around ventilating slots in the cover.

Check occasionally that the springs are holding the brushes firmly in contact with the slip rings and that they move freely in their holders. Renew any brush that is worn to less than $\frac{3}{8}$ inch. It should be sufficient to clean the slip rings with a cloth moistened in petrol, but if they are very dirty very fine glasspaper may be used, preferably while spinning in a lathe.

12:4 The starter motor

Sectioned views of the starter motor are shown in **FIG 12:2** and the components in **FIG 12:3**. When the ignition switch is turned to the starter position, current flows through the solenoid windings 11 and the plunger 12 is drawn in. This motion makes the operating lever 9, engaging in the sleeve 8, move the pinion 5 into mesh with the teeth of the ring on the engine flywheel. The splines 7 along which the drive pinion assembly moves are spiralled to give slight initial rotation, locking under drive and rapid throwout. Further movement of the plunger 12 closes the contacts 30 and allows heavy current to flow from the terminal 13 to the starter motor. The motor then operates to start the engine. A clutch 6 is fitted to the drive assembly and when the engine starts this clutch releases so that the engine does not drive the motor at high speed, with possible damage by centrifugal force. The lever has a wide slot so that there is some lost motion and this ensures that the current is cut off before the drive pinion is disengaged.

Maintenance:

At intervals of 20,000 miles (30,000 km), remove the starter motor and dismantle it for inspection of the brush gear and lubrication. The spiral splines should be lubricated with Fiat VS.10 W oil (engine oil) and the steel buffer ring with Fiat MR3 grease (Lithium-NLGI No. 3).

Starter fails to operate correctly:

1 Check the condition of the battery terminals and state of charge of the battery. Dirt at the heavy duty connections is the most frequent cause of poor starter motor operations. Do not forget to check the earth points for the battery on the chassis, though usually this does not become defective unless there is extensive body corrosion. If when operated the horn sounds weak or the lights are dim, it is likely that the battery is low in charge.

2 Switch on some lights that can be seen from the driving seat and again operate the starter switch. If the lights go dim, the starter motor is taking current. One cause can be that the starter is jammed in mesh. Select a gear and rock the car backwards and forwards. If this fails to free the starter motor, it must be removed for further examination. If the motor is free but still taking current, it will have to be removed for examination.

3 If the lights do not go dim, the starter is not taking current. Disconnect the thin supply lead to the spade terminal on the solenoid and connect it to earth through a suitable test bulb. Operate the ignition switch and check that the bulb lights when the switch is in the starter position. If the bulb does not light, check back through the various terminals in the circuit until the fault or break is found. If the lamp does light, short across the heavy duty terminals of the solenoid with a thick piece of metal. The starter now spinning freely shows that the solenoid is defective and must be renewed. If the solenoid operates without action from the starter motor, the motor will have to be removed for examination.

Dismantling:

Free the lead of the starter motor from the lower heavy duty terminal of the solenoid by removing the nuts. Take off the nut 10 so that the solenoid can be removed, unhooking the plunger pin from the lever.

Remove the cover from around the brushes. Carefully lift the springs 25 off the ends of the brushes 14 and withdraw the brushes from their holders.

Remove the nuts 17 and take off the commutator end plate 18, collecting the thrust washers.

The body housing complete with the field coils can then be drawn off over the armature, and the armature and drive assembly can be freed from the mounting end plate 4 and lever 9. Reassemble the starter motor in the reverse order of removal after cleaning, examination and renewal of worn parts.

Brush gear:

Check the brushes for wear and renew them if they are excessively worn or contaminated. If the brushes stick in their holders, polish the sides of the brushes with a fine file and clean the brush holder with a piece of rag moistened with fuel or methylated spirits.

The commutator should have a smooth polished surface which is dark in appearance. Wiping over with a piece of cloth moistened with methylated spirits or fuel will be sufficient cleaning. Light burn marks or scores can be polished off with fine grade glasspaper (**never use emery cloth as this leaves particles imbedded in the copper**). Deeper damage may be skimmed off in a lathe, at high speed and using a very sharp tool. A diamond tipped tool should be used for a light final cut.

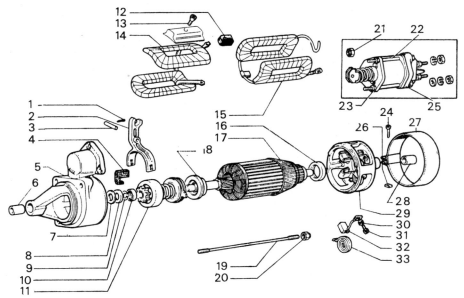

FIG 12:3 The components of the starter motor

Key to Fig 12:3   1 Splitpin   2 Lever   3 Spindle   4 Pad   5 End cover   6 Bush   7 Washer   8 Washer   9 Circlip
10 Stop   11 Drive unit   12 Retainer   13 Screw   14, 15 Field coils   16 Distance piece   17 Armature   18 Sleeve
19 Through-bolt   20 Nut   21 Nut   22 Tie rod   23 Nut   24 Screw   25 Solenoid   26 Nut   27 Shield   28 Bush
29 Brush carrier   30 Nut   31 Screw   32 Brush   33 Brush spring

Starter drive:

This can be removed from the armature shaft after driving down the collar with a suitable piece of tube and removing the snap ring covered by the collar.

Light damage to the pinion teeth can be cleaned off with a fine file or oilstone, but deeper damage necessitates renewal of the complete drive assembly.

Check that the clutch takes up drive instantaneously but slips freely in the opposite direction. Again, the complete drive assembly must be renewed if the clutch is defective.

The armature:

Check the armature for charred insulation, loose segments or laminations and for scored laminations. Shortcircuited windings may be suspected if individual commutator segments are badly burnt. No repairs can be carried out to a defective armature and renewal is the only cure.

Field coils:

The field coils and pole pieces are held in place by special screws which cannot be slackened or fully tightened with an ordinary screwdriver. For this reason, renewal of the field coils should be left to an agent.

The field coils can be checked for continuity using a test lamp and battery. A better method is to check the resistance using an ohmmeter. The resistance can also be checked using a 12-volt battery and ammeter (voltage divided by current equals resistance).

Bearings:

If the bushes are excessively worn, they should be renewed by a service station as press equipment and very accurate mandrels are required to install the new bushes.

Insulation and cleaning:

Blow away all loose dust and dirt with an air line. Use a small brush to clean out crevices. Fuel or methylated spirits may be used to help in cleaning the metal parts but the field coils, armature and drive assembly must under no circumstances be soaked with solvent.

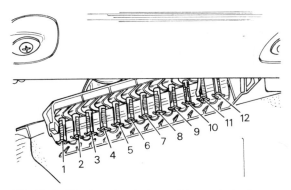

FIG 12:4   The fuse box is located beneath the instrument panel

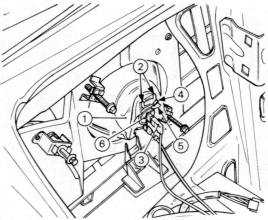

FIG 12:5   Renewing headlamp bulbs

Key to Fig 12:5   1 Dust boot   2 Retainer   3 Plug
connector   4 Spring   5 Retaining hook   6 Cup

A suitable test lamp and 12-volt battery may be used for testing purposes, though a better check will be to use a neon bulb and 110 AC volt supply. In neither case should the bulb light when connected across the insulations.

12:5 The fuses

On early cars twelve fuses are fitted into a fuse box located beneath the instrument panel on the righthand side, as shown in **FIG 12:4**; on later cars there are fourteen fuses located in the glove box. The removable cover is snap fastened to the housing. Fuses are rated at either 8, 16 or 25 amps according to the circuit they protect.

If a fuse blows, briefly check the circuit that it protects and install a new fuse. Check each circuit in turn and if the new fuse does not blow, it is likely that the old one had weakened with age. Do not forget that some circuits are 'live' only when the ignition is switched on. If the fuse blows, carefully check the circuit that was live at the time

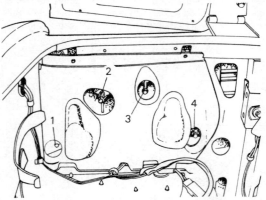

FIG 12:6   Lamp beam setting screws

Key to Fig 12:6   1 Low beam horizontal adjustment
screw   2 Low beam vertical adjustment screw   3 High
beam vertical adjustment screw   4 High beam horizontal
adjustment screw

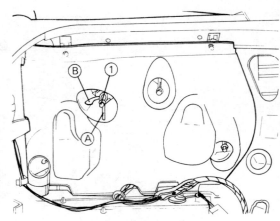

FIG 12:7   Dipped beam manual adjuster

Key to Fig 12:7   1 Low beam vertical adjustment screw
A Manual adjuster in no-load and half-load position
B Manual adjuster in full-load position

and do not fit another fuse until the fault has been found and repaired. A fuse that blows intermittently will make it more difficult to correct the fault, but try shaking the wiring loom, as the fault is likely to be caused by chafed insulation making intermittent contact with engine vibration or road shocks.

Never fit a fuse of higher rating than that specified. The fuse is designed to be the weak link in the circuit and if a higher rated fuse is installed the wiring may fail instead.

12:6 Headlamps

Bulb renewal:

Headlamp bulbs are accessible from the inside of the engine compartment. Refer to **FIG 12:5**. Fold up the dust boot 1 and fasten it to retainer 2, then slide out the plug connector 3. Press and slightly rotate spring 4 to free it from hook 5 and pull out the bulb.

Insert the new bulb, making sure that the two positioning dowels on cup 6 coincide with their seats on the lamp unit. Engage the bulb retaining spring 4 on hook 5, then turn down dust boot 1.

Headlamp beam setting:

The headlamp beam angles are adjusted by means of the horizontal and vertical adjustment screws which are fitted to each headlamp unit (see **FIG 12:6**), these screws being accessible from the inside of the engine compartment.

Headlamp main beams should be set so that, when the car is normally loaded the main beams are parallel to each other and to the road. The dipped beams should be set so that they provide a good spread of light to the front and nearside of the car without dazzling oncoming drivers. Accurate beam-setting is best left to a service station having special optical equipment.

The headlamp dipped beams are equipped with manual adjusters to enable the driver to set the beams vertically in two positions according to the loading of the car, as shown in **FIG 12:7**. Under normal conditions, the adjusters should be set in position A. When the car is fully loaded, move the adjuster to position B. Both adjusters should be set to the same position. The adjusters should always be set to position A when adjusting headlamp beam-setting as described previously.

The adjusting devices on 132 GLS models are disposed a little differently from those shown, but the general principles are the same.

12:7 Lighting circuits

Lamps give insufficient light:

Refer to **Section 12:2** and check the condition of the battery, recharging it if necessary. Check the setting of the headlamps as described in **Section 12:6** and renew any lamp units or bulbs which have darkened with age.

Bulbs burn out frequently:

Have the regulator setting checked by an auto-electrical service station.

Lamps light when switched on but gradually fade:

Refer to **Section 12:2** and check the battery, as it is not capable of supplying current for any length of time.

Lamp brilliance varies with the speed of the car:

Check the condition of the battery and its connections. Make sure that the connections are clean and tight and renew any faulty cables.

12:8 Fault diagnosis

(a) Battery discharged

1 Terminal connection loose or dirty
2 Shorts in lighting circuits
3 Alternator not charging
4 Regulator faulty
5 Battery internally defective

(b) Insufficient charge rate

1 Check 1 and 4 in (a)
2 Drive belt slipping
3 Alternator diodes defective

(c) Battery will not hold charge

1 Low electrolyte level
2 Battery plates sulphated
3 Electrolyte leakage from cracked case
4 Battery plate separators defective

(d) Battery overcharged

1 Regulator faulty

(e) Alternator output low or nil

1 Belt broken or slipping
2 Regulator needs adjusting
3 Brushes sticking, springs weak or broken
4 Defective rotor or stator windings
5 Defective diode(s)

(f) Starter motor lacks power or will not turn

1 Battery discharged, loose cable connections
2 Starter switch or solenoid faulty
3 Brushes worn or sticking, leads detached or shorting
4 Commutator dirty or worn
5 Starter shaft bent
6 Engine abnormally stiff, perhaps due to rebore

(g) Starter runs but will not turn engine

1 Pinion engagement mechanism faulty
2 Broken teeth on pinion or flywheel gears

(h) Noisy starter when engine is running

1 Pinion return mechanism faulty

(j) Starter motor inoperative

1 Check 1 and 4 in (f)
2 Armature or field coils faulty

(k) Starter motor rough or noisy

1 Mounting bolts loose
2 Pinion engagement mechanism faulty
3 Damaged pinion or flywheel teeth

(l) Lamps inoperative or erratic

1 Battery low, bulbs burned out
2 Faulty earthing of lamps or battery
3 Lighting switch faulty, loose or broken connections

(m) Wiper motor sluggish, taking high current

1 Wiper motor defective internally
2 Lack of lubrication
3 Linkage worn or binding
4 Wiper motor fixing bolts loose

(n) Wiper motor runs but does not drive arms

1 Wiper linkage faulty
2 Wiper transmission components worn

(o) Gauges do not work

1 Check wiring for continuity
2 Check instruments and transmitters for continuity

NOTES

CHAPTER 13

THE BODYWORK

13:1 Bodywork finish

Large scale repairs to body panels are best left to expert panel beaters. Even small dents can be tricky, as too much hammering will stretch the metal and make things worse instead of better. If panel beating is to be attempted, use a dolly on the opposite side of the panel. The head of a large hammer will suffice for small dents, but for large dents a heavy block of metal will be necessary. Use light hammer blows to reshape the panel, pressing the dolly against the opposite side of the panel to absorb the blows. If this method is used to reduce the depth of dents, final smoothing with a suitable filler will be easier, although it may be better to avoid hammering minor dents and just use the filler.

Clean the area to be filled, making sure that it is free from paint, rust and grease, then roughen the area with emerycloth or a file to ensure a good bond. Use a proprietary fibreglass filler paste mixed according to the instructions and press it into the dent with a putty knife. Allow the filler to stand proud of the surrounding area to allow for rubbing down after hardening. Use a file and emerycloth or a disc sander to blend the repaired area to the surrounding bodywork, using finer grade abrasives as the work nears completion. Apply a coat of primer surfacer and, when it is dry, rub down with 'Wet-or-Dry'

paper lubricated with soapy water, finishing with 400 grade. Apply more primer and repeat the operation until the surface is perfectly smooth. Take time in achieving the best finish possible at this stage as it will control the final effect.

The touching-up of paintwork can be carried out with self-spraying cans of paint, these being available in a wide range of colours. Use a piece of newspaper or board as a test panel to practice on first, so that the action of the spray will be familiar when it is used on the panel. Before spraying the panel, remove all traces of wax polish. Mask off large areas such as windows with newspaper and masking tape. Small areas such as trim strips or door handles can be wrapped with masking tape or carefully coated with grease or Vaseline. Apply the touching-up paint, spraying with short bursts and keeping the spray moving. Do not attempt to cover the area in one coat, applying several successive coats with a few minutes drying time between each. If too much paint is applied at one time, runs will develop. If so, do not try to remove the run by wiping, but wait until it is dry and rub down as before.

After the final coat has been applied, allow a few hours of drying time before blending the new finish to the old with fine cutting compound and a cloth, buffing

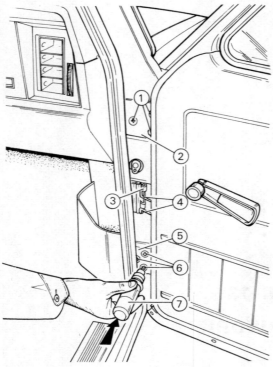

FIG 13:1 Front door removal

Key to Fig 13:1 1 Upper hinge screws 2 Upper hinge
3 Check link hinge 4 Check link 5 Lower hinge
6 Lower hinge screws 7 Impact screwdriver

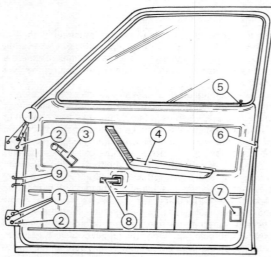

FIG 13:2 Removing window regulator handle and
lock control escutcheon

Key to Fig 13:2 1 Door hinge holes 2 Hinges
3 Window regulator handle 4 Armrest 5 Lock button
6 Lock 7 Reflector 8 Remote control handle 9 Check
link

with a light, circular motion. Leave the paint to harden
for a period of weeks rather than days before applying
wax polish.

13:2 Maintenance

Regular washing and waxing not only makes the car
look better but it also preserves the finish. Washing
removes the industrial grime which would otherwise
etch and damage the paintwork, while waxing fills the
pores and prevents moisture and dirt from creeping under
the paint to attack the metal. Chrome finish also benefits,
for the same reasons, from regular waxing.

When washing the car it is equally important to wash
the underside. Use a fine spray from a hose to soften
salt and mud deposits then remove them with a high
pressure jet. This is particularly important after winter,
as the salt spread on the roads rapidly corrodes the
underside. Wax-based oils and other compounds are
available for spraying on the underside of the vehicle to
protect it from salt and grit, the best time to apply these
being at the beginning of winter. **Care must be taken to
protect the brake units and flexible hoses from
any underbody treatments.**

Lubrication:

This should be carried out at intervals of 6000 miles
(10,000 km). The door lock barrels should be lubricated
with a little powdered graphite, blown in through the
key slot. Door hinges, seat mountings and pivots, and all
locks and stays should be lubricated with engine oil. The
bonnet catch and boot lock should be lubricated with
petroleum jelly. The seat runners should be lubricated
with Lithium-based grease. Avoid excessive lubrication
which could cause the staining of clothes or upholstery.

13:3 Front door components

Door removal and refitting:

Refer to **FIG 13:1**. Remove the door check link 4 from
its hinge 3. Scribe round the door hinge plates so that
they can be refitted to the body in their original positions.
Using an impact screwdriver, such as tool A.81011,
loosen the upper and lower door hinge attachment
screws 1 and 6. Support the door and remove the hinge
screws fully.

When refitting the door, make sure that it is properly
centred in the opening, aligning the hinges with the
scribe marks made previously. Adjust the position of the
door in the body aperture, if necessary, by slackening
screws 1 and 6 and moving the hinges as required.

Removing door components:

Refer to **FIG 13:2**. Using tool A.78034 or similar,
remove the attachment spring to release the window
regulator handle. Use a screwdriver to lever off the lock
control escutcheon. Take out the fixing screws and
remove the armrest assembly. Remove the door trim
panel as shown in **FIG 13:3**, pulling the plastic clips
from their locations in the door panel.

To remove the window glass and regulator mechanism,
make sure that the glass is fully lowered and remove the
joint covers, both inner and outer door window frames
and the rubber strip as shown in **FIG 13:4**. Refer to

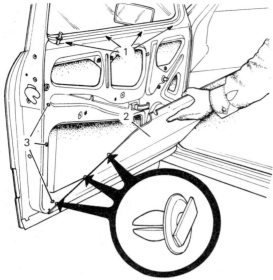

FIG 13:3   Removing door trim panel

Key to Fig 13:3   1 Upper attachment holes   2 Trim
panel   3 Retainer holes

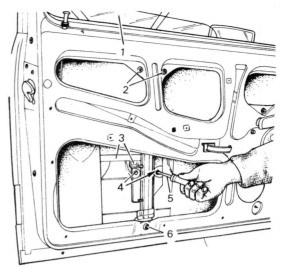

**FIG 13:5   Removing the window channel from the
regulator assembly**

Key to Fig 13:5   1 Window glass   2 Regulator upper
attachment screws   3 Window lift channel   4 Lift channel
to regulator screws   5 Phillips screwdriver   6 Regulator
lower attachment screw

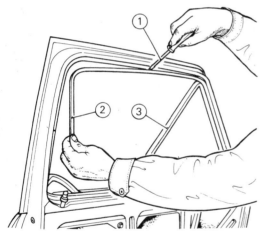

**FIG 13:4   Removing the window frames and rubber
strip**

Key to Fig 13:4   1 Screwdriver   2 Inner frame
3 Rubber strip

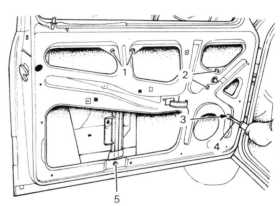

**FIG 13:6   The window regulator attachment screws
and nuts**

Key to Fig 13:6   1 Regulator upper attachment screws
2 Regulator handle plate nut   3 Regulator to door
attachment nut   4 Wrench   5 Regulator to door
attachment screw

FIG 13:5 and loosen screws 4 to separate the window
lift channel from the window regulator. Lift the glass and
channel to remove it from the top of the door panel.
Remove screws 1 and 5 and the nuts 2 and 3 as shown
in **FIG 13:6**, then remove the window regulator
assembly through the bottom of the door panel. If
necessary, the window rear guide channel can be
removed after loosening the two screws in the edge of
the door panel.

To remove the door lock and remote control assembly,
refer to **FIG 13:7**. Disconnect the rod which connects the

inside handle with the outside handle lock cylinder.
Disconnect the rod end from the lock and retainer, then
slide out the control rod and button from above. Loosen
the screws at positions 2 and 3 that secure the lock and
remote control handle. Slide out the components as
shown in the illustration.

To remove the outside door handle, loosen the attachment nuts from inside the door panel and detach the
handle and gasket from the outside of the door.

Reassemble the door components in the reverse order
of dismantling, adjusting the inside remote control lock

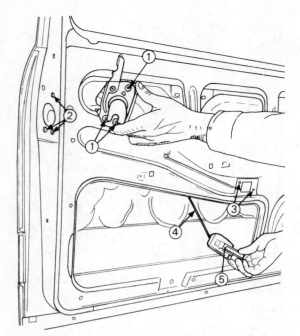

FIG 13:7   Door lock and remote control assembly

Key to Fig 13:7   1 Lock attachment screw holes
2 Attachment holes on door pillar   3 Slotted holes
4 Connecting link   5 Remote control handle

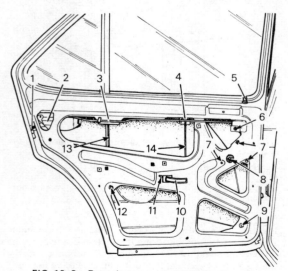

FIG 13:8   Rear door component attachments

Key to Fig 13:8   1 Lock   2 Door handle   3 Channel
upper attachment screw   4 Lift channel   5 Lock knob
6 Retaining nut   7 Regulator attachment nut   8 Regulator
handle attachment   9 Lower sheave attachment nut
10 Remote control handle   11 Attachment screw   12 Side
channel lower attachment screw   13 Side channel
14 Regulator cable

FIG 13:9   Bonnet removal

Key to Fig 13:9   1 Prop sliding sheave   2 Washer
3 Cotterpin   4 Prop   5 Bushes   6 Left hinge   7 Hinge to
bonnet screw   8 Hinge to body screw   9 Hinge to
bonnet screw   10 Hinge   11 Hinge to body screw

handle by means of the slotted holes 3 shown in **FIG
13:7**. It will be necessary to rewind the regulator
mechanism for front doors before installation.

On GLS models the window regulator is a little
different from that described and the interior trim is in
two sections, the upper section being retained by four
rivets which must be drilled out if removal is required.
Otherwise the doors are similar.

13:4 Rear door components

Door removal and refitting and the dismantling of door
components is carried out in a similar manner to that
described for front doors in **Section 13:3**, noting the
following points.

Before removing the trim panel, the ashtray must be
removed from its base plate by pressing down on the

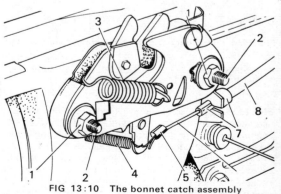

FIG 13:10   The bonnet catch assembly

Key to Fig 13:10   1 Attachment nuts   2 Stud
3 Latch return spring   4 Latch stop return spring
5 Release cable retainer   6 Release cable   7 Cable sheath
terminal   8 Cable sheath

metal tag, then the base plate removed by loosening the single screw.

FIG 13:8 shows the rear door components and attachments with the trim panel removed. To remove the window regulator, remove the lower sheave attachment nuts 9 and the window regulator attachment nuts 7, then remove the regulator assembly from the door panel aperture.

On GLS models the rear doors also have the two-piece trimming as on the front, the upper section being secured by the three rivets and a screw behind the ash tray.

A child safety catch is also fitted to each door lock below the striker. The catch is in the on, safe, position when pressed downwards.

13:5 Bonnet removal

Scribe around the hinges so that the bonnet can be refitted in its original position. Refer to **FIG 13:9**. Have an assistant steady the bonnet while the hinge screws are removed. Unhook the centre prop, then lift the bonnet from the car.

Refitting is a reversal of the removal procedure, centring the bonnet in the body aperture if necessary by adjusting the position of the hinge plates. If the bonnet fails to lock properly in the closed position, refer to **FIG 13:10** and loosen the attachment nuts 1. Move the latch assembly to the required position, then tighten the attachment nuts firmly.

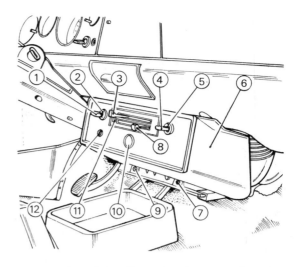

FIG 13:11   Heater housing removal

Key to Fig 13:11   1 Heater fan switch   2 Ring nut
3 Control lever   4 Demister switch   5 Ring nut   6 Heater
housing   7 Screw   8 Control lever   9 Screw   10 Cigar
lighter housing   11, 12 Plates

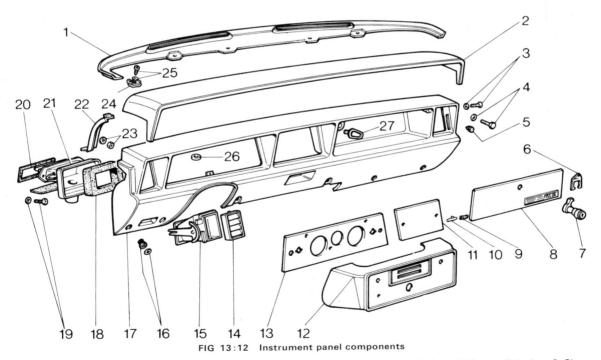

FIG 13:12   Instrument panel components

Key to Fig 13:12   1 Upper panel   2 Upper pad   3, 4 Screws and lockwashers   5 Buffer   6 Fork   7 Lock   8 Glove
compartment lid   9 Spring   10 Pin   11 Radio recess panel   12 Heater housing   13 Instrument cluster panel   14, 15 Adjustable
air outlets   16 Bush and lockwasher   17 Main instrument panel   18 Gasket   19 Screw and washer   20 Gasket   21 Air duct
22 Side brace   23 Nut and lockwasher   24 Plate   25 Screw and lockwasher   26 Spacer   27 Glove compartment light
plate

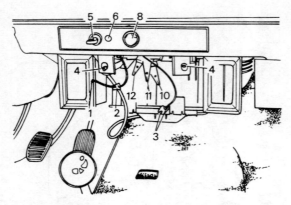

FIG 13:13 Removing the instrument panel (132 GLS). Console and tunnel tray removed

Key to Fig 13:13   1 Ideogram illumination light point
2 Light point clamp   3 Ash tray illumination point and clamp
4 Console retaining nuts and studs   5 Heater fan switch
6 Heater fan switch ideogram   8 Cigar lighter housing
10 Air distribution control (knob removed)   11 Heater
temperature control (knob removed)   12 Fresh air control
(knob removed)

13:6 Facia removal

Remove the instrument panel from the facia as described in **Chapter 10**, **Section 10:3**. Refer to **FIG 13:11** and remove the heater fan and rear window demister switch ring nuts 2 and 5. Using a screwdriver, remove the knobs from the heater control levers. Remove the two lower screws that secure the heater housing to the body. Open the glove compartment lid. Refer to **FIG 13:12** and remove the nuts and screws which secure the instrument panel to the body.

Refitting is a reversal of the removal procedure.

132 GLS models:

Remove the instrument panel trim by unscrewing the two light switch ring nuts and the three retaining screws.

Disconnect the speedometer cable and the connector plugs.

Undo the two retaining screws and lift off the radio recess cover. The grille over the loudspeaker recess is a snap-on fit.

Of the three upper nuts retaining the panel, two are behind the steering wheel and one in the speaker recess. Remove these.

Pull out the ash tray. Use a screwdriver to release the three knobs on the heater control levers and then pull out the centre console trim panel by the tongue at centre bottom.

Undo two retaining screws and remove the tunnel tray front panel, then remove the exposed screw securing the console and tray to the tunnel.

Refer to **FIG 13:13**. Disconnect the clamp 2 and light point 1 from the console trim and also the light point 3 from the ash tray by releasing its clamp. Remove the retaining nuts 4 and lift off the console.

Remove the two upper screws inside the lid retaining the glove box to the instrument panel. Remove the six panel to body retaining screws and take off the panel.

Refitting is carried out by reversing the above procedure.

APPENDIX

TECHNICAL DATA

Engine   Fuel system   Ignition system   Cooling system
Clutch   Transmission   Suspension   Steering   Brakes
Electrical system   Weights   Wheels and tyres   Capacities
Torque wrench settings

WIRING DIAGRAMS

HINTS ON MAINTENANCE AND OVERHAUL

GLOSSARY OF TERMS

INDEX

Inches	Decimals	Milli-metres	Inches to Millimetres		Millimetres to Inches	
			Inches	mm	mm	Inches
1/64	.015625	.3969	.001	.0254	.01	.00039
1/32	.03125	.7937	.002	.0508	.02	.00079
3/64	.046875	1.1906	.003	.0762	.03	.00118
1/16	.0625	1.5875	.004	.1016	.04	.00157
5/64	.078125	1.9844	.005	.1270	.05	.00197
3/32	.09375	2.3812	.006	.1524	.06	.00236
7/64	.109375	2.7781	.007	.1778	.07	.00276
1/8	.125	3.1750	.008	.2032	.08	.00315
9/64	.140625	3.5719	.009	.2286	.09	.00354
5/32	.15625	3.9687	.01	.254	.1	.00394
11/64	.171875	4.3656	.02	.508	.2	.00787
3/16	.1875	4.7625	.03	.762	.3	.01181
13/64	.203125	5.1594	.04	1.016	.4	.01575
7/32	.21875	5.5562	.05	1.270	.5	.01969
15/64	.234375	5.9531	.06	1.524	.6	.02362
1/4	.25	6.3500	.07	1.778	.7	.02756
17/64	.265625	6.7469	.08	2.032	.8	.03150
9/32	.28125	7.1437	.09	2.286	.9	.03543
19/64	.296875	7.5406	.1	2.54	1	.03937
5/16	.3125	7.9375	.2	5.08	2	.07874
21/64	.328125	8.3344	.3	7.62	3	.11811
11/32	.34375	8.7312	.4	10.16	4	.15748
23/64	.359375	9.1281	.5	12.70	5	.19685
3/8	.375	9.5250	.6	15.24	6	.23622
25/64	.390625	9.9219	.7	17.78	7	.27559
13/32	.40625	10.3187	.8	20.32	8	.31496
27/64	.421875	10.7156	.9	22.86	9	.35433
7/16	.4375	11.1125	1	25.4	10	.39370
29/64	.453125	11.5094	2	50.8	11	.43307
15/32	.46875	11.9062	3	76.2	12	.47244
31/64	.484375	12.3031	4	101.6	13	.51181
1/2	.5	12.7000	5	127.0	14	.55118
33/64	.515625	13.0969	6	152.4	15	.59055
17/32	.53125	13.4937	7	177.8	16	.62992
35/64	.546875	13.8906	8	203.2	17	.66929
9/16	.5625	14.2875	9	228.6	18	.70866
37/64	.578125	14.6844	10	254.0	19	.74803
19/32	.59375	15.0812	11	279.4	20	.78740
39/64	.609375	15.4781	12	304.8	21	.82677
5/8	.625	15.8750	13	330.2	22	.86614
41/64	.640625	16.2719	14	355.6	23	.90551
21/32	.65625	16.6687	15	381.0	24	.94488
43/64	.671875	17.0656	16	406.4	25	.98425
11/16	.6875	17.4625	17	431.8	26	1.02362
45/64	.703125	17.8594	18	457.2	27	1.06299
23/32	.71875	18.2562	19	482.6	28	1.10236
47/64	.734375	18.6531	20	508.0	29	1.14173
3/4	.75	19.0500	21	533.4	30	1.18110
49/64	.765625	19.4469	22	558.8	31	1.22047
25/32	.78125	19.8437	23	584.2	32	1.25984
51/64	.796875	20.2406	24	609.6	33	1.29921
13/16	.8125	20.6375	25	635.0	34	1.33858
53/64	.828125	21.0344	26	660.4	35	1.37795
27/32	.84375	21.4312	27	685.8	36	1.41732
55/64	.859375	21.8281	28	711.2	37	1.4567
7/8	.875	22.2250	29	736.6	38	1.4961
57/64	.890625	22.6219	30	762.0	39	1.5354
29/32	.90625	23.0187	31	787.4	40	1.5748
59/64	.921875	23.4156	32	812.8	41	1.6142
15/16	.9375	23.8125	33	838.2	42	1.6535
61/64	.953125	24.2094	34	863.6	43	1.6929
31/32	.96875	24.6062	35	889.0	44	1.7323
63/64	.984375	25.0031	36	914.4	45	1.7717

UNITS	Pints to Litres	Gallons to Litres	Litres to Pints	Litres to Gallons	Miles to Kilometres	Kilometres to Miles	Lbs. per sq. In. to Kg. per sq. Cm.	Kg per sq Cm. to Lbs. per sq. In.
1	.57	4.55	1.76	.22	1.61	.62	.07	14.22
2	1.14	9.09	3.52	.44	3.22	1.24	.14	28.50
3	1.70	13.64	5.28	.66	4.83	1.86	.21	42.67
4	2.27	18.18	7.04	.88	6.44	2.49	.28	56.89
5	2.84	22.73	8.80	1.10	8.05	3.11	.35	71.12
6	3.41	27.28	10.56	1.32	9.66	3.73	.42	85.34
7	3.98	31.82	12.32	1.54	11.27	4.35	.49	99.56
8	4.55	36.37	14.08	1.76	12.88	4.97	.56	113.79
9		40.91	15.84	1.98	14.48	5.59	.63	128.00
10		45.46	17.60	2.20	16.09	6.21	.70	142.23
20				4.40	32.19	12.43	1.41	284.47
30				6.60	48.28	18.64	2.11	426.70
40				8.80	64.37	24.85		
50					80.47	31.07		
60					96.56	37.28		
70					112.65	43.50		
80					128.75	49.71		
90					144.84	55.92		
100					160.93	62.14		

UNITS	Lb ft to kgm	Kgm to lb ft	UNITS	Lb ft to kgm	Kgm to lb ft
1	.138	7.233	7	.967	50.631
2	.276	14.466	8	1.106	57.864
3	.414	21.699	9	1.244	65.097
4	.553	28.932	10	1.382	72.330
5	.691	36.165	20	2.765	144.660
6	.829	43.398	30	4.147	216.990

TECHNICAL DATA

Dimensions are in millimetres (inches) unless otherwise stated

ENGINE

Designation:
- 1600 pre 1975 . . . . 132.A.000 or 132.B.000
- 1600 from 1975 . . . . 132.C.000 or 132.C6.000
- 1800 . . . . 132.A1.000 or 132.B1.000
- 2000 . . . . 132.C2.000

Bore and stroke:
- 1600 pre 1975 . . . . 80 × 79.2 (3.15 × 3.12)
- 1600 from 1975 . . . . 84 × 71.5 (3.31 × 2.81)
- 1800 . . . . 84 × 79.2 (3.31 × 3.12)
- 2000 . . . . 84 × 90 (3.31 × 3.54)

Capacity:
- 1600 pre 1975 . . . . 1592 cc (97.1 cu in)
- 1600 from 1975 . . . . 1585 cc (96.7 cu in)
- 1800 . . . . 1756 cc (107.1 cu in)
- 2000 . . . . 1995 cc (121.7 cu in)

Compression ratio:
- 1600 . . . . 9 : 1 or 7.77 : 1
- 1800 . . . . 8.9 : 1
- 2000 . . . . 8.9 : 1

Power output (DIN):
- 1600 (9 : 1 CR) . . . . 72 kW (98 BHP at 5600 rev/min
- 1600 (7.77 : 1 CR) . . . . 65.5 kW (89 BHP) at 6000 rev/min
- 1800 . . . . 81 kW (111 BHP) at 5600 rev/min
- 2000 . . . . 82.4 kW (112 BHP) at 5600 rev/min

Cylinder bores:
- Standard diameter:
  - 80 mm nominal . . . . 80.00 to 80.05 (3.1496 to 3.1516)
  - 84 mm nominal . . . . 84.00 to 84.05 (3.3070 to 3.3090)
- Maximum wear, taper or ovality . . . . . . .15 (.006)

Pistons:
- Diameter, 80 mm bore:
  - Class A . . . . 79.92 to 79.93 (3.1464 to 3.1468)
  - Class C . . . . 79.94 to 79.95 (3.1472 to 3.1476)
  - Class E . . . . 79.96 to 79.97 (3.1479 to 3.1483)
  - Oversizes . . . . +.2, +.4, +.6 (+.008, +.016, +.024)
- Diameter, 84 mm bore:
  - Class A . . . . 83.92 to 83.93 (3.3039 to 3.3043)
  - Class C . . . . 83.94 to 83.95 (3.3047 to 3.3051)
  - Class E . . . . 83.96 to 83.97 (3.3055 to 3.3059)
  - Oversizes . . . . +.2, +.4, +.6 (+.008, +.016, +.024)

Piston rings:
- Side clearance:
  - Top ring . . . . .045 to .077 (.0018 to .0030)
  - Second ring . . . . .030 to .070 (.0011 to .0027)
  - Third ring . . . . .030 to .062 (.0011 to .0024)
- Fitted gap, 80 mm bore:
  - Top ring . . . . .30 to .45 (.0118 to .0177)
  - Second ring . . . . .20 to .35 (.0078 to .0137)
  - Third ring . . . . .20 to .35 (.0078 to .0137)
- Fitted gap, 84 mm bore:
  - Top ring . . . . .30 to .45 (.0118 to .0177)
  - Second ring . . . . .30 to .45 (.0118 to .0177)
  - Third ring . . . . .25 to .40 (.0098 to .0157)

Crankshaft:

Main journal diameter	52.985 to 53.005 (2.0860 to 2.0868)
Main bearing clearance:	
Early 1600, 1800	.050 to .095 (.0020 to .0037)
Later 1600, 2000	.032 to .077 (.0013 to .0030)
Crankpin diameter, grade A:	
Early 1600, 1800, 2000	50.792 to 50.802 (1.9997 to 2.0001)
Later 1600	48.234 to 48.244 (1.8990 to 1.8994)
Crankpin diameter, grade B:	
Early 1600, 1800, 2000	50.782 to 50.792 (1.9993 to 1.9997)
Later 1600	48.224 to 48.234 (1.8986 to 1.8990)
Big-end bearing clearance	.030 to .075 (.0012 to .0029)

Camshaft:

Journal bore diameter:	
Front	30.009 to 30.034 (1.184 to 1.1824)
Centre	45.800 to 45.825 (1.8031 to 1.8042)
Rear	46.200 to 46.225 (1.8189 to 1.8198)
Journal diameter:	
Front	29.944 to 29.960 (1.1788 to 1.1795)
Centre	45.755 to 45.771 (1.8013 to 1.8020)
Rear	46.155 to 46.171 (1.8171 to 1.8178)
Running clearance:	
Front	.049 to .090 (.0019 to .0035)
Centre	.029 to .070 (.0011 to .0027)
Rear	.029 to .070 (.0011 to .0027)

Auxiliary drive shaft:

Journal bore diameter:	
Front	51.120 to 51.150 (2.0126 to 2.0138)
Rear	42.030 to 42.060 (1.6547 to 1.6559)
Inside diameter of bore bushes:	
Front	48.084 to 48.104 (1.8930 to 1.8938)
Rear	39.000 to 39.020 (1.5354 to 1.5362)
Journal diameter:	
Front	48.013 to 48.038 (1.8903 to 1.8913)
Rear	38.929 to 38.954 (1.5326 to 1.5336)

Tappets:

Tappet bore	37.000 to 37.025 (1.4567 to 1.4576)
Tappet diameter	36.975 to 36.995 (1.4557 to 1.4565)
Clearance	.005 to .050 (.0002 to .0020)

Valves and guides:

Seat angle on valve	45 deg. 30 min ± 5 min
Seat angle in head	45 deg. ± 5 min
Seat width in head	2 (.079)
Inner diameter of valve guide	8.022 to 8.040 (.3158 to .3165)
Valve stem diameter	7.974 to 7.992 (.3139 to .3146)
Valve stem clearance	.030 to .066 (.0012 to .0026)

Valve clearances cold:

Inlet	.45 (.018)
Exhaust	.60 (.024)

FUEL SYSTEM

Carburetter calibration:

Weber 34 DMS:

	Primary	Secondary
Bore	34 (1.338)	34 (1.338)
Venturi	24 (.945)	26 (1.023)
Auxiliary venturi	4.50 (.177)	4.50 (.177)
Main jet	1.25 (.049)	1.55 (.061)

Main air metering jet	..	..	..	..	1.80 (.071)	1.80 (.071)
Emulsion tube	..	..	..	..	F61	F61
Idle jet	..	..	..	..	.50 (.019)	.70 (.027)
Idle air metering jet	..	..	..	..	1.05 (.041)	.70 (.027)
Pump jet	..	..	..	..	.50 (.019)	–
Pump discharge	..	..	..	..	.40 (.016)	–
Power jet	..	..	..	..	1.10 (.043)	–
Power air metering jet	..	..	..	..	1.30 (.051)	–
Power mixture jet	..	..	..	..	1.10 (.043)	–
Needle valve seat	..	..	..	..	1.75 (.069)	–
Float level	..	..	..	..	7 (.275)	–

Weber 34 DMS 1 :

As above except :

Venturi	..	..	..	..	22 (.86)	24 (.94)
Main jet	..	..	..	..	1.15 (.045)	1.30 (.051)
Air correction jet	..	..	..	..	1.55 (.061)	1.70 (.067)
Emulsion tube	..	..	..	..	F61	F61
Idle air metering jet	..	..	..	..	.90 (.035)	.70 (.027)
Power jet	..	..	..	..	1.30 (.051)	–
Power air jet	..	..	..	..	1.00 (.039)	–

Weber 34 DMS 2 :

As above except :

Main jet	..	..	..	..	1.25 (.049)	1.50 (.059)
Air correction jet	..	..	..	..	1.50 (.059)	1.50 (.059)
Emulsion tube	..	..	..	..	F15	F15
Idle air metering jet	..	..	..	..	.90 (.035)	.70 (.027)
Power jet	..	..	..	..	1.30 (.051)	–
Power air jet	..	..	..	..	1.00 (.039)	–

Solex C 34 EIES 4 :

Bore	..	..	..	..	34 (1.338)	34 (1.388)
Venturi	..	..	..	..	24 (.945)	27 (1.063)
Auxiliary venturi	..	..	..	..	4.50 (.177)	4.50 (.177)
Main jet	..	..	..	..	1.25 (.049)	1.50 (.059)
Main air metering jet	..	..	..	..	1.50 (.059)	1.50 (.059)
Emulsion tube	..	..	..	..	3.50 (.138)	3.50).138)
Idle jet	..	..	..	..	.47 (.018)	.80 (.031)
Idle air metering jet	..	..	..	..	.90 (.035)	1.10 (.043)
Pump jet	..	..	..	..	.55 (.021)	–
Needle valve seat	..	..	..	..	1.80 (.071)	–
Float level	..	..	..	..	Use gauge A.95134	

Solex C 34 EIES 8 :

As above except:

Venturi	..	..	..	..	22 (.86)	25 (.98)
Main jet	..	..	..	..	1.125 (.044)	1.30 (.051)
Air correction jet	..	..	..	..	1.60 (.063)	1.60 (.063)
Idle jet	..	..	..	..	.50 (.019)	.60 (.024)
Idle air jet	..	..	..	..	.90 (.035)	1.10 (.043)
Pump jet	..	..	..	..	.55 (.022)	–
Power jet	..	..	..	..	–	1.05 (.041)
Float level (with gauge A.95144)	..	..	20.5 (.807)	

Solex C 34 EIES 9 :

As above except :

Venturi	..	..	..	..	24 (.94)	27 (1.06)
Main jet	..	..	..	..	1.30 (.051)	1.35 (.053)
Air correction jet	..	..	..	..	1.50 (.059)	1.50 (.059)
Idle jet	..	..	..	..	.525 (.021)	.60 (.024)

Weber 32 ADF 2/200, 2/100, 2/250, 2/150 :

Bore	..	..	..	..	32	32
Venturi	..	..	..	..	22	24
Auxiliary venturi	..	..	..	..	4.5	4.5
Main jet	..	..	..	..	1.10	1.25
Air correction jet	..	..	..	..	1.50	1.60

Emulsion tube	F52	F52
Slow-running jet	.50	.80
Slow-running air bleed	.80	.70
1st progression orifice	1.00	1.20
2nd progression orifice	1.10	1.20
3rd progression orifice	1.10	–
4th progression orifice	1.00	–
Accelerator pump jet	.45	–
Pump output (20 strokes)	19 cc	
Pump excess discharge	.40	
Power jet	–	1.30
Power mixture outlet	–	2.50
Crankcase vent orifice	1.40	–
Needle valve sent	1.75	
Float level	6	

Weber 32 ADF 4/200, 4/100 : As above except :

Venturi	23	25
Main jet	1.15	1.30
Air correction jet	1.65	1.90
Emulsion tube	F 20	F 20
Slow-running air bleed	1.35	.70
2nd progression orifice	1.00	1.20
3rd progression orifice	1.20	–
4th progression orifice	–	–

Weber 32 ADF 19/251 : As above except :

Slow-running jet	.50	.50
Slow-running air bleed	.80	1.00
Accelerator pump jet	.50	–
Power jet	–	1.00

Weber 34 ADF 250, 150 : As above except :

Bore	34	34
Venturi	24	26
Main jet	1.20	1.35
Air correction jet	1.45	1.80
Emulsion tube	F 20	F 5
Slow-running jet	.50	.90
Slow-running air bleed	.90	.70
2nd progression orifice	1.20	1.20
3rd progression orifice	1.20	–
Crankcase vent orifice	1.50	–

IGNITION SYSTEM

Firing order .. .. 1 – 3 – 4 – 2
Static advance setting .. .. .. 10 deg. BTDC
Centrifugal advance .. .. .. 28 deg. ± 2 deg.
Distributor contact gap .. .. .. .37 to .43 (.0145 to .0169)
Capacitor .. .. .20 to .25 microfarad
Sparking plugs :
    Thread and reach .. .. .. M14 × 1.25
    Type (132 and 132 Special) .. .. Bosch W.230.T.30, Marelli CW.8.LP, Champion N6Y
    Type (132 GL and 132 GLS) .. .. Bosch W.200.T.30, Marelli CW.78.LP, Champion N7Y
Plug gap (conventional ignition) .. .. .5 to .6 (.020 to .024)
Plug gap (electronic ignition) .. .. .6 to .7 (.024 to .028)

COOLING SYSTEM

Fan thermostatic switch :
Cuts in at	90 to 94°C (194 to 201°F)
Cuts out at	85 to 89°C (185 to 192°F)

Thermostat :
Starts opening	81 to 85°C (178 to 185°F)
Minimum opening at 92°C (198°F)	7.5 (.29)
Radiator cap valve opening pressure	.8 kg/sq cm (11.4 lb/sq inch)

CLUTCH

Type	Single dry plate, diaphragm spring
Operation	Mechanical

Pedal free travel :
1600 pre 1977	12.5 to 25.0 (.492 to .984)
1800	25.0 (.984)
Later cars	Nil (see text)

TRANSMISSION

Manual transmission :

Type	Four-speed or five-speed gearbox with synchromesh on all forward speeds

Gear ratios, pre 1975 :	First	Second	Third	Fourth	Fifth	Reverse
Four-speed	3.667	2.100	1.361	1	–	3.526
Five-speed	3.667	2.100	1.361	1	.881	3.526
Five-speed (optional) ..	3.554	2.175	1.410	1	.913	3.652
Gear ratios, from 1975 :						
Four-speed	3.612	2.045	1.357	1	–	3.244
Five-speed	3.612	2.045	1.375	1	.870	3.244

Automatic transmission :

Type	G.M.S. three-speed with torque converter

Gear ratios :
First	2.4
Second	1.48
Third	1
Reverse	1.92
Transmission fluid	Fiat GL/A or ATF type DEXRON

Rear axle :
Type	Hypoid. Optional limited slip differential

Ratio, pre 1977 :
Manual	4.1
Automatic	4.1 or 3.727

Ratio, from 1977 :
Manual	3.727
Automatic	3.416

SUSPENSION

Front suspension geometry :
Steering knuckle inclination	6 deg. ± 20 min

Castor angle :
Unloaded	3 deg. 25 min ± 15 min
Loaded (four persons)	4 deg. ± 30 min

STEERING

Front wheel toe-in:
Unloaded	5 ± 2 (.20 ± .08)
Loaded (four persons)	3 ± 2 (.12 ± .08)

BRAKES

Operation :
Footbrake	Hydraulic, on all four wheels
Handbrake	Mechanical, on rear wheels only
Brake adjustment	Automatic
Handbrake cable adjustment	Threaded rod at equaliser
Minimum pad lining thickness	1.5 (.06)
Maximum disc runout	.10 (.004)
Minimum disc thickness	10 (.39)
Brake fluid	Fiat Blue Label Brake Fluid, or Heavy Duty fluid meeting SAE.J.1703b specification

ELECTRICAL SYSTEM

Type	12-volt, negative earth

Battery :
Capacity	45 amp/hr at 20 hour rate
Heavy discharging rating	185 amps at − 18°C

Alternator :
Type	Fiat A.12.M.124/12/42.M or A.124-14.V-44.A (early). Marelli or Bosch (later)
Regulator	RC.2/12.B or D (early). Integral on late type alternators

Starter motor :
Type	Fiat E.100-1.3/12 or Bosch GF 12V 1.IPS
Engagement	Solenoid
Drive	Overrunning clutch

WEIGHTS

Kerb weight :
Manual transmission	2359 lb (1070 kg)
Automatic transmission	2403 lb (1090 kg)
Load capacity	Five persons plus 110 lb (50kg) luggage
Towing capacity	1980 lb (900 kg) maximum

WHEELS AND TYRES

Wheels (pre 1975)	Disc wheels, rim size 5J × 13
Tyres	Radial-ply 175 SR × 13
	170 SR × 13
Wheels (1975-77)	5½J × 13
Tyres	185/70 × 13
Wheels (from 1977)	5½J × 14
Tyres	175/70 SR 14

Tyre pressures, 13 inch rims :
Front	25.5 lb/sq inch (1.8 kg/sq cm)
Rear	27 lb/sq inch (1.9 kg/sq cm)

Tyre pressures, 14 inch rims :
Front	27 lb/sq inch (1.9 kg/sq cm)
Rear	28 lb/sq inch (2 kg/sq cm)

CAPACITIES

Fuel tank	12 gall. (56 litre)
Cooling system	1.75 gall (8 litre)
Engine and filter :	
Refill capacity	7 pint (4 litre)
Total capacity	8.4 pint (4.8 litre)
Transmission :	
Four-speed manual	2.25 pint (1.28 litre)
Five-speed manual	2.70 pint (1.53 litre)
Automatic	10 pint (5.6 litre)
Rear axle	2.90 pint (1.65 litre)
Steering gear	.44 pint (.25 litre)

TORQUE WRENCH SETTINGS

	Torque	
	lb ft	kgm
Engine:		
Front main bearing cap screw	58	8
Main bearing cap self-locking screw	83	11.5
Engine breather mounting screw	18	2.5
Cylinder head hold-down screw	61	8.5
Nut, upper cylinder head stud	14.5	2
Nut, intake and exhaust manifold to cylinder head stud	18	2.5
Connecting rod bearing cap screw nut	36	5
Flywheel to crankshaft screw	61.5	8.5
Camshaft sprocket screw	87	12
Belt tensioner nut	32.5	4.5
Alternator and water pump drive pulley nut	181	25
Self-locking, nylon-lined nut, alternator lower support stud	32.5	4.5
Alternator upper bracket screw	40	5.5
Alternator lower mounting nut	50	7
Self-locking, nylon-lined nut, alternator to upper bracket	32.5	4.5
Spark plug	29	4
Oil pressure switch	25	3.5
Electric heat gauge sending unit (water temperature)	36	5
Power plant mounting:		
Nut, insulator to mount screw	22	3
Nut, insulator to crossmember screw	25	3.5
Nut, mount to engine	18	2.5
Screw, rear crossmember to body	22	3
Nut, power plant rear insulator to crossmember screw	18	2.5
Nut, insulator to manual transmission rear cover stud	22	3
Screw, insulator to automatic transmission rear cover	36	5
Transmission:		
Manual 4-speed:		
Back-up light press switch	32.5	4.5
Screw, shifter shaft detent ball retainer cover	18	2.5
Screw, front cover lower attachment to engine	61.5	8.5
Screw, front cover upper attachment to engine	61.5	8.5
Nut, rear cover to transmission case attachment stud	18	2.5
Nut, front cover to transmission case attachment stud	36	5
Nut, front cover to transmission case attachment stud	18	2.5
Nut, flexible joint sleeve to mainshaft	58	8
Screw, countershaft front bearing	69	9.5
Screw, shifter fork and gear selection lever	14.5	2
Manual 5-speed:		
Screw, shifter shaft detent ball retainer cover	18	2.5
Back-up light press switch	32.5	4.5
Screw, front cover lower attachment to engine	61.5	8.5
Screw, front cover upper attachment to engine	61.5	8.5

	lb ft	kgm
Nut, front cover to transmission case attachment stud	36	5
Nut, rear cover to transmission case attachment stud	18	2.5
Nut countershaft rear bearing	87	12
Nut, flexible joint sleeve to mainshaft	108.5	15
Screw, countershaft front bearing	69	9.5
Screw, shifter fork	14.5	2
Nut, gear shifter and selection lever shaft retainer cover	7	1
Screw, lug to shifter rod	14.5	2
Nut, gearshift support screw	18	2.5
Self-locking nut, type S, inner cup to gearshift lever lower stem	11	1.5

Automatic transmission:

	lb ft	kgm
Screw, front cover lower attachment to engine	61.5	8.5
Screw, front cover upper attachment to engine	61.5	8.5
Indented screw, converter to flywheel	47	6.5
Self-locking nut, type S, gear selection rod lever	14.5	2
Indented screw, gearshift support lever	11	1.5

Propeller shaft:

	lb ft	kgm
Flange nut, yoke to support	21	3
Self-locking, nylon-lined nut, flexible joint to transmission and to propeller shaft screw	51	7
Self-locking nylon-lined nut, propeller shaft to rear axle screw	25	3.5
Screw, propeller shaft pillow block	18	2.5
Screw, propeller shaft pillow block to body	18	2.5

Rear axle:

	lb ft	kgm
Nut, brake backing and bearing retainer plate screw	18	2.5
Screw, differential carrier to axle housing *	32.5	4.5
Screw, caps to differential carrier	69	9.5
Screw, ring gear to differential case	72	10
Wheel stud	51	7
Screw, brake caliper bracket	36	5
Screw, brake caliper bleeder	3.5	0.5
Connector on body, rear wheel brake hose	14.5	2
Connector on caliper, rear wheel brake hose	14.5	2

Coat thread with Loctite before screwing in

Pedals:

	lb ft	kgm
Nut, brake and clutch pedals screw	22	3
Nut, brake pedal support screw	22	3
Nut, pedal support strut to floor screw	11	1.5
Nut, power brake to body attachment brace lower screw	11	1.5

Hydraulic brake system:

	lb ft	kgm
Nut, master cylinder screw	25	2.5
Screw, brake regulator to bracket on body	14.5	2

Power brake:

	lb ft	kgm
Nut, power brake attachment screw	18	2.5
Nut, power brake support screw	11	1.5
Self-locking nylon-lined nut, power brake control lever pivot screw	11	1.5

	Torque	
	lb ft	kgm
Handbrake:		
Self-locking nut, type S, handbrake idler lever ..	14.5	2
Self-locking nut, type S, handbrake idler lever pin	25	3.5
Steering:		
Nut, steering wheel to shaft	36	5
Nut, universal joint yoke screw	18	2.5
Screw, steering column bracket front attachment to body	7	1
Self-locking nut, type S, steering box to body ..	22	3
Screw, worm thrust cover	14.5	2
Screw, steering gear cover	14.5	2
Nut, Pitman arm	174	24
Self-locking nut, type S, idler arm damper to body	22	3
Nut, tie rod clamp screw	14.5	2
Nut with cotterpin, tie rod ball joint	43	6 *

Whenever, upon tightening to the specified torque, the castellation slot on the nut fails to coincide with the hole in the screw, tighten further the nut until the cotterpin can be driven home (angle less than 60 deg.)

Front suspension:		
Front wheel stud	65	9
Screw, upper control arm front attachment ..	43	6
Nut, lower control arm strut	72	10
Nut, upper control arm support to body screw ..	36	5
Nut, lower control arm to crossmember screw ..	65	9
Nut, upper control arm to support rear attachment screw	65	9
Self-locking nylon-lined nut, strut to lower control arm	47	6.5
Screw, crossmember to body	54	7.5
Self-locking nylon-lined nut, ball joints to knuckle	87	12
Nut, shock absorber upper mounting	29	4
Nut, shock absorber lower mounting screw ..	36	5
Nut, shock absorber upper mounting support ..	11	1.5
Nut, brake backing plate to knuckle screw ..	36	5
Nut, brake backing plate and steering arm to knuckle screw	36	5
Screw, front brake caliper bracket	36	5
Connector, front brake hose	22	3
Rear suspension:		
Nut, shock absorber upper mounting	29	4
Self-locking nylon-lined nut, shock absorber lower mounting support screw	14.5	2
Nut, shock absorber lower mounting screw ..	36	5
Self-locking nut, type S, strut attachment screw ..	32.5	4.5
Nut, upper struts front support to body	40	5.5

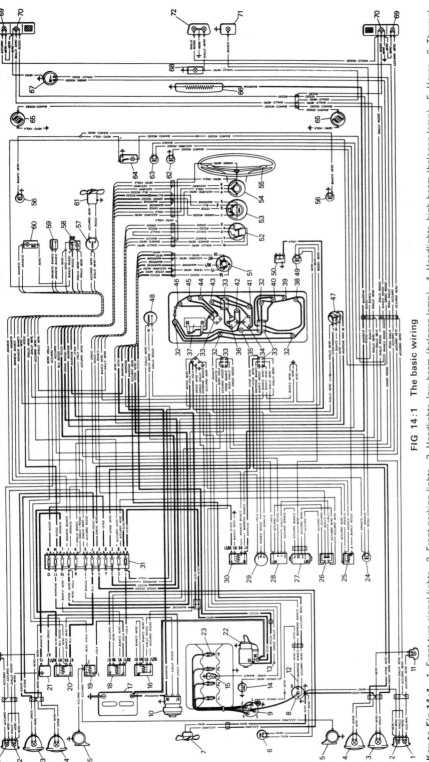

FIG 14:1   The basic wiring

Key to Fig 14:1   1 Front turn signal lights   2 Front parking lights   3 Headlights, low beam (halogen lamp)   4 Headlights, high beam (halogen lamp)   5 Horns   6 Thermal switch for motor 7   7 Engine radiator cooling fan motor   8 Ignition coil   9 Ignition distributor   10 Alternator   11 Turn signal side repeaters   12 Cable, preset for fitting engine tachometer   13 Cable, preset for fitting oil gauge   14 Low oil pressure indicator switch   15 Water temperature gauge sending unit   16 Relay for indicator 43   17 Battery   18 Relay for motor 7   19 Horn relay   20 Relay for lighting headlights 3 and 4 simultaneously   21 Voltage regulator   22 Starting motor   23 Spark plugs   24 Stop light press switch   25 Handbrake 'on' flasher   26 Windshield washer and wiper push button   27 Windshield wiper motor   28 Windshield wiper intermitter   29 Turn signal flasher   30 Relay for demister 66 (optional)   31 Fuses   32 Junction, wiring harness to cluster   34 Fuel gauge   35 Turn signal indicator (green)   36 Water temperature gauge   37 Electric clock   38 Parking light indicator (green)   39 Demister 66 indicator (optional)   40 High beam indicator (blue)   41 Low fuel warning light (red)   42 Spare indicator   43 No-charge warning light (red)   44 Handbrake 'on' flashing indicator (red)   45 Choke 'on' indicator push button switch   46 Low oil pressure warning light (red)   47 Exterior lighting three-position switch   48 Instrument cluster light switch   49 Choke 'on' indicator push button switch   50 Inspection lamp power socket   51 Ignition and starting switch   52 Windshield wiper three-position switch   53 Exterior lighting selector switch and low beam flasher   54 Turn signal selector switch   55 Horn buttons   56 Front courtesy light switches on front doors   57 Three-position switch for motor 61   58 Cigar lighter (with spot light)   59 Switch for demister 66 (optional)   60 Glove box light, with push button switch   61 Two-speed electrofan, interior ventilation   62 Handbrake 'on' push button switch   63 Back-up light push button switch   64 Front interior light, with built-in switch   65 Rear interior lights, with built-in switch   66 Rear window demister (optional)   67 Fuel gauge sending unit   68 Trunk compartment light   69 Rear turn signal lights   70 Tail and stop lights   71 Back-up light   72 Licence plate lights

Variants to the wiring diagram for model 132 (1600)

The red cable between terminal 3 of fuse box 31 and terminal (d) of switch 53 is suppressed
The blue cable of relay 20 terminal 87 is connected to terminal 3 of fuse box 31
Headlights are equipped with regular double filament bulbs. Outboard lights are both high and low beam, inboard lights high beam only

Key to colour code (all diagrams)

Nero Black   **Bianco** White   **Rosso** Red   **Azzurro** Light blue   **Verde** Green   **Giallo** Yellow   **Grigio** Grey   **Arancio** Orange

Rosa Pink   **Marrone** Brown   **Viola** Violet   **Blu** Dark blue

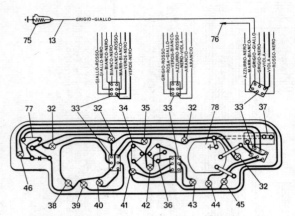

FIG 14:2 Engine tachometer and oil gauge

Key to Fig 14:2   13 Oil gauge cable   32 Instrument cluster lights   33 Junctions, wiring harness to cluster 34 Fuel gauge   35 Turn signal indicator (green) 36 Water temperature gauge   37 Electric clock   38 Parking lights indicator (green)   39 Rear window demister indicator (optional)   40 High beam indicator (blue)   41 Low fuel warning light (red)   42 Spare indicator   43 No-charge warning light (red)   44 Handbrake 'on' flashing indicator (red)   45 Choke 'on' indicator (amber)   46 Low oil pressure warning light (red)   75 Oil gauge sending unit   76 To terminal D of ignition coil 8   77 Oil gauge 78 Electronic engine tachometer

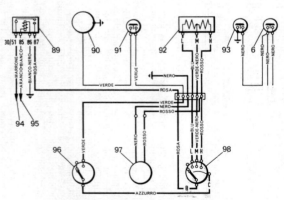

FIG 14:3 Air conditioner

Key to Fig 14:3   6 Thermal switch in radiator for motor 7 89 Air conditioner relay   90 Refrigerator compressor   91 Low pressure switch (on constant pressure valve)   92 Resistor, for regulating speed of motor 97   93 Thermal switch in condenser for motor 7   94 To terminal (M) of fuse block 31 95 To terminal (I) of fuse block 31   96 Knob for switching in refrigerator and regulating temperature of car interior   97 Air conditioner blower motor (replaces motor 61)   98 Knob for regulating speed of motor 97

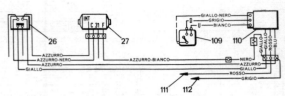

FIG 14:4 Electronic windscreen wiper intermitter

Key to Fig 14:4   26 Windshield washer and wiper push button   27 Windshield wiper motor   109 Three-position switch for intermitter 110   110 Electronic windshield wiper intermitter (replaces device 28)   111 To terminal (o) of switch 52   112 To terminal (p) of switch 52

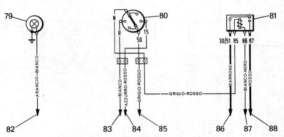

FIG 14:5 Automatic transmission

Key to Fig 14:5   79 Gear engagement indicator   80 Starter inhibitor and reverse switch (replaces back-up light switch 63) 81 Starter inhibitor relay   82 To terminal (I) of fuse block 31   83 To back-up light   84 To terminal (G) of fuse block 31   85 To terminal (50) of key switch 51   86 To terminal (30) of alternator 10   87 To ground of voltage regulator 21   88 To terminal (50) of starting motor 22

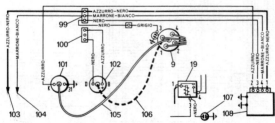

FIG 14:6 Electronic ignition

Key to Fig 14:6   9 Ignition distributor   19 Horn relay 99 Junction in electronic ignition position   100 Junction for emergency ignition   101 Electronic ignition coil 102 Emergency ignition coil   103 To terminal (15) of key switch 51   104 To junction (33) on instrument cluster 105 High voltage cable in electronic ignition position   106 High voltage cable in emergency ignition position   107 Radio interference suppressor capacitor for horns   108 Electronic ignition unit

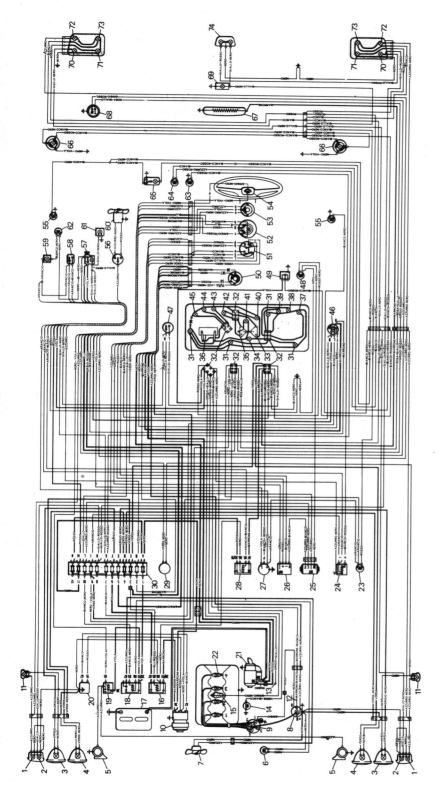

FIG 14:7 Wiring diagram, 132 GLS

Key to Fig 14:7   1 Front direction indicators   2 Side lights   3 Halogen headlamps, dipped beam   4 Halogen headlamps, main beam   5 Horns   6 Radiator fan control switch   7 Radiator fan motor   8 Ignition coil   9 Distributor   10 Alternator   11 Repeater lights   12 Tachometer lead   13 Oil pressure gauge lead   14 Oil pressure transmitter   15 Water temperature transmitter   16 Headlamp relay   17 Battery   18 Radiator fan relay   19 Horn relay   20 Voltage regulator   21 Starter   22 Spark plugs   23 Stop light switch   24 Handbrake warning flasher   25 Wiper motor   26 Wiper interrupter relay   27 Direction indicator flasher   28 Heated backlight relay (optional)   29 Wiper pump   30 Fuse unit   31 Panel lights   32 Connectors   33 Fuel gauge   34 Direction indicator warning light   35 Water temperature gauge   36 Clock   37 Side light warning light   38 Heated backlight warning light   39 Headlamp warning light   40 Fuel warning light   41 Spare warning light   42 Ignition warning light   43 Handbrake warning light   44 Choke warning light   45 Oil pressure warning light   46 Lighting switch   47 Panel light switch   48 Choke warning transmitter   49 Power point   50 Ignition switch   51 Wiper/washer switch   52 Headlamp switch   53 Direction indicator switch   54 Horn switch   55 Front door pillar switch   56 Heater fan switch   57 Cigar lighter/light   58 Heated backlight switch   59 Glove box light   60 Heater fan motor   61 Ideogram lamp   62 Glove box switch   63 Handbrake warning transmitter   64 Reversing light switch   65 Courtesy light/switch   66 Rear interior lights/switches   67 Heated backlight (optional)   68 Fuel transmitter   69 Boot light   70 Rear lights   71 Stop lights   72 Reversing lights   73 Rear direction indicators   74 Number plate lights

On 132 GL models: Twin tungsten double filament headlamps, outer lamps operate on main and dipped beams, inner lamps on main beam only.

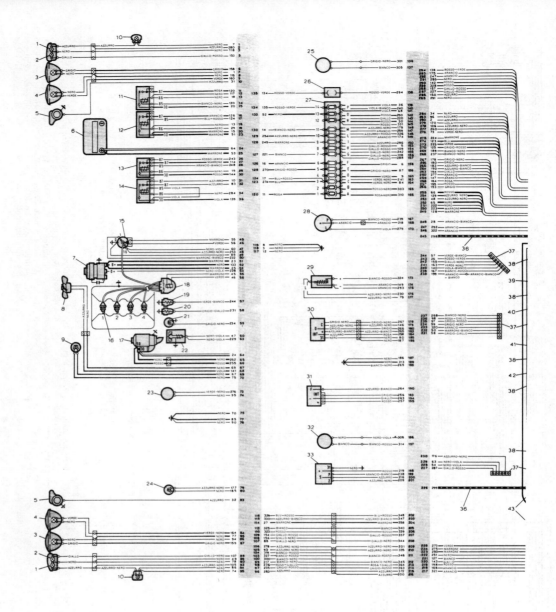

FIG 14 : 8   Wiring diagram 132 '1600' and '2000' April 1977 onwards

Key to Fig 14 : 8   1 Front direction indicators   2 Side lamps   3 Dipped beams   4 Main beams   5 Horns   6 Battery
7 Alternator   8 Radiator fan motor   9 Radiator fan control switch   10 Repeater lamps   11 Electric window relay   12 Dipped
beam relay   13 Heated backlight relay   14 Horn relay   15 Electronic control box and coil   16 Spark plugs   17 Starter motor
18 Ignition distributor and reluctor   19 Engine coolant temperature gauge transmitter   20 Engine oil pressure transmitter
21 Engine oil pressure warning transmitter   22 Idle stop solenoid (2000cm³ and 1600cm³ regular petrol)   23 Windscreen washer
pump   24 Brake fluid level indicator   25 Front righthand window motor   26 Fuse holder for radio power lead   27 Fuse unit
28 Direction indicator flasher   29 Handbrake warning flasher   30 Windscreen wiper   31 Wiper interruptor   32 Front lefthand
window motor   33 Hazard warning flasher   34 Aerial lead   35 Loudspeaker lead   36 Ideogram illumination light guide cables
37 Connectors   38 Panel lights   39 Engine coolant temperature gauge   40 Fuel gauge   41 Oil pressure gauge   42 Tachometer
43 Lighting switch   44 Heated backlight switch   45 Quartz crystal clock   46 Direction indicator warning light   47 Hazard warning
light   48 Headlamp warning lamp   49 Rear fog lamp warning light   50 Side lamp warning light   51 Spare warning light

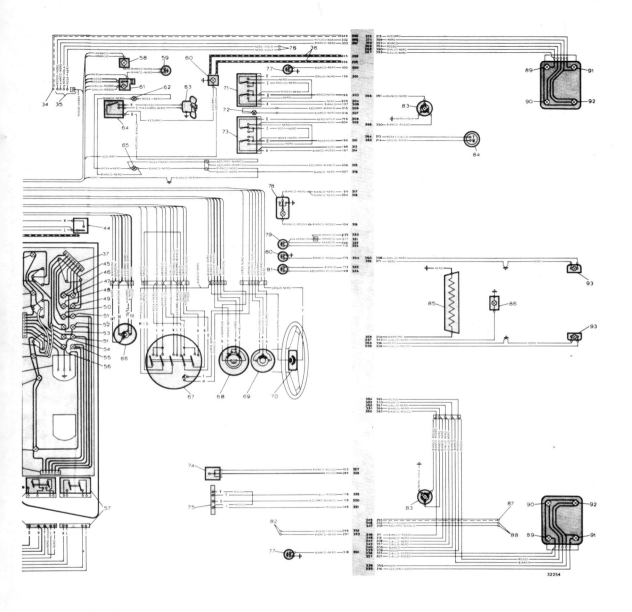

52 Handbrake warning light   53 Heated backlight warning light   54 Fuel warning light   55 Ignition warning light   56 Oil pressure
warning light   57 Hazard warning switch   58 Glovebox light   59 Glovebox light switch   60 Ideogram illumination light guide source
61 Cigar lighter/light   62 Ideogram illumination lamp   63 Heater fan   64 Heater fan switch   65 Ideogram illumination lamp
66 Ignition switch   67 Wiper/washer three-position switch   68 Headlamp switch   69 Direction indicator switch   70 Horn control
71 Front righthand window switch   72 Ideogram illumination lamp   73 Front lefthand window switch   74 Power point
75 Aerial motor switch   76 Righthand speaker leads   77 Front door pillar switches   78 Front courtesy light   79 Stop lamp switch
80 Handbrake warning switch   81 Reversing lamp switch   82 Lefthand speaker leads   83 Rear courtesy lights/switches
84 Fuel gauge   85 Heated backlight   86 Boot light   87 Aerial lead   88 Aerial motor leads   89 Rear lamps   90 Stop lamps
91 Rear direction indicators   92 Reversing lamps   93 Number plate lights

Explanatory Note: Each wire section ends in an identification number. Actual wiring can be traced by looking for the wire
number in the adjacent shaded strip, where wire path is resumed.

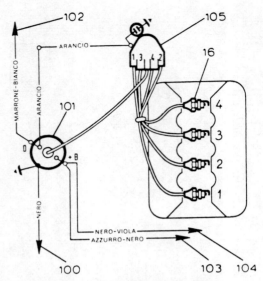

FIG 14 : 9   Ignition system '1600' engine

Key to Fig 14 : 9   100 To lefthand side lamp unit   102 To tachometer   103 To terminal 15/54 of ignition switch   104 To idle stop solenoid

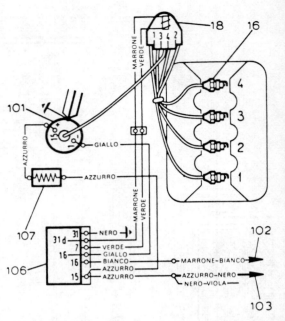

FIG 14 : 10   Bosch electronic ignition system '2000' engine

Key to Fig 14 : 10   102 To tachometer   103 To terminal 15/54 of ignition switch   106 Electronic control box 107 Resistor

HINTS ON MAINTENANCE AND OVERHAUL

There are few things more rewarding than the restoration of a vehicle's original peak of efficiency and smooth performance.

The following notes are intended to help the owner to reach that state of perfection. Providing that he possesses the basic manual skills he should have no difficulty in performing most of the operations detailed in this manual. It must be stressed, however, that where recommended in the manual, highly-skilled operations ought to be entrusted to experts, who have the necessary equipment, to carry out the work satisfactorily.

Quality of workmanship :

The hazardous driving conditions on the roads to-day demand that vehicles should be as nearly perfect, mechanically, as possible. It is therefore most important that amateur work be carried out with care, bearing in mind the often inadequate working conditions, and also the inferior tools which may have to be used. It is easy to counsel perfection in all things, and we recognise that it may be setting an impossibly high standard. We do, however, suggest that every care should be taken to ensure that a vehicle is as safe to take on the road as it is humanly possible to make it.

Safe working conditions :

Even though a vehicle may be stationary, it is still potentially dangerous if certain sensible precautions are not taken when working on it while it is supported on jacks or blocks. It is indeed preferable not to use jacks alone, but to supplement them with carefully placed blocks, so that there will be plenty of support if the car rolls off the jacks during a strenuous manoeuvre. Axle stands are an excellent way of providing a rigid base which is not readily disturbed. Piles of bricks are a dangerous substitute. Be careful not to get under heavy loads on lifting tackle, the load could fall. It is preferable not to work alone when lifting an engine, or when working underneath a vehicle which is supported well off the ground. To be trapped, particularly under the vehicle, may have unpleasant results if help is not quickly forthcoming. Make some provision, however humble, to deal with fires. Always disconnect a battery if there is a likelihood of electrical shorts. These may start a fire if there is leaking fuel about. This applies particularly to leads which can carry a heavy current, like those in the starter circuit. While on the subject of electricity, we must also stress the danger of using equipment which is run off the mains and which has no earth or has faulty wiring or connections. So many workshops have damp floors, and electrical shocks are of such a nature that it is sometimes impossible to let go of a live lead or piece of equipment due to the muscular spasms which take place.

Work demanding special care :

This involves the servicing of braking, steering and suspension systems. On the road, failure of the braking system may be disastrous. Make quite sure that there can be no possibility of failure through the bursting of rusty brake pipes or rotten hoses, nor to a sudden loss of pressure due to defective seals or valves.

Problems :

The chief problems which may face an operator are :

1 External dirt.
2 Difficulty in undoing tight fixings.
3 Dismantling unfamiliar mechanisms.
4 Deciding in what respect parts are defective.
5 Confusion about the correct order for reassembly.
6 Adjusting running clearance.
7 Road testing.
8 Final tuning.

Practical suggestions to solve the problems :

1 Preliminary cleaning of large parts – engines, transmissions, steering, suspensions, etc, – should be carried out before removal from the car. Where road dirt and mud alone are present, wash clean with a high-pressure water jet, brushing to remove stubborn adhesions, and allow to drain and dry. Where oil or grease is also present, wash down with a proprietary compound (Gunk, Teepol etc,) applying with a stiff brush – an old paint brush is suitable – into all crevices. Cover the distributor and ignition coils with a polythene bag and then apply a strong water jet to clear the loosened deposits. Allow to drain and dry. The assemblies will then be sufficiently clean to remove and transfer to the bench for the next stage.

On the bench, further cleaning can be carried out, first wiping the parts as free as possible from grease with old newspaper. Avoid using rag or cotton waste which can leave clogging fibres behind. Any remaining grease can be removed with a brush dipped in paraffin. Avoid using paraffin or petrol in large quantities for cleaning in enclosed areas, such as garages, on account of the high fire risk.

When all exteriors have been cleaned, and not before, dismantling can be commenced. This ensures that dirt will not enter into interiors and orifices revealed by dismantling. In the next phases, where components have to be cleaned, use a special solvent or petrol and keep the containers covered except when in use. After the components have been cleaned, plug small holes with tapered hard wood plugs cut to size and blank off larger orifices with greaseproof paper and masking tape. Do not use soft wood plugs or matchsticks as they may break.

2 It is not advisable to hammer on the end of a screw thread, but if it must be done, first screw on a nut to protect the thread, and use a lead hammer. This applies particularly to the removal of tapered cotters. Nuts and bolts seem to 'grow' together, especially in exhaust systems. If penetrating oil does not work, try the judicious application of heat, but be careful of starting a fire. Asbestos sheet or cloth is useful to isolate heat.

Tight bushes or pieces of tail-pipe rusted into a silencer can be removed by splitting them with an open-ended hacksaw. Tight screws can sometimes be started by a tap from a hammer on the end of a suitable screwdriver. Many tight fittings will yield to the judicious use of a hammer, but it must be a soft-faced hammer, if damage is to be avoided, use a heavy block on the opposite side to absorb shock. Any parts of the steering system which have been damaged should be renewed, as attempts to repair them may lead to cracking and subsequent failure, and steering ball joints should be disconnected using a recommended tool to prevent damage.

3 It often happens that an owner is baffled when trying to dismantle an unfamiliar piece of equipment. So many modern devices are pressed together or assembled by spinning-over flanges, that they must be sawn apart. The intention is that the whole assembly must be renewed. However, parts which appear to be in one piece to the naked eye may reveal close-fitting joint lines when inspected with a magnifying glass, and this may provide the necessary clue to dismantling. Lefthanded screw threads are used where rotational forces would tend to unscrew a righthanded screw thread.

Be very careful when dismantling mechanisms which may come apart suddenly. Work in an enclosed space where the parts will be contained, and drape a piece of cloth over the device if springs are likely to fly in all directions. Mark everything which might be reassembled in the wrong position, scratched symbols may be used on unstressed parts, or a sequence of tiny dots from a centre punch can be useful. Stressed parts should never be scratched or centre-popped as this may lead to cracking under working conditions. Store parts which look alike in the correct order for reassembly. Never rely upon memory to assist in the assembly of complicated mechanisms, especially when they will be dismantled for a long time, but make notes, and drawings to supplement the diagrams in the manual, and put labels on detached wires. Rust stains may indicate unlubricated wear. This can sometimes be seen round the outside edge of a bearing cup in a universal joint. Look for bright rubbing marks on parts which normally should not make heavy contact. These might prove that something is bent or running out of truth. For example, there might be bright marks on one side of a piston, at the top near the ring grooves, and others at the bottom of the skirt on the other side. This could well be the clue to a bent connecting rod. Suspected cracks can be proved by heating the component in a light oil to approximately 100°C, removing, drying off, and dusting with french chalk. If a crack is present the oil retained in the crack will stain the french chalk.

4 In determining wear, and the degree, against the permissible limits set in the manual, accurate measurement can only be achieved by the use of a micrometer. In many cases, the wear is given to the fourth place of decimals; that is in ten-thousandths of an inch. This can be read by the vernier scale on the barrel of a good micrometer. Bore diameters are more difficult to determine. If, however, the matching shaft is accurately measured, the degree of play in the bore can be felt as a guide to its suitability. In other cases, the shank of a twist drill of known diameter is a handy check.

Many methods have been devised for determining the clearance between bearing surfaces. To-day the best and simplest is by the use of Plastigage, obtainable from most garages. A thin plastic thread is laid between the two surfaces and the bearing is tightened, flattening the thread. On removal, the width of the thread is compared with the scale supplied with the thread and the clearance is read off directly. Sometimes joint faces leak persistently, even after gasket renewal. The fault will then be traceable to distortion, dirt or burrs. Studs which are screwed into soft metal frequently raise burrs at the point of entry. A quick cure for this is to chamfer the edge of the hole in the part which fits over the stud.

5 **Always check a replacement part with the original one before it is fitted.**

If parts are not marked, and the order for reassembly is not known, a little detective work will help. Look for marks which are due to wear to see if they can be mated. Joint faces may not be identical due to manufacturing errors, and parts which overlap may be stained, giving a clue to the correct position. Most fixings leave identifying marks especially if they were painted over on assembly. It is then easier to decide whether a nut, for instance, has a plain, a spring, or a shakeproof washer under it. All running surfaces become 'bedded' together after long spells of work and tiny imperfections on one part will be found to have left corresponding marks on the other. This is particularly true of shafts and bearings and even a score on a cylinder wall will show on the piston.

6 Checking end float rocker clearances by feeler gauge may not always give accurate results because of wear. For instance, the rocker tip which bears on a valve stem may be deeply pitted, in which case the feeler will simply be bridging a depression. Thrust washers may also wear depressions in opposing faces to make accurate measurement difficult. End float is then easier to check by using a dial gauge. It is common practice to adjust end play in bearing assemblies, like front hubs with taper rollers, by doing up the axle nut until the hub becomes stiff to turn and then backing it off a little. Do not use this method with ballbearing hubs as the assembly is often preloaded by tightening the axle nut to its fullest extent. If the splitpin hole will not line up, file the base of the nut a little.

Steering assemblies often wear in the straight-ahead position. If any part is adjusted, make sure that it remains free when moved from lock to lock. Do not be surprised if an assembly like a steering gearbox, which is known to be carefully adjusted outside the car, becomes stiff when it is bolted into place. This will be due to distortion of the case by the pull of the mounting bolts, particularly if the mounting points are not all touching together. This problem may be met in other equipment and is cured by careful attention to the alignment of mounting points.

When a spanner is stamped with a size and A/F it means that the dimension is the width between the jaws and has no connection with ANF, which is the designation for the American National Fine thread. Coarse threads like Whitworth are rarely used on cars to-day except for studs which screw into soft aluminium or cast iron. For this reason it might be found that the top end of a cylinder head stud has a fine thread and the lower end a coarse thread to screw into the cylinder block. If the car has mainly UNF threads then it is likely that any coarse threads will be UNC, which are not the same as Whitworth. Small sizes have the same number of threads in Whitworth and UNC, but in the $\frac{1}{2}$ in size for example, there are twelve threads to the inch in the former and thirteen in the latter.

7 After a major overhaul, particularly if a great deal of work has been done on the braking, steering and suspension systems, it is advisable to approach the problem of testing with care. If the braking system has been overhauled, apply heavy pressure to the brake pedal and get a second operator to check every possible source of leakage. The brakes may work extremely well, but a leak could cause complete failure after a few miles.

Do not fit the hub caps until every wheel nut has been checked for tightness, and make sure that the tyre pressures are correct. Check the levels of coolant, lubricants and hydraulic fluids. Being satisfied that all is well, take the car on the road and test the brakes at once. Check the steering and the action of the handbrake. Do all this at moderate speeds on quiet roads, and make sure there is no other vehicle behind you when you try a rapid stop.

Finally, remember that many parts settle down after a time, so check for tightness of all fixings after the car has been on the road a hundred miles or so.

8 It is useless to tune an engine which has not reached its normal running temperature. In the same way, the tune of an engine which is stiff after a rebore will be different when the engine is again running free. Remember too, that rocker clearances on pushrod operated valve gear will change when the cylinder head nuts are tightened after an initial period of running with a new head gasket.

Trouble may not always be due to what seems the obvious cause. Ignition, carburation and mechanical condition are interdependent and spitting back through the carburetter, which might be attributed to a weak mixture, can be caused by a sticking inlet valve.

For one final hint on tuning, never adjust more than one thing at a time or it will be impossible to tell which adjustment produced the desired result.

NOTES

GLOSSARY OF TERMS

Allen key   Cranked wrench of hexagonal section for use with socket head screws.

Alternator   Electrical generator producing alternating current. Rectified to direct current for battery charging.

Ambient temperature   Surrounding atmospheric temperature.

Annulus   Used in engineering to indicate the outer ring gear of an epicyclic gear train.

Armature   The shaft carrying the windings, which rotates in the magnetic field of a generator or starter motor. That part of a solenoid or relay which is activated by the magnetic field.

Axial   In line with, or pertaining to, an axis.

Backlash   Play in meshing gears.

Balance lever   A bar where force applied at the centre is equally divided between connections at the ends.

Banjo axle   Axle casing with large diameter housing for the crownwheel and differential.

Bendix pinion   A self-engaging and self-disengaging drive on a starter motor shaft.

Bevel pinion   A conical shaped gearwheel, designed to mesh with a similar gear with an axis usually at 90 deg. to its own.

bhp   Brake horse power, measured on a dynamometer.

bmep   Brake mean effective pressure. Average pressure on a piston during the working stroke.

Brake cylinder   Cylinder with hydraulically operated piston(s) acting on brake shoes or pad(s).

Brake regulator   Control valve fitted in hydraulic braking system which limits brake pressure to rear brakes during heavy braking to prevent rear wheel locking.

Camber   Angle at which a wheel is tilted from the vertical.

Capacitor   Modern term for an electrical condenser. Part of distributor assembly, connected across contact breaker points, acts as an interference suppressor.

Castellated   Top face of a nut, slotted across the flats, to take a locking splitpin.

Castor   Angle at which the kingpin or swivel pin is tilted when viewed from the side.

cc   Cubic centimetres. Engine capacity is arrived at by multiplying the area of the bore in sq cm by the stroke in cm by the number of cylinders.

Clevis   U-shaped forked connector used with a clevis pin, usually at handbrake connections.

Collet   A type of collar, usually split and located in a groove in a shaft, and held in place by a retainer. The arrangement used to retain the spring(s) on a valve stem in most cases.

Commutator   Rotating segmented current distributor between armature windings and brushes in generator or motor.

Compression ratio   The ratio, or quantitative relation, of the total volume (piston at bottom of stroke) to the unswept volume (piston at top of stroke) in an engine cylinder.

Condenser   See capacitor.

Core plug   Plug for blanking off a manufacturing hole in a casting.

Crownwheel   Large bevel gear in rear axle, driven by a bevel pinion attached to the propeller shaft. Sometimes called a 'ring gear'.

'C'-spanner   Like a 'C' with a handle. For use on screwed collars without flats, but with slots or holes.

Damper   Modern term for shock-absorber, used in vehicle suspension systems to damp out spring oscillations.

Depression   The lowering of atmospheric pressure as in the inlet manifold and carburetter.

Dowel   Close tolerance pin, peg, tube, or bolt, which accurately locates mating parts.

Drag link   Rod connecting steering box drop arm (pitman arm) to nearest front wheel steering arm in certain types of steering systems.

Dry liner   Thinwall tube pressed into cylinder bore

Dry sump   Lubrication system where all oil is scavenged from the sump, and returned to a separate tank.

Dynamo   See Generator.

Electrode   Terminal, part of an electrical component, such as the points or 'Electrodes' of a sparking plug.

Electrolyte   In lead-acid car batteries a solution of sulphuric acid and distilled water.

End float   The axial movement between associated parts, end play.

EP   Extreme pressure. In lubricants, special grades for heavily loaded bearing surfaces, such as gear teeth in a gearbox, or crownwheel and pinion in a rear axle.

Fade	Of brakes. Reduced efficiency due to overheating.
Field coils	Windings on the polepieces of motors and generators.
Fillets	Narrow finishing strips usually applied to interior bodywork.
First motion shaft	Input shaft from clutch to gearbox.
Fullflow filter	Filters in which all the oil is pumped to the engine. If the element becomes clogged, a bypass valve operates to pass unfiltered oil to the engine.
FWD	Front wheel drive.
Gear pump	Two meshing gears in a close fitting casing. Oil is carried from the inlet round the outside of both gears in the spaces between the gear teeth and casing to the outlet, the meshing gear teeth prevent oil passing back to the inlet, and the oil is forced through the outlet port.
Generator	Modern term for 'Dynamo'. When rotated produces electrical current.
Grommet	A ring of protective or sealing material. Can be used to protect pipes or leads passing through bulkheads.
Grubscrew	Fully threaded headless screw with screwdriver slot. Used for locking, or alignment purposes.
Gudgeon pin	Shaft which connects a piston to its connecting rod. Sometimes called 'wrist pin', or 'piston pin'.
Halfshaft	One of a pair transmitting drive from the differential.
Helical	In spiral form. The teeth of helical gears are cut at a spiral angle to the side faces of the gearwheel.
Hot spot	Hot area that assists vapourisation of fuel on its way to cylinders. Often provided by close contact between inlet and exhaust manifolds.
HT	High Tension. Applied to electrical current produced by the ignition coil for the sparking plugs.
Hydrometer	A device for checking specific gravity of liquids. Used to check specific gravity of electrolyte.
Hypoid bevel gears	A form of bevel gear used in the rear axle drive gears. The bevel pinion meshes below the centre line of the crownwheel, giving a lower propeller shaft line.
Idler	A device for passing on movement. A free running gear between driving and driven gears. A lever transmitting track rod movement to a side rod in steering gear.
Impeller	A centrifugal pumping element. Used in water pumps to stimulate flow.
Journals	Those parts of a shaft that are in contact with the bearings.
Kingpin	The main vertical pin which carries the front wheel spindle, and permits steering movement. May be called 'steering pin' or 'swivel pin'.
Layshaft	The shaft which carries the laygear in the gearbox. The laygear is driven by the first motion shaft and drives the third motion shaft according to the gear selected. Sometimes called the 'countershaft' or 'second motion shaft.'
lb ft	A measure of twist or torque. A pull of 10 lb at a radius of 1 ft is a torque of 10 lb ft.
lb/sq in	Pounds per square inch.
Little-end	The small, or piston end of a connecting rod. Sometimes called the 'small-end'.
LT	Low Tension. The current output from the battery.
Mandrel	Accurately manufactured bar or rod used for test or centring purposes.
Manifold	A pipe, duct, or chamber, with several branches.
Needle rollers	Bearing rollers with a length many times their diameter.
Oil bath	Reservoir which lubricates parts by immersion. In air filters, a separate oil supply for wetting a wire mesh element to hold the dust.
Oil wetted	In air filters, a wire mesh element lightly oiled to trap and hold airborne dust.
Overlap	Period during which inlet and exhaust valves are open together.
Panhard rod	Bar connected between fixed point on chassis and another on axle to control sideways movement.
Pawl	Pivoted catch which engages in the teeth of a ratchet to permit movement in one direction only.
Peg spanner	Tool with pegs, or pins, to engage in holes or slots in the part to be turned.
Pendant pedals	Pedals with levers that are pivoted at the top end.
Phillips screwdriver	A cross-point screwdriver for use with the cross-slotted heads of Phillips screws.
Pinion	A small gear, usually in relation to another gear.
Piston-type damper	Shock absorber in which damping is controlled by a piston working in a closed oil-filled cylinder.
Preloading	Preset static pressure on ball or roller bearings not due to working loads.
Radial	Radiating from a centre, like the spokes of a wheel.

Radius rod	Pivoted arm confining movement of a part to an arc of fixed radius.
Ratchet	Toothed wheel or rack which can move in one direction only, movement in the other being prevented by a pawl.
Ring gear	A gear tooth ring attached to outer periphery of flywheel. Starter pinion engages with it during starting.
Runout	Amount by which rotating part is out of true.
Semi-floating axle	Outer end of rear axle halfshaft is carried on bearing inside axle casing. Wheel hub is secured to end of shaft.
Servo	A hydraulic or pneumatic system for assisting, or, augmenting a physical effort. See 'Vacuum Servo'.
Setscrew	One which is threaded for the full length of the shank.
Shackle	A coupling link, used in the form of two parallel pins connected by side plates to secure the end of the master suspension spring and absorb the effects of deflection.
Shell bearing	Thinwalled steel shell lined with anti-friction metal. Usually semi-circular and used in pairs for main and big-end bearings.
Shock absorber	See 'Damper'.
Silentbloc	Rubber bush bonded to inner and outer metal sleeves.
Socket-head screw	Screw with hexagonal socket for an Allen key.
Solenoid	A coil of wire creating a magnetic field when electric current passes through it. Used with a soft iron core to operate contacts or a mechanical device.
Spur gear	A gear with teeth cut axially across the periphery.
Stub axle	Short axle fixed at one end only.
Tachometer	An instrument for accurate measurement of rotating speed. Usually indicates in revolutions per minute.

TDC	Top Dead Centre. The highest point reached by a piston in a cylinder, with the crank and connecting rod in line.
Thermostat	Automatic device for regulating temperature. Used in vehicle coolant systems to open a valve which restricts circulation at low temperature.
Third motion shaft	Output shaft of gearbox.
Threequarter floating axle	Outer end of rear axle halfshaft flanged and bolted to wheel hub, which runs on bearing mounted on outside of axle casing. Vehicle weight is not carried by the axle shaft.
Thrust bearing or washer	Used to reduce friction in rotating parts subject to axial loads.
Torque	Turning or twisting effort. See 'lb ft'.
Track rod	The bar(s) across the vehicle which connect the steering arms and maintain the front wheels in their correct alignment.
UJ	Universal joint. A coupling between shafts which permits angular movement.
UNF	Unified National Fine screw thread.
Vacuum servo	Device used in brake system, using difference between atmospheric pressure and inlet manifold depression to operate a piston which acts to augment brake pressure as required. See 'Servo'.
Venturi	A restriction or 'choke' in a tube, as in a carburetter, used to increase velocity to obtain a reduction in pressure.
Vernier	A sliding scale for obtaining fractional readings of the graduations of an adjacent scale.
Welch plug	A domed thin metal disc which is partially flattened to lock in a recess. Used to plug core holes in castings.
Wet liner	Removable cylinder barrel, sealed against coolant leakage, where the coolant is in direct contact with the outer surface.
Wet sump	A reservoir attached to the crankcase to hold the lubricating oil.

NOTES

INDEX

150

NOTES